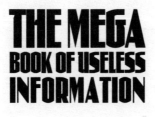

THE MEGA
BOOK OF USELESS
INFORMATION

THE MEGA
BOOK OF USELESS
INFORMATION

**AN OFFICIAL USELESS INFORMATION
SOCIETY PUBLICATION**

NOEL BOTHAM

JOHN BLAKE

Published by John Blake Publishing Ltd,
3 Bramber Court, 2 Bramber Road,
London W14 9PB, UK

www.johnblakepublishing.co.uk

First published in hardback in 2008

ISBN: 978-1-84454-666-4

British Library Cataloguing-in-Publication Data:
A catalogue record for this book is available from the British Library.

Design by www.envydesign.co.uk

Printed in the UK by CPI William Clowes Beccles NR34 7TL

3 5 7 9 10 8 6 4 2

Text copyright © Noel Botham, 2008

Papers used by John Blake Publishing are natural, recyclable products made from
wood grown in sustainable forests. The manufacturing processes conform to the
environmental regulations of the country of origin.

Every attempt has been made to contact the relevant copyright-holders, but some
were unobtainable. We would be grateful if the appropriate people could contact us.

As always, to my wife, Lesley Lewis, with love

CONTENTS

THE WORLD AND ITS PEOPLE

THE WORLD AND ITS PEOPLE

* Kemo Sabe means 'soggy shrub' in Navajo.

* Napoleon carried chocolate on all his military campaigns.

* In 1973, Swedish confectionery salesman Roland Ohisson was buried in a coffin made entirely of chocolate.

* Someone's gender can be guessed with 95 per cent accuracy just by smelling his or her breath.

* On average, Elizabeth Taylor has remarried every four years and five months.

* Pontius Pilate was born in Scotland.

* When he was young, Leonardo da Vinci drew a picture of a horrible monster and placed it near a window in order to surprise his father. The drawing was so convincing that, upon seeing it, his father believed it to be real and set out to protect his family until the boy showed him it was just a picture. Da Vinci's father then enrolled his son in an art class.

* Ten per cent of Star Trek fans replace the lenses on their glasses every five years, whether they need to or not.

THE WORLD AND ITS PEOPLE

- Ancient Romans at one time used human urine as an ingredient in their toothpaste.

- People who are lying to you tend to look up and to the left.

- The middle name of Jimmy Hoffa is Riddle. The legendary American union figure disappeared without trace on 30 July 1975.

- Boys who have unusual first names are more likely to have mental health problems than boys with conventional names.

- One in three consumers pays off his or her credit card bill every month.

- Pop star Justin Timberlake's half-eaten French toast sold for over $3,000 on eBay.

- One in three snakebite victims is drunk. One in five is tattooed.

- Michelangelo was harshly criticized by a Vatican official for the nudity in his fresco *The Last Judgement*, which hangs on the walls of the Sistine Chapel in Rome. In retaliation, the artist made some changes to his work: he painted in the face of the complaining clergyman and added donkey's ears and a snake's tail.

THE WORLD AND ITS PEOPLE

- More than 50 per cent of lottery players go back to work after winning the jackpot.

- Children who are breast-fed tend to have an IQ seven points higher than children who are not.

- Male hospital patients fall out of bed twice as often as female hospital patients.

- Fewer than ten per cent of criminals commit about 67 per cent of all crime.

- We inhale about 700,000 of our own skin flakes each day.

- A pickled snake bit Li of Suzhou, China, when he opened a bottle of rice wine.

- As his body was never found, a German court officially declared Hitler dead as recently as 1956.

- More than 50 per cent of the world's population have never made or received a telephone call.

- The average human eats eight spiders at night during their lifetime.

- All the chemicals in the human body have a combined value of approximately £4.

—— THE WORLD AND ITS PEOPLE ——

- Smokers eat more sugar than non-smokers.

- In ancient Sparta, Greece, married men were not allowed to live with their wives until they turned 30.

- Dorothy Parker wanted 'This is on me' inscribed on her tombstone.

- Half the world's population is under 25 years of age.

- In 1994, Chicago artist Dwight Kalb sent US talk-show host David Letterman a statue of Madonna, made of 180lb (82kg) of ham.

- The people killed most often during bank robberies are the robbers.

- An exocannibal eats only enemies, while an indocannibal eats only friends.

- Howard Hughes, the American billionaire businessman, aviator and film producer, never once attended a board of directors meeting, or any sort of meeting, at any of the companies he owned.

- Although Howard Hughes had 15 personal attendants and three doctors on full-time duty, he died of neglect and malnutrition, caused by his intense desire to be left alone.

THE WORLD AND ITS PEOPLE

* King Louis XIV of France established in his court the position of 'Royal Chocolate Maker to the King'.

* The Nestlés haven't run Nestlé since 1875.

* Astronauts get taller when they are in space.

* When a person is wide awake, alert, and mentally active, they are still only 25 per cent aware of what various parts of their body are doing.

* It has been estimated that men have been riding horses for over 3,000 years.

* The make-up entrepreneur Elizabeth Arden's real name was Florence Nightingale Graham, but she changed it once her company became successful at the beginning of the 1900s.

* Heavyweight boxing champion George Foreman has five sons named George; George Jnr, George III, George IV, George V and George VI.

* A five-and-a-half-year-old weighing 250lb (113kg) was exhibited at a meeting of the Physical Society of Vienna on 4 December 1894. She ate a normal diet and was otherwise in good health but she wasn't able to sweat.

——— **THE WORLD AND ITS PEOPLE** ———

* People who have computers in their homes tend to watch 40 per cent less television than average.

* A German soldier was riding in the back seat of a World War I plane when the engine suddenly stalled and he fell out of his seat while over two miles (3 km) above ground. As he was falling, the plane started falling too, and he was blown back into his own seat by the wind and was able to land the plane safely.

* Queen Elizabeth I named a man as the 'Official Uncorker of Bottles', and passed a law that stated all bottles found washed up on beaches had to be opened by him and no one else, in case they contained sensitive military messages. The penalty for anyone else opening a bottle was death.

* Afraid of growing old, Countess Bathory of Hungary became convinced that if she bathed in the blood of young girls, she could stay young for ever, and so for ten years she drained the blood of imprisoned girls so that she could take 'blood baths' in a huge iron vat. After one intended victim escaped, the King of Hungary ordered his soldiers to storm her castle. When they found many dead and some still-alive bodies, they locked the countess inside her room and bricked up the entrance, leaving only a small opening through which she was given food until she died.

THE WORLD AND ITS PEOPLE

* People overwhelmingly tend to marry partners who live near them.

* Charles Darwin cured his snuff habit by keeping his snuffbox in the basement and the key for the snuffbox in the attic.

* Voltaire drank between 50 and 65 cups of coffee every day.

* Manfredo Settala (1600–1680) is the only person in all recorded history to have been killed by a meteorite.

* Rembrandt died penniless with a friend coming up with the £2.85 it cost to bury him.

* Young children are poisoned by houseplants more often than by detergents and other chemicals.

* An Indian emperor was given four wives when he inherited the throne at the age of eight.

* Riverdance star Michael Flatley is also an accomplished concert flute player, a champion boxer and a chess master. He has been listed by the National Geographic Society as a 'Living Treasure'.

* Pablo Picasso has sold more works of art individually costing over $1 million than any other artist, with 211

THE WORLD AND ITS PEOPLE

Picasso pieces topping the million dollar mark, well ahead of the 168 Pierre-Auguste Renoir works.

- When there is no one else waiting to use a public phone, callers average 90 seconds' talking, but if someone is waiting, the callers average four minutes per call.

- Men more often dream about their male heroes, bosses, friends or role models than about women.

- Howard Hughes became so compulsive about germs that he used to spend hours swabbing his arms over and over again with rubbing alcohol.

- In 1949, Jack Wurm, an unemployed man, was aimlessly walking on a California beach when he came across a washed-up bottle containing this message: 'To avoid confusion, I leave my entire estate to the lucky person who finds this bottle and to my attorney, Barry Cohen, share and share alike. Daisy Alexander, June 20, 1937.' It was not a hoax and Mr Wurm received over $6 million from the Alexander estate.

- W C Fields used to open savings accounts everywhere he went. He put over £500,000 in 700 different banks but couldn't remember where many of his accounts were.

THE WORLD AND ITS PEOPLE

* Railroad worker Phineas P Gage was working with some dynamite that exploded unexpectedly and a metre-long iron bar weighing 13lb (6kg) went clear through his brain. He remained conscious, but was unable to see out of his left eye. After a while, his sight returned and he fully recovered.

* In November 1972, student skydiver Bob Hail jumped from his plane then discovered that both his main parachute and his back-up parachute had failed. He dropped 3,300 ft (1,006 m) at a rate of 80 mph (129 kph), and smashed into the ground face first. A few moments after landing, however, he got up and walked away with only minor injuries.

* Comedy team Abbott and Costello had an insurance policy to cover themselves financially in the event they had an argument with each other.

* A Japanese priest set a kimono on fire in Tokyo in 1657 because it carried bad luck. The flames spread until over 10,000 buildings were destroyed and 100,000 people died.

* Taxi drivers in London are required to pass a training test based on *The Blue Book*, with preparation for this test taking between two and four years. Of ten drivers who start, eight or nine drop out before completion.

—— **THE WORLD AND ITS PEOPLE** ——

- The most children born from the same mother, at one time, were decaplets. Born in Brazil, in 1946, eight girls and two boys were delivered.

- The most popular topic of public speakers is motivation at 23 per cent, followed by leadership at 17 per cent.

- One lady had her husband's ashes made into an egg timer so that, even in death, he can still 'help' in the kitchen.

- The most popular form of hair removal among women is shaving, with 70 per cent of women who remove hair doing so by this method.

- All pilots on international flights identify themselves in English, regardless of their country of origin.

- The disgraced Lord Jeffrey Archer once worked as a deckchair attendant during the holiday season in Weston-super-Mare in Somerset.

- Karl Marx rarely took a bath and suffered from boils most of his life.

- Early students of forensics hoped that by photographing the eyes of murder victims they would see a reflection of the murderer lingering in the victim's eyes.

THE WORLD AND ITS PEOPLE

- Some odour technicians in the perfume trade have the olfactory skill to distinguish 20,000 odours at 20 levels of intensity.

- Each morning more than a third of all adults hit their alarm clock's 'snooze' button an average of three times before they get up. Those most guilty of snatching some extra sleep are those in the 25–34 age bracket, at 57 per cent.

- Teenagers often have episodes of anger and negativity in which they slam doors and scream tirades, most of these lasting an average of 15 minutes.

- Adults spend an average of 16 times as many hours selecting clothes (145.6 hours a year) as they do on planning their retirement.

- Iraqi terrorist Khay Rahnajet, didn't pay enough postage on a letter bomb. It came back with 'return to sender' stamped on it. Forgetting it was the bomb; he opened it and was blown to bits.

- Peter the Great hated the Kremlin, where, as a child, he had witnessed the brutal torture and murder of his mother's family.

- The shortest human on record was Pauline Musters of the Netherlands. She measured 12 inches (30cm) at

THE WORLD AND ITS PEOPLE

her birth in 1876, and was 23 inches (58cm) tall with a weight of 9lb (4kg) at her death in 1885.

- Two German motorists each guiding their car at a snail's pace near the centre of the road, due to heavy fog near the town of Guetersloh, had an all-too-literal head-on collision. At the moment of impact their heads were both out of the windows when they smacked together. Both men were hospitalized with severe head injuries, though their cars weren't scratched.

- About 18 per cent of animal owners share their bed with their pets.

- Two animal rights protesters were protesting at the cruelty of sending pigs to a slaughterhouse in Bonn. Suddenly the pigs – all 2,000 of them – escaped through a broken fence and stampeded, trampling the two helpless protesters to death.

- Couples who diet while on holiday argue three times more often than those who don't; and those who don't diet have three times as many romantic interludes.

- Two out of every three women in the world are illiterate.

- In Britain, two women were killed in 1999 by lightning conducted through their under-wired bras.

THE WORLD AND ITS PEOPLE

* Women who snore are at an increased risk of high blood pressure and cardiovascular disease.

* Astronauts Neil Armstrong and Buzz Aldrin ate roast turkey from foil packets for their first meal on the moon.

* About 24 per cent of alcoholics die in accidents, falls, fires or suicides.

* US Army doctor D W Bliss had the unique role of attending to two US presidents after they were shot. In 1865, he was one of 16 doctors who tried to save Abraham Lincoln; in 1881, Bliss supervised the care of James Garfield.

* King John did not sign the Magna Carta in 1215, as he could not write his name. Instead he placed his seal on it.

* Notorious bootlegger Al Capone made £34,000,000 during Prohibition.

* One in ten people admit that they would buy an outfit intending to wear it once and return it.

* Only 29 per cent of married couples agree on most political issues.

THE WORLD AND ITS PEOPLE

- It is estimated that 74 billion human beings have been born and died in the last 500,000 years.

- Thirty-nine per cent of people admit that, as guests, they have snooped in their host's medicine cabinets.

- Trying to prevent ageing, Charlie Chaplin, Winston Churchill and Christian Dior all had injections of foetal lamb cells. The process failed.

- In a test of Russian psychic Djuna Davitashvili's powers, a computer randomly selected a San Francisco landmark for her to predict. However, not only had she managed to predict it correctly six hours before it made the selection, Djuna also gave an incredibly detailed description of the site, though she was 6,000 miles away in Moscow at the time.

- A psychology student in New York rented out her spare room to a carpenter in order to nag him constantly and study his reactions. After weeks of needling, he snapped and beat her repeatedly with an axe, leaving her mentally retarded.

- The average person receives eight birthday cards annually.

- More than 50 per cent of adults say that children should not be paid money for getting good grades in school.

THE WORLD AND ITS PEOPLE

* Robert Todd Lincoln, son of Abraham Lincoln, was present at the assassinations of three presidents: his father's, President Garfield's, and President McKinley's. After the last shooting, he refused ever to attend a state affair again.

* Leonardo da Vinci wrote notebook entries in backwards script, a trick that kept many of his observations from being widely known until decades after his death. It is believed that he was hiding his scientific ideas from the powerful Roman Catholic Church, whose teachings sometimes disagreed with what Da Vinci observed.

* Peter the Great of Russia was almost 7 ft (2 m) tall.

* On his way home to visit his parents, a Harvard student fell between two rail-road cars at the station in Jersey City, New Jersey, and was rescued by an actor on his way to visit a sister in Philadelphia. The student was Robert Lincoln, heading for 1600 Pennsylvania Avenue. The actor was Edwin Booth, the brother of the man who, a few weeks later, would murder the student's father.

* When a thief was surprised while burgling a house in Antwerp, Belgium, he fled out of the back door, clambered over a 9-ft (3 m) wall, dropped down and found himself in the city prison.

--------- **THE WORLD AND ITS PEOPLE** ---------

- A flower shop entrepreneur named O'Banion held the greatest ever funeral for a gangster in Chicago. The shop, at the corner of State and Superior Streets, was a front for O'Banion's bootlegging and hijacking operations. Ten thousand mourners were in attendance, and the most expensive wreath, costing $1,000, came from Al Capone, who had ordered that O'Banion be killed.

- When a thief was surprised while burgling a house in Antwerp, Belgium, he fled out of the back door, clambered over a 9-ft (3 m) wall, dropped down and found himself in the city prison.

- About 25 per cent of alcoholics are women.

- Levi Strauss was paid £3.35 in gold dust for his first pair of jeans.

- Adolf Hitler's third-grade school report remarked that he was 'bad tempered' and fancied himself as a leader.

- Robert Peary, discoverer of the North Pole, included a photograph of his nude mistress in a book about his travels.

- The first women flight attendants in 1930 were required to be unmarried, trained nurses, and weigh no more than 115lb (52kg).

THE WORLD AND ITS PEOPLE

* One of Napoleon's drinking cups was made from the skull of the famous Italian adventurer Cagliostro.

* When King Edward II was deposed from the throne in the 14th century, there were strict instructions that no one should harm him. To avoid leaving marks on his body when he was murdered, a deer horn was inserted into his rectum then a red-hot poker was placed inside it.

* Pamela Anderson is Canada's Centennial Baby, being the first baby born on the centennial anniversary of Canada's independence.

* A woman weighing less than 100lb (45kg) ran a fever of 114°F (45.5°C) and survived without brain damage or physiological after-effects.

* Seventy-five per cent of people who play the car radio while driving also sing along with it.

* While 1950s Hollywood actor Jack Palance was serving in the US Air Corps, during World War II, he was shot down in flames. Although Palance survived the crash, he received severe facial burns that required major plastic surgery.

* Three per cent of adults use toilet paper to clean a child's hands and/or face.

THE WORLD AND ITS PEOPLE

- Lincoln's assassin, John Wilkes Booth, was a famous actor who belonged to one of the most distinguished theatrical families of the 19th century. He received 100 fan letters a week.

- Orson Welles' ghost is said to haunt Sweet Lady Jane's restaurant in Los Angeles, where customers and employees have reported seeing Welles' caped apparition sitting at his favourite table, often accompanied by the scent of his favourite brandy and cigars.

- French chemist Louis Pasteur had an obsessive fear of dirt and infection. He would never shake hands, always carefully wipe his plate and glass before dining, and sneak a microscope into friends' houses under his coat and then examine the food they served to make sure it was safe from germs.

- Pope Innocent VIII drank the blood of three young donors thinking it would prevent ageing, and died shortly after.

- Three per cent of adults use toilet paper to clean a child's hands and/or face.

- Tsar Nicholas II considered the construction of an electric fence around Russia and expressed interest in building a bridge across the Bering Straits.

THE WORLD AND ITS PEOPLE

- Andrew Carnegie, one of the richest Americans ever, never carried cash. He was once sent off a London train because he did not have the fare.

- Purple is by far the favourite ink colour in pens used by bingo players.

- The average person spends 30 years being angry with a family member.

- Thirty per cent of all marriages occur because of friendship.

- Seventy per cent of women would rather have chocolate than sex.

- Before going into the music business, Frank Zappa was a greetings-card designer.

- University graduates live longer than people who did not complete school.

- Richard Wagner was known to dress in historical costumes while composing his operas.

- In 1981, near Pisa, 42-year-old Romolo Ribolla was so depressed about not being able to find a job, he sat in his kitchen with a gun in his hand threatening to

THE WORLD AND ITS PEOPLE

kill himself. His wife pleaded for him not to do it, and after about an hour he burst into tears and threw the gun to the floor. It went off and killed his wife.

- Humphrey Bogart's ashes are in an urn that also contains a small gold whistle. Lauren Bacall had the whistle inscribed, 'If you need anything, just whistle' – the words she spoke to him in their first film together, To Have and Have Not (1944).

- Of devout coffee drinkers, about 62 per cent of those who are 35 to 49 years of age say they become upset if they don't have a cup of coffee at their regular time. Only 50 per cent of those under age 35 become upset.

- Leonardo da Vinci was the first person to suggest using contact lenses for vision, in 1508.

- Napoleon's haemorrhoids contributed to his defeat at Waterloo, as they prevented him from surveying the battlefield on horseback.

- The lightest human adult ever was Lucia Xarate, from Mexico. At the age of 17, in 1889, she weighed 4lb 11oz (2.13kg).

- Isaac Newton's only recorded utterance while he was a Member of Parliament was a request to open the window.

THE WORLD AND ITS PEOPLE

- Sixty per cent of men spit in public.

- Men who are exposed to a lot of toxic chemicals, high heat and unusual pressures, such as jet pilots and deep-sea divers, are more prone to father girls than boys.

- Cleopatra tested the efficacy of her poisons by giving them to slaves.

- Only about 30 per cent of teenage males consistently apply sun-protection lotion compared with 46 per cent of female teens.

- American showman P T Barnum had his obituary published before his death.

- Lawrence of Arabia's ghost is said to be heard riding his motorbike near his house in Dorset, England, where he died in a motorbike accident.

- With 382,650 babies being born and 144,902 people dying, the world population increases by about 237,748 people a day.

- The spirit of silent-screen star Rudolph Valentino is said to haunt Paramount Studios in Hollywood, with the Sheik's shimmering spectre seen floating among old garments in the costume department.

THE WORLD AND ITS PEOPLE

- Gioacchino Antonio Rossini covered himself with blankets when he composed, and could only find inspiration by getting profoundly drunk.

- Alcoholics are twice as likely to confess a drinking problem to a computer than to a doctor.

- Henry Ford was obsessed with soy-beans. He once wore a suit and tie made from soy-based material, served a 16-course meal made entirely from soy-beans, and ordered many Ford auto parts to be made from soy-derived plastic.

- Albert Einstein reportedly had a huge crush on film star Marilyn Monroe.

- People who eat fresh fruit daily have 24 per cent fewer heart attacks and 32 per cent fewer strokes than those that don't.

- Marcel Proust worked in bed, and only in a soundproof room.

- King Charles VIII of France was obsessed with the idea of being poisoned. As his phobia grew, the monarch ate so little that he died of malnutrition.

- After the death of Alexander the Great, his remains were preserved in a huge crock of honey.

THE WORLD AND ITS PEOPLE

- In 1979, David Booth had a series of recurring nightmares about a plane crashing, and on 25 May 1979 his premonitions came true. Departing from Chicago's O'Hare Airport, a DC-10 flew half a mile then turned on its side and slammed into the ground, exploding on impact. All 272 people on board died. Booth's dreams began on 16 May, and continued for seven nights. Having seen the name of the airline in his dreams, Booth went and told the airport authorities. They took note of what he'd said, but claimed they couldn't just ground a whole airline, so flights went on as usual – and Booth's nightmares came true.

- Albert Einstein was reluctant to sign autographs, and charged people a dollar before signing anything. He gave the dollars to charity.

- It's been estimated that an opera singer burns an average of more than two calories per minute during a performance.

- Lady Diana Spencer was the first Englishwoman commoner in 300 years to marry an heir to the British throne.

- Elderly women are more likely to live alone than elderly men; 17 per cent of men 65 years or older are living alone, compared with 42 per cent of women the same age.

THE WORLD AND ITS PEOPLE

- As a boy, Charles Darwin was so enamoured with chemistry that his young friends nicknamed him 'Gas'.

- Paul Cézanne was 56 years old when he had his first one-man exhibition.

- Julius Caesar and Dostoyevsky were epileptics.

- Napoleon suffered from ailurophobia, the fear of cats.

- Viscount Horatio Nelson chose to be buried in St Paul's Cathedral in London rather than in the national shrine of Westminster Abbey because he had heard that Westminster was sinking into the Thames River.

- A fierce gust of wind blew 45-year-old Vittorio Luise's car into a river near Naples, Italy, in 1983. He managed to break a window, climb out and swim to shore, where a tree blew over and killed him.

- Six per cent of motorists said they sometimes leave their keys in the ignition of their unattended car.

- Napoleon Bonaparte was always depicted with his hand inside his jacket because he suffered from 'chronic nervous itching' and often scratched his stomach sores until they bled.

—— THE WORLD AND ITS PEOPLE ——

* The younger of Albert Einstein's two sons was a schizophrenic.

* More than 20 per cent of men and ten per cent of women say they've forgotten their wedding anniversary at least once.

* Catherine II of Russia kept her wigmaker in an iron cage in her bedroom for more than three years.

* One in three male motorists picks his nose while driving.

* The average housewife walks 10 miles (16km) a day around the house doing her chores. In addition, she walks nearly 4 miles (6km) and spends 25 hours a year making beds.

* Over 80 per cent of professional boxers have suffered brain damage.

* Emerson Moser, Crayola's senior crayon maker, revealed upon his retirement that he was blue-green colour-blind and couldn't see all the colours.

* Nearly half of all psychiatrists have been attacked by one of their patients.

* Xerxes, King of Persia, became so angry at the sea

THE WORLD AND ITS PEOPLE

when it destroyed his two bridges of boats during a storm, he had his army beat it with sticks.

- The Marquis de Sade was only 5 ft 3 in (about 1.6m) tall.

- Using a fine pen and a microscope, James Zaharee printed Abraham Lincoln's Gettysburg Address on a human hair less than 3 inches (8 cm) long.

- Men change their minds two to three times more than women. Women tend to take longer to make a decision, but once they do, they are more likely to stick to it.

- Believing that he could end his wife's incessant nagging by giving her a good scare, Hungarian Jake Fen built an elaborate harness to make it look as if he had hanged himself. When his wife came home and saw him, she fainted. Hearing a disturbance, a neighbour came over and, finding what she thought were two corpses, seized the opportunity to loot the place. As she was leaving the room, her arms laden, the outraged and suspended Mr Fen kicked her stoutly on the backside. This so surprised the lady that she dropped dead of a heart attack. Happily, Mr Fen was acquitted of manslaughter and he and his wife were reconciled.

—— THE WORLD AND ITS PEOPLE ——

* About 25 per cent of all adolescent and adult males never use deodorant.

* Only one person walked from the church to the cemetery with Mozart's coffin.

* Some publishers claim that science-fiction readers are better educated than the average book buyer.

* Jeff Bezos, founder of Amazon.com, takes at least one snapshot a day to chronicle his life.

* Women comprise less than 2 per cent of the total death row population in America's prisons.

* Martha Jane Burke, better known as Calamity Jane, was married 12 times.

* Telephone inventor Alexander Graham Bell had an odd habit of drinking his soup through a glass straw.

* Victoria Woodhall, the radical feminist who ran for the US presidency in 1872, feared that she would die if she went to bed in her old age. She spent the last four years of her life sitting in a chair.

* Jesse James would run back home to his mother following a crime. His obsessive love for his mother extended to him marrying a woman called Zerelda,

THE WORLD AND ITS PEOPLE

the same name as his mother and one that was
uncommon in the 1800s.

- In 1983, a woman was laid out in her coffin, presumed
  dead of heart disease. As mourners watched, she
  suddenly sat up. Her daughter dropped dead of fright.

- When he was a boy, Thomas Edison suffered a
  permanent hearing loss following a head injury. One
  of his ears was pulled roughly as he was being lifted
  aboard a moving train.

- While sleeping, one man in eight snores, and one in
  ten grinds his teeth.

- The most celebrated levitator in history was St Joseph
  of Copertino, a dim-witted monk who would
  allegedly soar into the air whenever he felt religious
  ecstasy. He had no control over his 'flights', which
  could last for minutes and were attested to by scores
  of witnesses, including the Pope.

- Mozart once composed a piano piece that required a
  player to use two hands and a nose in order to hit all
  the correct notes.

- When Napoleon wore black silk handkerchiefs around
  his neck during a battle, he always won. At Waterloo,
  he wore a white cravat and lost.

THE WORLD AND ITS PEOPLE

- The Roman emperor Nero married his male slave Scorus in a public ceremony.

- The shortest place names in the USA are 'L', a lake in Nebraska, 'T', a gulch in Colorado, 'D', a river in Oregon flowing from Devil's Lake to the Ocean, and 'Y', a city in Arkansas, each named after its shape.

- In Europe, 'E' is a river in Perthshire, Scotland; there are villages called 'Å' in Norway, Sweden and Denmark, and a 'Y' in France.

- The Pacific Caroline Islands has a place named 'U' and a peak in Hong Kong is called 'A'.

- Benjamin Franklin was first to suggest daylight saving.

- The most abundant metal in the Earth's crust is aluminium.

- It snowed in the Sahara Desert on 18 February 1979.

- Captain Cook was the first man to set foot on all continents except Antarctica.

- 200 million years ago, the Earth contained one land mass called Pangaea.

- It is illegal to swim in Central Park, New York.

THE WORLD AND ITS PEOPLE

- At the deepest point (11.034km), an iron ball would take more than an hour to sink to the ocean floor.

- The largest wave ever recorded was 85m high near the Japanese Island of Ishigaki in 1971.

- Antarctic means 'opposite the Arctic'.

- The largest iceberg recorded, in 1956, was 200 miles long and 60 miles wide, larger than the country of Belgium.

- The surface of the Dead Sea is 400m below the surface of the Mediterranean Sea, which is only 75km away.

- The country of Benin changed its name from Dahomey in 1975.

- The Nova Zemlya Glacier in the former USSR is over 400km long.

- Canada (9,970,610 sq km) is larger than China (9,596,961 sq km) which is larger than the USA (9,363,130 sq km).

- The coldest temperature ever recorded was -70°C in Siberia.

- The second largest US state in the 1950s was California.

—————— **THE WORLD AND ITS PEOPLE** ——————

- Maryland was named after Queen Henrietta Maria.

- The only country to register zero births in 1983 was the Vatican City.

- Florida first saw the cultivation of oranges in 1539.

- The world's largest National Park is Wood Buffalo National Park in Canada.

- The world's largest exporter of sugar is Cuba.

- There are no rivers in Saudi Arabia.

- England's Stonehenge is 1,500 years older than Rome's Colosseum.

- In 1896, Britain and Zanzibar were at war for 38 minutes.

- The Eskimo language has over 20 words to describe different kinds of snow.

- Numbering houses in London streets only began in 1764.

- More than 75 per cent of all the countries in the world are north of the equator.

THE WORLD AND ITS PEOPLE

- Less than one per cent of the Caribbean Islands are inhabited.

- Fulgurite is formed when lightning strikes sand.

- Mountains are formed by a process called orogeny.

- Obsidian, used by American Indians for tools, weapons and ornaments, is dark volcanic glass.

- Eighty-two per cent of the workers on the Panama Canal suffered from malaria.

- In May 1948, New Zealand's Mount Ruapehu and Mount Ngauruhoe both erupted simultaneously.

- The Incas and the Aztecs were able to function without the wheel.

- The tree on the Lebanese flag is a Cedar.

- Tokyo was once called Edo.

- The Atlantic Ocean covers the world's longest mountain range.

- In 1825, Upper Peru became Bolivia.

- New York City contains 920km of shoreline.

THE WORLD AND ITS PEOPLE

- There are three Great pyramids at Giza.

- The southwestern tip of the Isle of Man is called 'The Calf of Man'.

- The world's largest Delta was created by the River Ganges.

- The Scottish city Edinburgh is nicknamed 'Auld Reekie' meaning 'Old Smoky'.

- The inhabitants of Papua New Guinea speak about 700 languages (including localized dialects, which are known to change from village to village), approximately 15 per cent of the world's total.

- The world's first National Park was Yellowstone National Park.

- Sixty per cent of all US potato products originate in Idaho.

- The northernmost country claiming part of Antarctica is Norway.

- The 'DC' in Washington DC stands for District of Columbia.

- New York's Central Park opened in 1876.

THE WORLD AND ITS PEOPLE

- The inhabitants of Monaco are known as Monegasques.

- The East Alligator River in Australia's Northern Territory was misnamed. It contains crocodiles, not alligators.

- France contains the greatest length of paved roads.

- The city of Istanbul straddles two separate continents, Europe and Asia.

- Rio de Janeiro translates to 'River of January'.

- The furthest point from any ocean is in China.

- The percentage of the population that walks to work is higher in the state of Alaska that the rest of the United States.

- The busiest stretch of highway in the US is New York's George Washington Bridge.

- Ropesville, Lariat and Loop are all towns in Texas.

- Venetian blinds were invented in Japan.

- In Venice, Venetian blinds are known as 'Persian blinds'.

THE WORLD AND ITS PEOPLE

- If you head directly south from Detroit, the first foreign country you will enter is Canada.

- One in every three people in Israel uses a mobile phone.

- Sixty per cent of the country of Liechtenstein's GDP is generated from the sale of false teeth.

- In the US, 166,875,000,000 pieces of mail are delivered each year.

- Oklahoma is the US state with the highest population of Native Americans. It has no Indian Reservations.

- The Statue of Liberty's fingernails weigh about 100lb apiece.

- In Kenya, they don't drive on the right or left side of the street in particular, just on whichever side is smoother.

- The state of Maryland has no natural lakes.

- JELL-O [jelly] was declared the 'official state snack' of Utah in January 2001.

- Scandinavian folklore records that trolls only come out at night because sunlight would turn them to stone.

—— **THE WORLD AND ITS PEOPLE** ——

- 1,525,000,000 miles of telephone wire are strung across the Unites States.

- Wyoming Valley is so difficult to find because it is in Pennsylvania.

- After Canada and Mexico, Russia is the nearest neighbour to the United States. Siberia's easternmost point is just 56 miles from Alaska. In fact, in the middle of the Bering Strait, Russia's Big Diomede Island and the US's Little Diomede Island are only two miles apart.

- The parents of the groom pay for the weddings in Thailand.

- One US state no longer exists. In 1784, the US had a state called Franklin, named after Benjamin Franklin. But four years later, it was incorporated into Tennessee.

- In Tibet, there is actually a practice called 'polyandry' where many men, usually brothers, marry a single woman.

- The coastline around Lake Sakawea in North Dakota is longer than the California coastline along the Pacific Ocean.

- Brooklyn is the Dutch name for 'broken valley'.

--------- **THE WORLD AND ITS PEOPLE** ---------

- Danishes are called Vienna cakes in Denmark, and Spanish rice is unknown in Spain.

- Birkenhead Park was the inspiration for New York's Central Park as it was the world's first urban park.

- The city of Nottingham was the first city to have Braille signs in the UK.

- Minnesota has 99 lakes named Mud Lake.

- At the turn of the century, the New Brighton Tower (located atop the tower ballroom) was higher than the Blackpool Tower. The steel tower was taken down between 1919 and 1921.

- Fort Worth Texas was never a fort.

- Legend has it that, when Burmese women are making beer, they need to avoid having sex or the beer will be bitter.

- Kitsap County, Washington, was originally called Slaughter County, and the first hotel there was called the Slaughter House.

- Bagpipes, although identified with Scotland, are actually a very ancient instrument, introduced into the British Isles by the Romans.

THE WORLD AND ITS PEOPLE

* Saunas outnumber cars in Finland.

* Although Argentina's name means 'Land of Silver', there is actually very little silver there. It was misnamed by explorers who thought they saw veins of the metal there.

* The state of California raises the most turkeys in the US.

* America's first stock exchange was the Philadelphia Stock Exchange, established in 1791.

* Antarctica is visited by over 10,000 tourists a year.

* The Pony Express, one of the most famous chapters in US history, only lasted one year, from 1860 to 1861.

* There are four states where the first letter of the capital city is the same letter as the first letter of the state: Dover, Delaware; Honolulu, Hawaii; Indianapolis, Indiana; and Oklahoma City, Oklahoma.

* Andorra, a tiny country on the border between France and Spain, has the longest average lifespan: 83.49 years.

* Oregon has the most ghost towns of any state.

──── THE WORLD AND ITS PEOPLE ────

- Construction of the Notre Dame Cathedral in Strasbourg started in 1015, but it was not until 1439 that the spire was completed.

- There are more Rolls-Royces in Hong Kong than anywhere else in the world.

- Japan has 130 times more people per square mile than the state of Montana.

- The most expensive commercial real estate in the world is in Tokyo. The second most expensive is 57th Street in New York City.

- Mt. Everest grows about 4mm a year: the two tectonic plates of Asia and India, which collided millions of years ago to form the Himalayas, continue to press against each other, causing the Himalayan peaks to grow slightly each year.

THE ANIMAL
WORLD

THE ANIMAL WORLD

- The ant always falls over to its right side when intoxicated.

- Starfish don't have brains.

- Turtles can breathe through their bottoms.

- Fish have no eyelids, as their eyes do not close.

- Seahorses are the only fish in which the head forms a right angle with the body.

- The pheasant originated in China.

- The arctic fox often follows the polar bear, feeding on the abandoned carcass of its kill.

- The stomach of a giraffe has four chambers.

- Baby squirrels are called kittens.

- A racoon appears to wash its food before eating it.

- The jaguar is the largest of the American big cats.

- The roadrunner is a member of the cuckoo family.

- The elephant is the only mammal able to kneel on all fours.

THE ANIMAL WORLD

- The nesting site of penguins is called a rookery.

- Desert-living gerbils never need to drink, as they obtain all the moisture they need from the overnight dew on their food.

- The elephant is the only mammal able to kneel on all fours.

- The feet of the puffin are red in summer and yellow in winter.

- Coyotes mate for life.

- A female walrus is called a cow.

- A male guinea pig is called a boar.

- The Falabella is the world's smallest breed of horse.

- Turkish van cats have a natural liking for water.

- A female mouse is called a doe.

- The dingo is the only carnivore native to Australia.

- In China the hedgehog is considered sacred.

- The Chinese crested dog is hairless.

THE ANIMAL WORLD

- Dolphins are the only species, barring humans, which have sex for pleasure.

- The anal glands of the African civet cat secrete a strong-smelling substance used in perfume manufacture.

- The part of a snail's body that remains inside the shell is called a mantle.

- The wolverine is sometimes known as the Glutton due to its enormous appetite.

- Lobsters are blue when alive and red when cooked.

- In ancient Canadian legend, the turtle was the oldest and wisest creature on earth before man came to the Americas.

- Monkeys fling faeces at each other when agitated.

- Ravens can learn to open a box to get a treat, and then teach others to do the same.

- Cockroaches can find their way in a dark room by dragging one antenna against the wall.

- A Brazilian MP has drawn up a new law to ban people from giving their pets 'human' names.

THE ANIMAL WORLD

- Finches practise songs in their sleep.

- Crickets hear through their knees.

- A Chinese man has trained his pet dog to walk on its hind legs for up to five miles.

- The heart of a blue whale only beats nine times a minute.

- Baboons and chimps dig for clean water when the surface water is polluted. Chimps even use sticks as digging tools.

- A weddell seal can hold its breath for seven hours.

- Conservation workers introduced an exercise regime for giant pandas in Chinese zoos because they were too fat to mate.

- Turkeys were first brought to Britain in 1526 by Yorkshireman William Strickland, who sold six, acquired from American Indians, for sixpence each, in Bristol.

- The Basenji, an African dog, is the only dog that does not bark.

- One in three dog owners say they have talked to their pets on the phone.

THE ANIMAL WORLD

* A Belgian company is producing ice cream specifically for dogs.

* A course teaching people how to perform the kiss of life on dogs has been launched in Chile.

* A church in Connecticut is giving Holy Communion to pets and offering them special worship services.

* Chimps live in groups that each has its own culture.

* The average American dog will cost its owner £9,000 in its lifetime.

* Only male turkeys gobble. Females make a clicking sound.

* The average pregnancy of an Indian elephant lasts 650 days.

* A geriatric dwarf mouse that lived at a university in Michigan became the world's oldest after celebrating his fourth birthday.

* A Swiss woman is offering lessons on how to talk with animals for £360 a time.

* Cows drink anywhere from 25 to 50 gallons of water each day.

THE ANIMAL WORLD

- The red kangaroo can produce two different types of milk at the same time from adjacent teats to feed both younger and older offspring.

- Firefighters in Florida are carrying oxygen masks for cats, dogs and even hamsters to help save pets suffering from smoke inhalation.

- A German basset hound with the longest dog ears in the world has had them insured for £30,000.

- Hard rock music makes termites chew through wood at twice their usual speed.

- Red squirrels are being given rope bridges to help them cross busy roads in Formby, Merseyside.

- A Michigan woman who runs a boutique for pets is stocking a special range of Halloween costumes for dogs.

- Domestic turkeys cannot fly because of their size and breeding but, in the wild, they can fly at up to 50mph over short distances and run at 20mph.

- The Giant African cricket enjoys eating human hair.

- Ninety-five per cent of the creatures on earth are smaller than a chicken egg.

THE ANIMAL WORLD

- The first known 'zeedonks' were the result of an accidental mating between a male Chapman's zebra and a female black ass (donkey) at Colchester Zoo in 1983.

- Ziggy, the largest and oldest elephant ever in captivity, was taught to play 'Yes, Sir, that's my baby' on the harmonica.

- The Antarctic notothenia fish has a protein in its blood that acts like antifreeze and stops the fish freezing in icy sea.

- Goat's eyes have rectangular pupils.

- The megalodon shark became extinct about 1.6 million years ago. Marine biologists have estimated the megalodon shark was double the size and weight of today's great white shark.

- Catfish are the only animals that naturally have an odd number of whiskers.

- Sheep can detect other sheep faces in the way that humans do. Researchers claim they can remember up to 50 sheep faces.

- Male bats have the highest rate of homosexuality of any mammal.

THE ANIMAL WORLD

- When mating, a hummingbird's wings beat 200 times a second.

- A cow gives nearly 200,000 glasses of milk in her lifetime.

- The average American bald eagle weighs about 9lb.

- Robins eat three miles of earthworms in a year.

- The beautiful Cone Shell Molluscs are just 2in long but have a deadly poison-filled harpoon-like tooth that spears their prey, injecting it with lethal toxins.

- A study has concluded that if a woodchuck could chuck wood it could chuck about 700lb.

- Baby elephants can drink over 80 litres of milk a day.

- An experiment in Canada determined that chickens lay most eggs when pop music is played.

- A cow has four stomachs.

- Two dogs were hanged for witchcraft during the Salem witch trials.

- All polar bears are left-handed.

THE ANIMAL WORLD

- A mother shark can give birth to as many as 70 baby sharks per litter.

- The top speed of a pigeon in flight is 90mph.

- An adult crocodile can go two years without eating.

- Emus cannot walk backwards.

- The oldest bird on record was Cocky, a cockatoo, who died in London Zoo at the age of 82.

- A chicken's top speed is 9mph.

- Both gorillas and housecats purr.

- Ostriches can run faster than horses and the males can roar like lions.

- Squirrels cannot see the colour red.

- If birds could sweat, they wouldn't be able to fly.

- The decapitated jaws of a snapping turtle can keep snapping for about a day.

- Jackrabbits got their name because their ears look like a donkey's (Jackass).

———— THE ANIMAL WORLD ————

- Sheep can survive up to two weeks buried in snowdrifts.

- The last animal in the dictionary is the zyzzyva, a tropical American weevil.

- The giraffe has the highest blood pressure of any animal.

- Armadillos can catch malaria.

- Baboons cannot throw overhand.

- Lions are the only cats that live in packs.

- To get a gallon of milk, it takes about 345 squirts from a cow's udder.

- A warthog has only four warts, all of which are on its head.

- The penalty for stealing a rabbit in 19th century England was seven years in prison.

- Even bloodhounds cannot smell the difference between identical twins.

- Cows and cats both get hairballs.

THE ANIMAL WORLD

* Camels are born without humps.

* Anteaters can flick their tongues 160 times a minute.

* Chimpanzees will hunt ducks if given the opportunity.

* Black sheep have a better sense of smell than white sheep.

* Whales and buffalos both stampede.

* A hibernating bear can go as long as six months without a toilet break.

* A bat can eat up to 1,000 insects per hour.

* Turkeys can reproduce without having sex. It's called parthenogenesis.

* Snakes have two sex organs.

* Male rhesus monkeys often hang from tree branches by their amazing prehensile penises.

* The English sparrow is not a sparrow and it comes from Africa, not England.

* One humped camels run faster than two humped camels.

THE ANIMAL WORLD

- A blue whale's testicles are the size of a family car.

- Skunks can accurately spray their fluid up to 10ft.

- Sheep snore.

- To maintain a chimpanzee in captivity for 60 years it would cost an estimated £200,000.

- An ant can detect movement through 5cm of earth.

- Lobsters like to eat lobster.

- The only time a turkey whistles is when it is panicking.

- A group of jellyfish is called a 'smack'.

- Camel hairbrushes are made from squirrel hair.

- Sloths sneeze slowly. They also give birth upside down slowly.

- A hippo can open its mouth wide enough to fit a 4ft child inside.

- A parrot that shouts 'Show us your t*ts' at women on board a Royal Navy ship is always taken ashore during royal visits.

THE ANIMAL WORLD

* The Andrex puppy has met a waxwork copy of itself at Madame Tussauds in London.

* A dog just over 7in long and weighing 27oz has been officially confirmed as the world's smallest living dog.

* Deer urine can turn blue when they become dehydrated in the winter.

* Cash-strapped bosses at Moscow Zoo are renting out animals for the day in a bid to boost funds.

* The London Zoo employs an 'entertainment director' for the animals.

* A German pot-bellied pig called Berta has passed an audition to star in an opera.

* A lonely and confused male flamingo has caused a stir at a Gloucestershire nature reserve by trying to incubate a pebble.

* Hook-tip moth caterpillars defend their territories by drumming out warnings.

* Chinese scientists are appealing to the Guinness Book of Records to recognize a 900kg pig which died earlier this month as the biggest ever porker.

THE ANIMAL WORLD

- Fish are much brainier than previously thought – and can learn quicker than dogs.

- A Chilean doctor is using alternative medicines to treat pets and their owners for mental conditions including depression.

- A Brazilian vet is offering plastic surgery and botox injections for pampered pets.

- Two polar bears have turned green at Singapore Zoo as a result of algae growing in their hair.

- The world's first restaurant for cats is about to open in New York.

- Moscow Zoo keepers are to fit televisions in the cages of their gorillas in a bid to make them 'think more'.

- Rescuers did a microchip scan on a stray cat that was wandering the streets of Oxford and found it had been registered in the USA.

- Scientists say they want to send 15 mice into space to help prepare for possible human missions to Mars.

- A chicken farm in Germany is claiming a new world record after a hen laid a giant egg weighing 6oz.

THE ANIMAL WORLD

* Conveners of an Australian agricultural show are so concerned at the rise of cosmetic surgery among cattle breeders that they have issued new rules forbidding it.

* A German businessman who trained his dog to do the Hitler salute was given 13 months' probation.

* Croat farmers staged a beauty contest for goats in a bid to publicize the fact that traditional goat farming is dying out.

* A Catholic priest has started holding masses for pets in the German city of Cologne.

* A German zoo has scrapped plans to break up homosexual penguin couples following protests from gay-rights groups.

* A Brazilian seaside town has built two toilets for dogs to try to stop pets fouling the beach.

* If an entire family is overweight, it is likely that the dog will be too.

* Homing pigeons are becoming increasingly lost because of mobile-phone masts, say racing enthusiasts.

* A Japanese researcher claims dogs can sense earthquakes before they happen.

--------------- **THE ANIMAL WORLD** ---------------

* A Brazilian man who bought a 6ft boa constrictor online faces charges after it was posted to him in a paper box.

* Ptarmigans help their chicks go out into the world by teaching them which plants are more nutritious.

* A goldfish believed to be the world's oldest in captivity is still swimming strongly – 44 years after it was won at a fairground.

* A marathon runner became the first human to win a horse-against-man race in the event's 25-year history.

* A Brazilian company is launching a chewing gum for dogs.

* The Amazon River is home to the world's only nut- and seed-eating fish.

* An elderly elephant in Thailand has been given a new lease of life after being fitted with custom-made dentures.

* New Zealand has abandoned plans for a flatulence tax on animals in the face of fierce opposition from farmers.

* A sea-hare can lay 40,000 eggs in one minute.

---------------- **THE ANIMAL WORLD** ----------------

- A three-year-old boxer is being dubbed the most allergic dog in the UK after being found to suffer severe allergies to grass, flowers, cotton, lamb, soya, white fish and most materials used in bedding.

- China has built a biscuit factory to cater exclusively for the nutritional needs of its captive giant pandas.

- British dog owners spend an average of £981 a year on their animals while cat owners shell out £476, researchers have concluded.

- A gozzard is a person who owns geese.

- A zoo in Russia is claiming a world record after a hippopotamus named Mary gave birth for the 24th time at the age of 47.

- The UK's first canine classroom assistant has been appointed to a school in Derbyshire.

- Armadillos get an average of 18.5 hours of sleep per day.

- After giving postmen training in dog psychology, the German Post Office claims attacks on them have been cut by 80 per cent.

- A gym exclusively for dogs has opened in Santiago, Chile.

THE ANIMAL WORLD

- When snakes are born with two heads, they fight each other for food.

- A zoo in India is serving brandy to bears to keep them warm in winter.

- Chocolate affects a dog's heart and nervous system; a few ounces are enough to kill a small dog.

- A flock of swallows have delayed more than 100 flights after taking over a runway at Beijing International Airport.

- A Canadian scientist claims to have proven that the world's most expensive coffee really does taste better because the beans it is produced from have been eaten and defecated by a wild cat.

- Former First Division footballer, ex-Crystal Palace and Middlesbrough defender Craig Harrison says he had dozens of dogs on a waiting list after opening a hydrotherapy pool for overweight hounds.

- The UK faces an invasion of parakeets, with the wild population likely to exceed 100,000 in a decade, experts are warning.

- Male and female rats may have sex twenty times a day.

THE ANIMAL WORLD

- Rabbits love liquorice.

- An Essex man believes he has the biggest cockerel in Britain – a 2ft monster called Melvin.

- Farm animals have been banned from council flats in Kiev after a survey found residents were keeping more than 3,000 pigs, 500 cows and 1,000 goats.

- Mosquitoes have teeth.

- Penguins can jump as high as 6 feet in the air.

- Scottish scientists have become the first in the world to breed a golden eagle chick from frozen sperm.

- A snake measuring more than 19ft long and weighing almost 16 stone was found inside a factory in Brazil.

- Polar bears' fur is not white, it's clear. Polar bear skin is actually black. Their hair is hollow and acts like fibre optics, directing sunlight to warm their skin.

- Italy has put border collies, corgis and St Bernards on a dangerous-dogs list that bans children and criminals from owning them.

- A Japanese department store cashed in on a pet boom by offering a special £145 New Year meal for dogs.

THE ANIMAL WORLD

- Princess Tamara Borbon and her five-year-old Yorkshire terrier Bugsy were top of the bill at a canine fashion show at Harrods.

- Thailand's prime minister has banned vagrant elephants from the streets of Bangkok in an effort to ease traffic chaos.

- Canada's entry in the world's most prestigious international art exhibition featured a video filmed by a Jack Russell puppy called Stanley.

- Trained hawks employed to keep pigeons from making a mess on visitors in a Manhattan park were grounded in August 2003 because one of the birds mistook a Chihuahua for its lunch.

- A British homing pigeon has become a star in the US after completing a 3,321-mile journey across the Atlantic.

- Giant rats have been trained to sniff out landmines in Tanzania.

- Most marine fish can survive in a tank filled with human blood.

- Most cows give more milk when they listen to music.

THE ANIMAL WORLD

- Poodles, dachshunds and Chihuahuas have strutted down the catwalk at a fashion show organized by a Tokyo department store.

- Some dogs can predict when a child will have an epileptic seizure, and even protect the child from injury. They're not trained to do this, but simply learn to respond after observing at least one attack.

- Rats destroy an estimated third of the world's food supply each year.

- The United States has never lost a war in which mules were used.

- International animal-rights groups are urged Thailand to ban orang-utan kickboxing fights being staged at a Bangkok safari park.

- A chain of gyms in the US has started offering yoga classes for dogs.

- Armadillos breed in July, but get pregnant in November after delaying implantation. This allows the young to be born during the spring when there is an abundance of food.

- The world's smallest winged insect is the Tanzanian parasitic wasp. It's smaller than the eye of a housefly.

THE ANIMAL WORLD

- The world's only robotic swimming shark is moving into an aquarium with four live sharks. The 2m-long creature called Roboshark2 will spend up to three years alongside sand tiger sharks at the National Marine Aquarium in Plymouth.

- In Tokyo, they sell wigs for dogs.

- Tarantulas can go up to two years without eating or drinking. Sea turtles can go up to 35 years without eating or drinking.

- Manatees possess vocal chords that give them the ability to speak like humans, but they don't do so because they have no ears with which to hear the sound.

- Homing pigeons use roads where possible to help find their way home.

- Authorities in New Delhi are planning to export cow dung and urine to the United States. The dung will be processed into compost while the urine will be converted into a biopesticide.

- Engineers in the East Midlands are fitting rubber boots to the top of pylons to save squirrels from electrocution and keep the power flowing.

ARTS AND ENTERTAINMENT

——— ARTS AND ENTERTAINMENT ———

* When Marlon Brando signed into hotels, he used the name Lord Greystoke, aka Tarzan.

* Batman actor Michael Keaton's real name is Michael Douglas.

* The largest number of fatalities on a film set is 40, occurring during the making of *The Sword of Tipu Sultan* (1989).

* Norma Talmadge made the first footprints in the Hollywood Walk of Fame outside Grauman's Chinese Theater in May 1927.

* *Some Like it Hot* (1959) was originally called 'Not Tonight, Josephine'.

* One of the actors in *Reservoir Dogs* (1992), Eddie Bunker (Mr Blue), was a real former criminal and was once on the FBI's Ten Most Wanted list.

* Michael Caine, Sean Connery, Steve McQueen, Cher and Tom Cruise never finished school.

* Brad Pitt once worked as a chicken for the El Pollo Loco restaurant chain.

* Marni Nixon provided the singing voice for Audrey Hepburn's character in *My Fair Lady* (1964).

ARTS AND ENTERTAINMENT

- Screen 6 at Atlanta's CNN Center has been showing *Gone with the Wind* twice a day, 365 times a year since the film's release in 1939.

- Elizabeth Taylor and Richard Burton first married in Canada in 1964, and then again in Botswana in 1975.

- The first film to show the sex act was *Extase* in 1932.

- The longest ever interval between an original film and its sequel is 46 years – between *The Wizard of Oz* and *Return to Oz*.

- Since 1989, to avoid offending losers, Oscar presenters say, 'And the Oscar goes to…' instead of 'And the winner is…'

- Darth Vader has advertised Duracell batteries.

- Charlie Chaplin first spoke on film in *The Great Dictator* (1940).

- James Dean recorded an album called Jungle Rhythm.

- Oliver Reed was once a bouncer for a strip club.

- Robert Duvall's character in *Apocalypse Now* (1979), Colonel Kilgore, was originally called Colonel Kharnage.

ARTS AND ENTERTAINMENT

- Bob Hope hosted the Academy Awards a record 16 times.

- As well as the handprints and footprints outside Grauman's Chinese Theater in Hollywood, you'll also find casts of Groucho Marx's cigar, Betty Grable's legs, Jimmy Durante's nose, Trigger's hooves, Harold Lloyd's glasses and Whoopi Goldberg's braids.

- Between 1990 and 1995, Holocaust films won four out of five Best Documentary Oscars.

- The Hollywood sign originally read 'Hollywoodland'.

- *Star Wars* character Yoda was originally called The Critter.

- John Wayne made an album entitled *America, Why I Love Her*.

- In *Superman*, when Superman discovers Lois Lane's body he lets out a scream, revealing his tooth fillings. Not very in keeping with his invincible image.

- Tom Selleck was originally cast as Indiana Jones.

- Meryl Streep, Dustin Hoffman, Gene Hackman and Burt Lancaster all started out as waiting staff.

—— **ARTS AND ENTERTAINMENT** ——

- Bruce Willis recently played with his band at the opening of a branch of Krispy Kreme Doughnuts.

- Goldie Hawn and Kurt Russell had a car stolen from their drive and didn't notice for three days.

- Sergeant Bilko's first name is Ernest.

- Paramount is the only major studio still based in Hollywood.

- After breaking up with his fiancée Winona Ryder, Johnny Depp had his tattoo 'Winona Forever' changed to 'Wino Forever'.

- Mickey Rooney's real name is Joe Yule Jnr.

- Bix Beiderbecke was the first white jazz musician.

- The melody of 'Twinkle, Twinkle Little Star' was composed by Mozart.

- The real name of *Batman* villain The Penguin is Oswald Chesterfield Cobblepot.

- A total of 364 gifts are given by the lover in 'The Twelve Days of Christmas' song.

- Sting's real name is Gordon Sumner.

ARTS AND ENTERTAINMENT

- Contralto is the lowest female singing voice.

- Engelbert Humperdinck's real name is Arnold Dorsey.

- Hank Williams was known as the 'Drifting Cowboy'.

- Kazatsky is a Russian folk dance characterized by a step in which a squatting dancer kicks out each leg alternately to the front.

- The taboo against whistling backstage comes from the pre-electricity era, when a whistle was the signal for the curtains and the scenery to drop. An unexpected whistle could cause an unexpected scene change.

- 'The Star-Spangled Banner' is ranked the most difficult national anthem to sing.

- The Writers' Guild of America Registration Office states that approximately 20,000 movie scripts are registered with the Guild each year and that, of these, less than one per cent are picked up by a studio and made into a film.

  Roger Moore is the only English actor to have played the role of James Bond. Sean Connery is Scottish, George Lazenby is Australian, Timothy Dalton is Welsh and Pierce Brosnan is Irish.

——— ARTS AND ENTERTAINMENT ———

* The names of the six Gummi bears are Gruffi, Cubbi, Tummi, Zummi, Sunni and Grammi.

* Whistler's best-known painting, often called Whistler's Mother, is actually titled Arrangement in Grey and Black: The Artist's Mother.

* The names of Popeye's four nephews are Pipeye, Peepeye, Pupeye and Poopeye.

* The Pac Man video arcade game featured coloured ghosts named Inky, Blinky, Pinky and Clyde.

* The Marlboro Man has appeared in more advertisements than any ad figure in history.

* The Hitchcock film *North by Northwest* (1959) takes its name from a Hamlet quote: 'I am but mad north-northwest.'

* Elizabeth Hurley checks into hotels under the name Rebecca de Winter.

* *Braveheart* (1995) director/producer Mel Gibson was investigated by RSPCA inspectors, who refused to believe the horses on the film weren't real but mechanical.

* An Oscar statuette is 34.3 cm tall.

ARTS AND ENTERTAINMENT

- On the set of *The Usual Suspects* (1995), Kevin Spacey glued his fingers together to keep his left hand consistently paralysed.

- Jane Seymour's real name is Joyce Penelope Wilhelmina Frankenberg.

- Hollywood actor Tony Curtis is great friends with Harrods owner Mohammed Al Fayed.

- The Roosevelt Hotel, in Hollywood, is apparently haunted by the ghost of Marilyn Monroe.

- Thora Birch, the actress who played Janie in *American Beauty* (1999), was only 17 during filming and so her nude scene had to be filmed in the presence of her parents and child labour representatives.

- Doris Day's dog was named after the beer Heineken.

- The Oscar award ceremony has never been cancelled.

- Both Richard Burton and Peter O'Toole have been Oscar nominated a record seven times without winning.

- Disney Studios has the record for the biggest global box-office year of all time, grossing over $3 billion in 2003.

——— ARTS AND ENTERTAINMENT ———

- Marilyn Monroe's ex-husband Jo DiMaggio had fresh roses delivered to her crypt three times a week for 20 years after her death.

- The real names of Dean Martin and Jerry Lewis were Dino Paul Croccetti and Jerome Levitch.

- 'Her virtue was that she said what she thought, her vice that what she thought didn't amount to much.' Peter Ustinov on Hollywood gossip columnist Hedda Hopper.

- A few witty remarks from comedienne actress Mae West:

  'Too much of a good thing can be wonderful.'

  'When I'm good I'm very good, but when I'm bad I'm better.'

  'There are no good girls gone wrong, just bad girls found out.'

  'When choosing between two evils, I always like to pick the one I've never tried before.'

- Inscription on Rodney Dangerfield's tombstone: 'There goes the neighbourhood.'

ARTS AND ENTERTAINMENT

- The most copied noses in Hollywood are those of Heather Locklear, Nicole Kidman and Catherine Zeta Jones.

- The longest film title was *Night of the Day of the Dawn of the Son of the Bride of the Return of the Revenge of the Terror of the Attack of the Evil, Mutant, Alien, Flesh Eating, Hellbound, Zombified Living Dead Part 2: In Shocking 2-D* released in 1991.

- Pete the Pup, a pit-bull mix that appeared in the *Our Gang* shorts, had a fresh circle drawn around his right eye before every shoot.

- Only 3 dogs have a star in the Hollywood Walk of Fame: Strongheart, Rin Tin Tin and Lassie.

- Cary Grant had been offered the role of James Bond, 007, and refused it before the producers offered it to Sean Connery.

- Marilyn Monroe had six toes on one foot.

- Actor Bill Murray doesn't have a publicist or an agent.

- During *The Empire Strikes Back's* famous asteroid scene, one of the deadly hurling asteroids is actually a potato.

───── ARTS AND ENTERTAINMENT ─────

- Rocker Ozzy Osbourne has had two smiley face tattoos etched on his kneecaps so he can talk to them when he's feeling lonely.

- Oasis singer Liam Gallagher has received the top prize in Nuts magazine's 'man boobs' awards.

- The sound effect for the light sabres in *Star Wars* was recorded by moving a microphone next to a television set.

- In 1979, Oscar-winning actress Shirley MacLaine used the podium to cheer up her sibling, Warren Beatty, who had lost out for *Heaven Can Wait*. 'I want to use this opportunity to say how proud I am of my little brother. Just imagine what you could accomplish if you tried celibacy!' He was not amused.

- A low-cut gown worn by Elizabeth Taylor in 1969 fetched £98,000 at auction.

- The youngest actor to win an Oscar was 29-year-old Adrien Brody in 2003 for *The Pianist*. Shirley Temple is the youngest actress. She won a special award in 1934 aged six.

- The song 'When Irish Eyes Are Smiling' was written by George Graff, who was German and was never in Ireland in his life.

ARTS AND ENTERTAINMENT

- Talk-show queen Oprah Winfrey and legendary singer Elvis Presley are distant cousins.

- The estates of 22 dead celebrities earned over £2.6 million in 2004. These celebrities include Elvis Presley, Dr Seuss, Charles Schulz, J R R Tolkien and John Lennon.

- CBS's fine for Janet Jackson's 'wardrobe malfunction' in the 2004 Super Bowl show was £286,000. This could be paid with only 7.5 seconds of commercial time during the same Super Bowl telecast.

- *Kill Bill* star Vivica A Fox ruined a diamond-encrusted dress worth $1.5 million with red wine.

- In 1938, Walt Disney won one full-sized Oscar and seven miniature Oscars for his classic *Snow White and the Seven Dwarfs*.

- Actor Gary Lucy thought he had paid £6,000 for one of Paul Weller's guitars at an auction, but got rugs belonging to Madonna instead.

- Nicole Kidman says when she was younger she used to pray she would be turned into a witch.

- Al Gore's roommate in college (Harvard, class of 1969) was Tommy Lee Jones.

——— ARTS AND ENTERTAINMENT ———

- The trucking company Elvis Presley worked at as a young man was owned by Frank Sinatra.

- Lenny Kravitz says he's happy Courtney Love is his neighbour – because she runs around naked.

- Britney Spears has more hate websites than Saddam Hussein.

- Calvin Klein model-turned-actor Travis Fimmel had to audition nine times before landing the title role in the new TV series *Tarzan*.

- Three Oscars have been refused by winners, including Marlon Brando in 1972, who rejected his second Oscar for *The Godfather*.

- The Strokes star Nikolai Fraiture once shamed his dad when he was caught trying to steal a Luke Skywalker doll from the Macy's store where his father worked as a security guard.

- Actress Rosie O'Donnell's lover Kelli Carpenter has founded a new travel company that helps gay and lesbian couples seek out the perfect getaway. R Family Vacations will specialize in gay cruises.

- The first Oscar went to Emil Jannings in 1929 for Best Actor. He didn't turn up for it.

ARTS AND ENTERTAINMENT

- US singer Shania Twain has started the day off the same way for the past ten years – with a fruit smoothie made with grapes and ginger.

- Pop hunk Justin Timberlake's links with McDonald's have paid off for the fast-food chain – profits are up 12 per cent since the *NSYNC star started endorsing the company by letting them use his 'I'm Lovin' It' tune for TV commercials.

- Posh frocks at the Oscars can mean huge publicity for designers. Valentino estimated that *Erin Brockovich* star Julia Roberts's appearance in one of his designs generated some £13 million worth of publicity.

- Jet-setting pop svengali Simon Fuller, creator of Pop Idol, spent £9 million on two aeroplanes and a helicopter because he was sick of flying 90,000 miles a year on commercial airlines.

- Hollywood veteran Jack Nicholson became addicted to baked beans on toast after discovering the snack when serving it to his son, Raymond.

- Malnourished magician David Blaine's first public meal after his self-imposed 44-day incarceration in a plastic box was a plate of chicken satay at Mr Chow's restaurant in Knightsbridge, London. He followed this with a big helping of dessert.

ARTS AND ENTERTAINMENT

- Former basketball ace Dennis Rodman claims the police have visited his Newport Beach, California, home over 80 times because of noise complaints.

- The first Oscar went to Emil Jannings in 1929 for Best Actor. He didn't turn up for it.

- Dennis Rodman claims he's pierced his penis three times.

- The Strokes star Julian Casablancas doesn't own a mobile phone, a computer or a watch.

- During a one-day shopping spree in Japan, US rapper Lil Kim spent £25,000 on clothes – and Barbie dolls.

- Hollywood stars Demi Moore and Ashton Kutcher spent the Halloween of 2003 dressed as rival supercouple Jennifer Lopez and Ben Affleck.

- Model-turned-actress Jerry Hall has appeared on stage 536 times in plays.

- It takes 12 people 20 hours to make one Oscar statuette.

- Indie rockers Coldplay like to keep in touch with their family and friends when they're touring – their backstage requirements include eight 'stamped, local postcards'.

ARTS AND ENTERTAINMENT

- Disney's *The Lion King* has become the most successful re-release ever, after three million copies of the new DVD sold in its first two days on release.

- Rocker Sting is *Titanic* star Leonardo DiCaprio's next-door neighbour in Malibu, California.

- Dustin Hoffman had to pass up the chance of appearing in a jury for the first time because he had to publicize his film *Runaway Jury*, in which he plays a lawyer.

- Friends star Courtney Cox is scared of dogs – unless they're her own. The actress owns three pooches.

- Pop star Jessica Simpson used to keep photographs of missing children under her pillow and pray for them every night when she was a teenager. She also tried to adopt a Mexican baby found in a dumpster when she was 16.

- Ex-pop couple Jessica Simpson and Nick Lachey had a television mounted in their shower.

- When Orson Welles won the Screenplay Oscar for his classic *Citizen Kane* in 1941, it wasn't a popular choice. The audience booed.

- *American Idol* star Clay Aiken is allergic to mushrooms, shellfish, chocolate, mint and coffee.

—————— **ARTS AND ENTERTAINMENT** ——————

- There was havoc on the shoot for Atomic Kitten video 'Ladies Night' – the British trio hired famous drag queen Lily Savage, real name Paul O'Grady, to star, but Savage stormed out when he discovered he was to be appearing alongside a troop of unknown female impersonators.

- Gravel-voiced singer Macy Gray has puffer fish pets named Justin Timberlake, Muhammad Ali and R Kelly.

- Rap mogul Sean 'P Diddy' Combs spends £625 on each of his haircuts. His personal barber sketches out styles before even touching Diddy's dome.

- Bad-boy rapper Eminem's two favourite places to tour are Amsterdam, The Netherlands, because of its liberal laws, and London, England, because of its food.

- Actress Gwyneth Paltrow is studying German, as she endeavours to conquer European languages. She's already fluent in Spanish, Italian and French.

- Super-rich movie beauty Cameron Diaz recently bought a £1.25 Californian lottery ticket – and won £3,125.

- Oscar winner Holly Hunter used to be a poultry judge in her native Georgia.

ARTS AND ENTERTAINMENT

- Austin Powers creator Mike Myers has two streets named after him in his native Toronto, Canada.

- Crooner Harry Connick Jr. quit smoking when his idol Mel Torme told him he'd never speak to him again until he was nicotine free.

- At £150 for just two ounces, Sex and the City's Sarah Jessica Parker's SJJL moisturizer contains gold and silver essence.

- Destiny's Child singer Kelly Rowland is so turned off by the cuisine whenever she's in Britain that she will only eat at the country's Caribbean restaurants and posh eatery Nobu.

- Notting Hill star Julia Roberts once had her own scent created for the Oscars. It cost £4,000 a litre.

- Friends star Jennifer Aniston ate the same lunch – consisting of lettuce, garbanzo beans, turkey and lemon dressing – for nine years.

- Hollywood actor Brad Pitt has topped a survey conducted by American condom makers Trojan as the celebrity women think is most well endowed. Despite his ladykiller reputation, ★NSYNC Justin Timberlake didn't make the list's top ten.

ARTS AND ENTERTAINMENT

- Legendary London nightspot Annabel's welcomed British beauty Elizabeth Hurley onto its management committee in an effort to give the club a sleeker image and encourage younger members to join.

- Soul star-turned-Reverend Al Green was so worried about including words like 'baby' and 'sugar' in songs on his album *I Can't Stop* that he asked for guidance from the congregation at his Tennessee church.

- The longest Oscars ceremony, in 2000, lasted a bum-numbing 256 minutes.

- Spanish crooner Julio Iglesias holds the record for selling more albums in more languages than any other singer.

- One Christmas, *Friends* stars Jennifer Aniston, Courtney Cox, Lisa Kudrow, Matt Leblanc, Matthew Perry and David Schwimmer gave plasma TVs to crew members who'd worked on the show for less than five years – while those who'd passed the five-year mark received Mini Cooper cars.

- Rapper Ice Cube's Navigator sports utility vehicle has six television screens in it.

- Before hitting acting success, *Everybody Loves Raymond* star Patricia Heaton worked in New York as a 6am room-service waitress at the Park Le Meridien hotel.

ARTS AND ENTERTAINMENT

- Hollywood star Tom Cruise had attended 15 schools by the time he was 14.

- Alfred Hitchcock directed the first talking film ever made in England. It was called *Blackmail* and was made in 1931.

- *Dynasty* star Joan Collins's late father once served as an agent for *X Factor's* Sharon Osbourne's dad Don Arden, who was a singer at the time.

- *24* star Kiefer Sutherland has his family's Scottish crest tattooed on his back. It's one of six tattoos the actor boasts.

- Patrick Swayze's first crush was on a dancer his mother taught, called Ellen Smith. The young girl later changed her name to Jaclyn Smyth and became an original Charlie's Angel.

- If you decide you don't want your Oscar, you are supposed to sell it back to the academy for $1.

- Former Destiny's Child singer Farrah Franklin's middle name is Destiny.

- Armourers created 9,000 arrows and 3,000 swords for historical epic *Alexander* starring Colin Farrell.

ARTS AND ENTERTAINMENT

- Late rapper Tupac Shakur – who was shot and killed at the age of 25 in 1996 – came up with his signature shaven hairstyle because he suffered from premature baldness.

- The red carpet at the 2004 Grammy Awards turned green because the event was sponsored by beer company Heineken.

- Singer Robbie Williams once posed as a beggar in New York's Times Square and gave £55 to the first person who gave him money.

- The oldest Oscar winner was 81-year-old Jessica Tandy, for *Driving Miss Daisy* in 1989. Gloria Stuart is the oldest nominee ever, nominated in 1997 for *Titanic*. She was 87.

- Singer-turned-children's author Madonna likes to sing 'Truly Scrumptious' from hit musical *Chitty Chitty Bang Bang* to her children Lourdes and Rocco.

- Hollywood star Tom Cruise insists on having his own stuntplane on standby whenever he's on location filming so he can take off and relax high above the earth.

- *Paycheck* star Aaron Eckhart has a pet dog named Dirty.

ARTS AND ENTERTAINMENT

- Wacky screenwriter and director Quentin Tarantino wrote a script called 'Captain Peachfuzz and The Anchovy Bandit' as a child.

- San Francisco-based Neil Diamond tribute group Super Diamond are the world's top covers band – they charge £8,820 per show.

- Destiny's Child star Beyonce Knowles's hit single 'Crazy In Love' was the best-selling mobile-phone ring tone in Britain in 2003.

- Sugar Ray rocker Mark McGrath has such an intense fear of elevators that he insists on taking the stairs if he has to travel 40 floors or less.

- Judi Dench clocked up the shortest screen time for an Oscar winner. She won Best Supporting Actress in 1998 for less than eight minutes on screen in *Shakespeare in Love*.

- Hollywood star Bruce Willis holds the record for the biggest payout for voiceover work, after receiving £5.5 million for 1990's *Look Who's Talking Too*.

- A man in Dallas, Texas, spent his entire life savings – £22,105 – on 6,000 seats for people to see Mel Gibson's movie *The Passion Of The Christ*, because he believes it will 'change' America.

———— ARTS AND ENTERTAINMENT ————

* Scottish band Texas were named after the 1984 film *Paris, Texas*.

* Mel Gibson and Johnny Depp refused offers by bosses at the 2004 Oscars to present awards because they admitted they'd be far too nervous.

* Rockers U2 use a sound system on tour which weighs 30 tons.

* Hollywood is being hit by a new fad – bio-degradable pants. The two Hobbits Elijah Wood and Sean Astin are fans and hip-hop legend Missy Elliott is meant to be partial to the bizarre bio pants.

* Hit thriller *Jaws 2* was originally going to be called 'More Jaws', but polling showed audiences assumed a film with that name would be a comic spoof.

* There are still two Oscar categories in which no women have ever won – Best Cinematography and the Best Sound.

* X-Men actor Hugh Jackman turned down a role in Australian soap opera *Neighbours* at the beginning of his career because he was auditioning for drama schools.

ARTS AND ENTERTAINMENT

- Inspired by Mel Gibson's controversial new movie *The Passion Of The Christ*, replicas of crucifixion nails are selling at select stores around America for £8.94.

- To mark young actor Tyler Hoechlin's 16th birthday, Tom Hanks – who played his father in *Road To Perdition* – sent him $16 (£9).

- The Used singer Bert McCracken has a pet Chihuahua named David Bowie.

- Kate Winslet gave birth to baby son Joe with the music of Rufus Wainwright in the background.

- British heir-to-the-throne Prince Charles has launched his own range of shampoos and conditioners under his company Duchy Originals.

- US Rapper Fat Joe is building a specially designed wardrobe in his new Miami mansion to house his 5,000-plus pairs of running shoes.

- Kathy Richards Hilton, mother of hotel heiress Paris Hilton, went to school with pop singer Janet Jackson.

- Potential Oscar winners are told to keep acceptance speeches to 45 seconds – unlike Greer Garson, whose 1942 speech clocked in at seven minutes.

——— ARTS AND ENTERTAINMENT ———

* British pop stars Busted helped cure a boy who was told he might never walk again. Seven-year-old Alex Harris had been wheelchair bound with a rare muscle-wasting disease, but tapped his toes after hearing the band for the first time – and now, four months on, he's dancing again.

* Hollywood star Tom Hanks's movies have amassed an impressive total in excess of £3 billion since his film career began in 1980.

* The average cost of making a Hollywood movie in 2003 was £57.2 million.

* Hollywood veterans Sophia Loren, Liz Taylor and Raquel Welch were all considered for the role of *Dynasty* TV bitch Alexis before Joan Collins landed the part.

* An English town is to name a street after The Darkness front man Justin Hawkins. The rock star's home of Lowestoft, Suffolk is planning on a Hawkins Way or a Justin Avenue.

* Gleneagles Hotel, the original hotel that inspire John Cleese's legendary sitcom *Fawlty Towers*, has been saved from demolition and is being turned into an official tourist landmark in Torquay, Devon, England.

——— ARTS AND ENTERTAINMENT———

- *Cabaret* star Liza Minnelli is the only Oscar winner with two Oscar-winning parents – her mum, Judy Garland, was a winner in 1939, and her dad, Vincente Minnelli, in 1958.

- Hotel heiress sisters Paris and Nicky Hilton are each expected to inherit £15.5 million.

- *Lord of the Rings* director Peter Jackson promised two of his Oscars to his children, because they want to use them as bedside objects.

- Bosses at vacuum cleaner company Dyson have treated *X Factor's* Sharon Osbourne to a brand new purple hoover, which they've created to pick up animal hair and excrement.

- US comedienne Ellen DeGeneres and singer Harry Connick Jr.'s fathers worked on a paper round together as children in their native New Orleans, Louisiana.

- Three generations of the Astin family have acted in director Peter Jackson's films. Sean Astin played Samwise Gamgee in *The Lord Of The Rings* trilogy; his young daughter Ali played his child in *The Return Of The King*, and his dad John Astin appeared in Jackson's 1996 movie *The Frighteners*.

——— ARTS AND ENTERTAINMENT ———

- Action hero Harrison Ford was so in love with fiancée Calista Flockhart that he drank out of a cup decorated with their pictures and names.

- Patrick Presley, 31, a cousin of rock legend Elvis, hanged himself while in jail in Mississippi over a fatal car accident.

- Justin Timberlake's 2003 Christmas show in Dublin, Ireland, sold out in 40 seconds.

- Around 5,800 people on the Academy of Motion Picture Arts and Sciences' panel vote for the Oscars.

- *Playboy* magnate Hugh Hefner auctioned off his address book containing the phone numbers of some of the most beautiful women in the world – along with memorabilia including portraits of Marilyn Monroe, Madonna and Brigitte Bardot – to mark the 50th anniversary of the men's magazine.

- Justin Timberlake was so impressed by Queen's 'Bohemian Rhapsody' as a child that he locked himself away in his bedroom for two days straight to listen to the track over and over again.

- *Bridget Jones* star Renee Zellweger carries two mobile phones around with her – one for calls from England and the other for American calls.

——— ARTS AND ENTERTAINMENT ———

- US talk-show legend Oprah Winfrey sleeps on Frette bed sheets, which boast a very high thread count and sell for up to £1,500 a set.

- Troubled singer Michael Jackson once paid £14,705 to hire two private jets – one for him to travel in and another as a decoy to confuse the press when he travelled from Las Vegas, Nevada, to Santa Barbara, California.

- Funnyman Mike Myers's wedding ring is his late father's 1956 Encyclopaedia Britannica Salesman of The Year gift.

- Singer-turned-actress Cher refuses to watch hit movie *Thelma & Louise* – she turned down Geena Davis's role.

- The original title of cult TV show *Charlie's Angels* was 'Alleycats'.

- *Catwoman* star Halle Berry's stint on American satire show *Saturday Night Live* was so chaotic that she appeared for the final curtain call with her boots on the wrong feet.

- Supermodel Claudia Schiffer was paid an incredible £200,000 to make a one-minute cameo in Hugh Grant's film *Love Actually*.

ARTS AND ENTERTAINMENT

- Accident-prone *Lord Of The Rings* star Orlando Bloom has broken his skull three times, both legs, a finger, a toe, a rib, an arm, a wrist, his nose and his back.

- US movie star Billy Bob Thornton once spent 18 months working in a Los Angeles pizza parlour. He was so good he worked his way up to assistant manager.

- The gun that killed outlaw Jesse James sold at auction in Anaheim, California, for £218,750 on 10 November 2003. The winning bid is a new record for a Western history firearm.

- The first thing *King Arthur* star Keira Knightley bought with her first movie paycheque was a doll's house.

- US rocker Pink has a ritual every time she releases a new album – she takes a bottle of champagne to New York's Virgin Megastore and buys the first copy.

- Singer Madonna once worked as a coat-check girl at New York's Russian Tea Room restaurant, but she was fired for wearing fishnet stockings.

- US singer and actress Jennifer Lopez stores her lavish pink diamond engagement ring in a safe when she's filming.

ARTS AND ENTERTAINMENT

- Hollywood star Denzel Washington and his wife Pauletta have a special trophy room in their California home to display all of their accolades. While Washington has won awards – including two Academy Awards – for his acting, his spouse has been honoured many times over as a concert pianist.

- Duran Duran frontman Simon Le Bon has historical controversy in his past – he can trace his family tree back to Europe's Huguenots who were forced to find refuge in England after being chased out of France by the Catholics for their Protestant beliefs.

- Teenage rap sensation Bow Wow's monthly allowance was £3,750.

- Roc-A-Fella hip-hop mogul Damon Dash – who owns more than 3,000 pairs of trainers – never wears the same clothes twice, and refuses to write in red ink because it signifies losing money.

- *Charlie's Angels* star Cameron Diaz insists on being environmentally friendly even when she's being ferried to awards shows and events – she uses Los Angeles' Evo Limo Luxury Car Service, where all vehicles run on natural gases.

- US actress Brooke Shields can trace her heritage back to King Henry IV of France and Lucrezia Borgia.

—— ARTS AND ENTERTAINMENT ——

- Legendary rocker Ozzy Osbourne and opera singer Sarah Brightman used to go to the same vocal coach in London.

- US diva Barbra Streisand insisted on spraying her black microphone white for her performance on the Oprah Winfrey Show so it matched her off-white outfit.

- Magician David Blaine opted to fast in a box above London's River Thames for 44 days because the number correlates with his birthday, 4 April.

- US rapper Lil Kim's manicurist charges up to £3,125 a day to wrap her nails in shredded $100 bills.

- Two of US actor Ashton Kutcher's toes on his right foot are stuck together.

- America's first reality-TV awards were scrapped because network bosses refused to offer clips to the organizers. Producer Don Mischer has cited lack of network co-operation for his decision to cancel the first Reality Awards.

- More than 2.2 million guests visited Dollywood, Dolly Parton's theme park, in 1998, making the park the most visited attraction in the state of Tennessee after the Great Smoky Mountains National Park.

THE THINGS
PEOPLE SAY

THE THINGS PEOPLE SAY

- 'I can't really remember the names of the clubs that we went to.'

- Shaquille O'Neal, on whether he had visited the Parthenon during his visit to Greece.

- 'It's nice, it gives you a feeling of security so that if something breaks we know we can always call a guy over and he'll bring a drill or something.'
  Brooke Shields, on why it was good to live in a co-ed dormitory when she was in college

- 'You don't have to be the Dalai Lama to tell people that life's about change.'
  John Cleese

- 'Hearthrobs are a dime a dozen.'
  Brad Pitt

- 'My weaknesses have always been food and men – in that order.'
  Dolly Parton

- 'Hugh Grant and I both laugh and cringe at the same things, worship the same books, eat the same food, hate central heating and sleep with the window open.

THE THINGS PEOPLE SAY

- 'I just want to conquer people and their souls.'
  Mike Tyson

- I thought these things were vital, but being two peas in a pod ended up not being enough.'
  Elizabeth Hurley

- 'I don't have a boyfriend right now. I'm looking for anyone with a job that I don't have to support.'
  Anna Nicole Smith

- 'I've never had a problem with drugs. I've had problems with the police.'
  Keith Richards

- 'Men cheat for the same reason that dogs lick their balls… because they can.'
  Kim Cattrall

- 'I always had a repulsive need to be something more than human.'
  David Bowie

- 'You don't realize how useful a therapist is until you see one yourself and discover you have more problems than you ever dreamed of.'
  Claire Danes

THE THINGS PEOPLE SAY

- 'Through years of experience I have found that air offers less resistance than dirt.'
  Jack Nicklaus

- 'You mean they've scheduled Yom Kippur opposite *Charlie's Angels*?'
  Fred Silverman, TV programmer, when told that Yom Kippur would fall on a Wednesday

- 'I don't think I'm too thin at all. I understand when people say, "Well, your face gets gaunt," but, to get your bottom half to be the right size, your face might have to be a little gaunt. You choose your battles.'
  Courtney Cox

- 'Well the joke is, of course, there is no British Empire left, is there? So I'm dame of a great big zero.'
  Helen Mirren, on receiving a Royal honour

- 'I think in 20 years I'll be looked at like Bob Hope. Doing those president jokes and golf shit. It scares me.'
  Eddie Murphy

- 'Real freedom is having nothing. I was freer when I didn't have a cent.'
  Mike Tyson

- 'From an early age I was aware of what America meant, and how the Marines at Camp Pendleton were

THE THINGS PEOPLE SAY

ready to defend us at a moment's notice. I also remember what fabulous bodies those troops had.'
Heather Locklear

- 'If you talk bad about country music, it's like saying bad things about my momma. Them's fightin' words.'
Dolly Parton

- 'Now I can wear heels.'
Nicole Kidman, on divorcing Tom Cruise

- 'I could serve coffee using my rear as a ledge.'
Jennifer Lopez

- 'I just don't like the idea of her singing my songs. Who the hell does she thinks she is? The world doesn't need another Streisand!'
Barbra Streisand, on Diana Ross

- 'I never thought I was wasted, but I probably was.'
Keith Richards

- 'Golf is a better game played downhill.'
Jack Nicklaus

- 'I will wear whatever and blow whomever I want as long as I can breathe and kneel.'
Kim Cattrall

THE THINGS PEOPLE SAY

* 'There are so many people out there taking the p★ss out of me that if I can't take the p★ss out of myself there's something going wrong.'
  Victoria Beckham

* 'There are two types of actors: those who say they want to be famous and those who are liars.'
  Kevin Bacon

* 'It's been seven years since I've had sex.'
  Anna Nicole Smith

* 'There's no drugs, no Tom in a dress, no psychiatrists.'
  Nicole Kidman

* 'Women don't want to hear what you think. Women want to hear what they think – in a deeper voice.'
  Bill Cosby

* 'I don't want to ever, ever do something in life that isn't fun. Ever.'
  Jennifer Love Hewitt

* 'I found my inner bitch and ran with her.'
  Courtney Love

* 'I don't want people to know what I'm actually like. It's not good for an actor.'
  Jack Nicholson

THE THINGS PEOPLE SAY

- 'I have got little feet because nothing grows in the shade.'
  Dolly Parton

- 'Mr Right's coming, but he's in Africa, and he's walking.'
  Oprah Winfrey

- 'I don't always wear underwear. When I'm in the heat, especially, I can't wear it. Like, if I'm wearing a flower dress, why do I have to wear underwear?'
  Naomi Campbell

- 'I hated singing. I wanted to be an actress. But I don't think I'd have made it any other way.'
  Barbra Streisand

- 'I'm afraid to be alone, I'm afraid not to be alone. I'm afraid of what I am, what I'm not, what I might become, what I might never become. I don't want to stay at my job for the rest of my life, but I'm afraid to leave. And I'm just tired, you know? I'm just so tired of being afraid.'
  Michelle Pfeiffer

- 'I hope there's a tinge of disgrace about me. Hopefully, there's one good scandal left in me yet.'
  Diana Rigg

--------- **THE THINGS PEOPLE SAY** ---------

- 'I'd like to design something like a city or a museum. I want to do something hands on rather than just play golf which is the sport of the religious right.'
  Brad Pitt

- 'If it's illegal to rock and roll, throw my ass in jail!'
  Kurt Cobain

- 'So you know what I'm gonna do? I'm gonna do something really outrageous, I'm gonna tell the truth.'
  John Travolta

- 'My mother never saw the irony in calling me a son-of-a-bitch.'
  Jack Nicholson

- 'Any idiot can get laid when they're famous. That's easy. It's getting laid when you're not famous that takes some talent.'
  Kevin Bacon

- 'I feel old when I see mousse in my opponent's hair.'
  Andre Agassi

- 'I don't think President Bush is doing anything at all about AIDS. In fact, I'm not sure he even knows how to spell AIDS.'
  Elizabeth Taylor

THE THINGS PEOPLE SAY

- 'Lots of people want to ride with you in the limo, but what you want is someone who will take the bus with you when the limo breaks down.'
  Oprah Winfrey

- 'I'm tough, ambitious, and I know exactly what I want. If that makes me a bitch, OK.'
  Madonna

- 'We are not that flash, me or the missus [Madonna]. In fact, we are quite low-maintenance.'
  Guy Ritchie

- 'I am not the archetypal leading man. This is mainly for one reason: as you may have noticed, I have no hair.'
  Patrick Stewart

- 'The English contribution to world cuisine – the chip.'
  John Cleese

- 'I miss New York. I still love how people talk to you on the street – just assault you and tell you what they think of your jacket.'
  Madonna

- 'I enjoy being a highly overpaid actor.'
  Roger Moore

—————— **THE THINGS PEOPLE SAY** ——————

• 'If you ever need anything please don't hesitate to ask someone else first.'
Kurt Cobain

• 'Being number two sucks.'
Andre Agassi

• 'Angelina Jolie may get him [Antonio Banderas] in bed for eight hours on a movie set, but I get him in bed every day.'
Melanie Griffith

• 'If you want to ask about my drug problem, go ask my big, fat, smart, ten-pound daughter, she'll answer any questions you have about it.'
Courtney Love

• 'Being English, I always laugh at anything to do with the lavatory or bottoms.'
Elizabeth Hurley

• 'When I get down on my knees, it is not to pray.'
Madonna

• 'I wasn't always black... There was this freckle, and it got bigger and bigger.'
Bill Cosby

THE THINGS PEOPLE SAY

- 'I can't believe people got so upset at the sight of a single breast! America is so parochial; I may just have to move to Europe where people are more mature about things like that!'
  Janet Jackson

- 'Sometimes you have to be a bitch to get things done.'
  Madonna

- 'Traffic signals in New York are just rough guidelines.'
  David Letterman

- 'In college I castrated 21 rats, and I got pretty good at it.'
  Lisa Kudrow

- 'My favourite thing in the world is a box of fine European chocolates which is, for sure, better than sex.'
  Alicia Silverstone

- 'I want a big house with a moat and dragons and a fort to keep people out!'
  Victoria Beckham

- 'Up until they go to school, they're relatively portable.'
  Elizabeth Hurley, on children

- 'Bitches. It's a very male-chauvinist word. I resent it deeply. A person who's a bitch would seem to be

THE THINGS PEOPLE SAY

mean for no reason. I'm not a mean person. Maybe I'm rude without being aware of it – that's possible.'
Barbra Streisand

* 'If it's hard to remember, it'll be difficult to forget.'
Arnold Schwarzenegger

* 'If I'm in the middle of hitting a most fantastic cross-court back hand top spin and someone says, 'Can you stop now and have sex?' I'll say, "No thanks!"'
Cliff Richard

* 'Always end the name of your child with a vowel, so that when you yell the name will carry.'
Bill Cosby

* 'Better to live one year as a tiger, then a hundred as sheep.'
Madonna

* 'Whatever side I take, I know well that I will be blamed.'
Keith Richards

* 'I'm going to marry a Jewish woman because I like the idea of getting up Sunday morning and going to the deli.'
Michael J Fox

THE THINGS PEOPLE SAY

- 'I'm not offended by dumb-blonde jokes because I know that I'm not dumb. I also know I'm not blonde.'
  Dolly Parton

- 'I veer away from trying to understand why I act. I just know I need to do it.'
  Ralph Fiennes

- 'If it bleeds, we can kill it.'
  Arnold Schwarzenegger

- 'You can get Indian food at three in the morning, but I personally don't want Indian food at three in the morning. I want to go for a walk in my nightgown!'
  Ashley Judd, on the pros and cons of living in New York

- 'I'm not used to the C word. That is sort of a new deal. It is so funny. C'mon, I was not raised to take myself that seriously.'
  Brittany Murphy, on the novelty of being a celebrity

- 'Officially, I am not a woman anymore. Dublin has turned me into a man.'
  Keira Knightley, on drinking with the boys while filming King Arthur in the Irish capital

- 'Craig David called me and said he'd written a song based on my song and asked if I'd like to come and sing on it. I asked my son, "Is that cool? Is he cool?",

THE THINGS PEOPLE SAY

and he was like, "Yes, Dad!", so I said, "Absolutely."'
Sting, on career advice from his hip kids

* 'Once you're famous, you realize for the rest of your life sex has to be in the bedroom.'
Sandra Bullock, on her pre-celebrity sexual tryst in a taxi

* 'I'm so pleased. I couldn't stand any of his stuff. He's always buying me things, but I never let him buy me furniture.'
Sir Elton John's mum Sheila, on her relief that her son is auctioning off some of his more flamboyant home furnishings

* 'The show was terrible because I didn't win!'
Frasier's David Hyde Pierce, on his 2003 Emmy Award failure

* 'My parents have been there for me, ever since I was about seven.'
David Beckham

* 'They didn't even shoot my butt. Every now and again, you'll see a breast. But, like, big whoops! It's like, have you seen an Evian poster lately? Big deal, right?'
Daryl Hannah, on her nude photo shoot for American men's magazine Playboy

* 'It was a really bad film, I'm really bad in it, and it was the hardest thing to go out there and promote it by

——— THE THINGS PEOPLE SAY ———

saying, "There are things about this that are fascinating."'
George Clooney, on his role in Batman & Robin

* 'We're pleased he doesn't want to listen to the Wiggles
  – he just asks for The Clash.'
  *Cate Blanchett, on her relief that her infant son Dashiell has
  good musical taste*

* 'People look back on it now with nostalgia and say it
  was great. It was bulls★★★.'
  Robert Carlyle, on the 1970s

* 'I have the same goal I've had ever since I was a girl.
  I want to rule the world.'
  Madonna

* 'Passing the vodka bottle. And playing the guitar.'
  Keith Richards, on how he keeps fit

* 'People say New Yorkers can't get along. Not true. I
  saw two New Yorkers, complete strangers, sharing a
  cab. One guy took the tyres and the radio; the other
  guy took the engine.'
  David Letterman

* 'You know the only people who are always sure about
  the proper way to raise children? Those who've never
  had any.'
  Bill Cosby

THE THINGS PEOPLE SAY

- 'I am my own experiment. I am my own work of art.'
  Madonna

- 'Smoking kills. If you're killed, you've lost a very important part of your life.'
  Brooke Shields

- 'I just use my muscles as a conversation piece, like someone walking a cheetah down 42nd Street.'
  Arnold Schwarzenegger

- 'Old is always 15 years from now.'
  Bill Cosby

- 'I cannot sing, dance or act; what else would I be but a talk-show host.'
  David Letterman

- 'I grew up with a lot of boys. I probably have a lot of testosterone for a woman.'
  Cameron Diaz

- 'You're about as useful as a one-legged man at an arse-kicking contest.'
  Rowan Atkinson

- 'It's a bit like going to heaven without having to die first.'
  Labour MP Tony Banks, on being made Minister for Sport

THE THINGS PEOPLE SAY

* 'People have been so busy relating to how I look,
  it's a miracle I didn't become a self-conscious blob
  of protoplasm.'
  Robert Redford

* 'I'm the master of low expectations.'
  US President George W Bush

* 'If your lifeguard duties were as good as your singing,
  a lot of people would be drowning.'
  Simon Cowell, judge on reality TV talent show Pop Idol

* 'I can still enjoy sex at 74 – I live at 75 so it's
  no distance.'
  Comic Bob Monkhouse

* 'The midfield is numerically outnumbered.'
  Football pundit Ron Atkinson

* 'Last week I stated that this woman was the ugliest
  woman I had ever seen. I have since been visited by
  her sister and now wish to withdraw that statement.'
  American writer Mark Twain

* 'Actually, it only takes one drink to get me loaded.
  Trouble is, I can't remember if it's the thirteenth or
  fourteenth.'
  US comic actor George Burns

THE THINGS PEOPLE SAY

* 'Common-looking people are the best in the world: that is the reason the Lord makes so many of them.'
US *President Abraham Lincoln*

* 'I bought a dog the other day... I named him Stay. It's fun to call him... "Come here, Stay! Come here, Stay!" He went insane. Now he just ignores me.'
US comic Stephen Wright

* 'The first thing that ran across my mind was to bite him back.'
Boxer Evander Holyfield, after rival Mike Tyson bit his ear off during a fight

* 'I'm not smart enough to lie.'
US *President Ronald Reagan*

* 'Hollywood is a place where they'll pay you 50,000 dollars for a kiss and 50 cents for your soul.'
Hollywood movie star Marilyn Monroe

* 'Being a celebrity is probably the closest to being a beautiful woman as you can get.'
US actor Kevin Costner

* 'You have to be a bastard to make it, and that's a fact. And the Beatles are the biggest bastards on earth.'
John Lennon, musician, writer, actor and activist

THE THINGS PEOPLE SAY

* 'You can see our respect for women by the fact that we have pledged to pay working women, even though they don't have to work.'
Taliban Information Minister Amir Khan Muttaqi

* 'If I die before my cat, I want a little of my ashes put in his food so I can live inside him.'
US actress Drew Barrymore

* 'If you're going through hell, keep going.'
US animator and film producer Walt Disney

* 'Every man wishes to be wise, and they who cannot be wise are almost always cunning.'
US actor Samuel L Jackson

* 'I want a man who's kind and understanding. Is that too much to ask of a millionaire?'
Hollywood actress Zsa Zsa Gabor

* 'The streets are safe in Philadelphia. It's only the people who make them unsafe.'
Frank Rizzo, ex-police chief and mayor of Philadelphia

* 'People used to throw rocks at me because of my clothes. Now they wanna know where I buy them.'
Singer Cyndi Lauper

THE THINGS PEOPLE SAY

- 'During the scrimmage, Tarkanian paced the sideline with his hands in his pockets while biting his nails.'
  Report describing basketball coach Jerry Tarkanian

- 'Give me a museum and I'll fill it.'
  Spanish Cubist painter and sculptor Pablo Picasso

- 'Military intelligence is a contradiction in terms.'
  Groucho Marx

- 'Giving up smoking is easy... I've done it hundreds of times.'
  Mark Twain

- 'Every time I look at you I get a fierce desire to be lonesome.'
  Oscar Levant

- 'Ever notice how it's a penny for your thoughts, yet you put in your two cents? Someone is making a penny on the deal!'
  US comic Stephen Wright

- 'If you steal from one author, it's plagiarism; if you steal from many, it's research.'
  US screenwriter Wilson Mizner

- 'Hull is very nice. The weather is very like home.'
  Hull City's Spanish footballer Antonio Doncel-Valcarcel

THE THINGS PEOPLE SAY

* 'The laziest man I ever met put popcorn in his pancakes so they would turn over by themselves.'
W C Fields

* 'There are three faithful friends: an old wife, an old dog, and ready money.'
Benjamin Franklin

* 'If people screw me, I screw back in spades.'
US billionaire Donald Trump

* 'I wasn't the cutest or the most talented, but I could get through the question-and-answer period.'
Talk-show presenter Oprah Winfrey, commenting on beauty pageants

* 'Charlie Brown is the one person I identify with. CB is such a loser. He wasn't even the star of his own Halloween special.'
US comic Chris Rock

* 'I never set out to hurt anybody deliberately unless it was, you know, important. Like a league game or something.'
American footballer Dick Butkus

* 'I dress for women, and undress for men.'
US actress Angie Dickinson

THE THINGS PEOPLE SAY

* 'The problem with people who have no vices is that generally you can be pretty sure they're going to have some pretty annoying virtues.'
  British actress Elizabeth Taylor

* 'If you suck on a tit, the movie gets an R rating. If you hack the tit off with an axe, it will be PG.'
  US actor Jack Nicholson

* 'I feel safe in white because, deep down inside, I'm an angel.'
  Rapper and producer P-Diddy

* 'I was like, "I want that one!" '
  US pop princess Jessica Simpson, speaking about her now ex-husband, Nick Lachey of boyband 98 Degrees

* 'By the time you're 80 years old you've learned everything. You only have to remember it.'
  George Burns

* 'Being married means I can break wind and eat ice-cream in bed.'
  US actor Brad Pitt

* 'How many husbands have I had? You mean apart from my own?'
  Zsa Zsa Gabor

THE THINGS PEOPLE SAY

- 'One man with courage is a majority.'
  US President Thomas Jefferson

- 'It's so sweet, I feel like my teeth are rotting when I listen to the radio.'
  Irish singer and activist Bono

- 'I think the team that wins Game 5 will win the series. Unless we lose Game 5.'
  Charles Barkley

- 'You're not drunk if you can lie on the floor without holding on.'
  US actor and singer Dean Martin

- 'We're going to move left and right at the same time.'
  Jerry Brown, Governor of California

- 'Don't stay in bed, unless you can make money in bed.'
  George Burns

- 'Denial ain't just a river in Egypt.'
  Mark Twain

- 'Sport is like the theatre. People want to see good-looking people who are dressed properly.'
  Tennis star Anna Kournikova

THE THINGS PEOPLE SAY

- 'Real happiness is when you marry a girl for love and find out later she has money.'
  Bob Monkhouse

- 'If the Cameroons get a goal back here, they're literally gonna catch on fire.'
  Ron Atkinson

- 'I was thrown out of college for cheating on the metaphysics exam: I looked into the soul of another boy.'
  Woody Allen

- 'I like pigs. Dogs look up to us. Cats look down on us. Pigs treat us as equals.'
  British Prime Minister Winston Churchill

- 'Who is General Failure, and why is he reading my hard disk?'
  US comic Stephen Wright

- 'I never forget a face, but in your case I'll make an exception.'
  Groucho Marx

- 'I am free of all prejudices. I hate everyone equally.'
  W C Fields

THE THINGS PEOPLE SAY

- 'They misunderestimated me.'
  George W Bush

- 'Anybody that walks can sing.'
  Michael Stipe, REM singer

- 'I once said cynically of a politician, "He'll double-cross that bridge when he comes to it." '
  Oscar Levant

- 'It's better to live one day as a lion, than a hundred as a sheep.'
  Italian Fascist statesman and Prime Minister Benito Mussolini

- 'It is full of interest. It has noble poetry in it; and some clever fables; and some blood-drenched history; and some good morals; and a wealth of obscenity; and upwards of a thousand lies.'
  Mark Twain on the Bible

- 'TV is more interesting than people. If it were not, we should have people standing in the corners of our rooms.'
  British satirist Alan Coren

- 'Chemistry is a class you take in high school or college, where you figure out two plus two is ten, or something.'
  Dennis Rodman, speaking about the Chicago Bull's team chemistry being overrated

THE THINGS PEOPLE SAY

- 'Golf is a game whose aim is to hit a very small ball into an even smaller hole, with weapons singularly ill-designed for the purpose.'
  Winston Churchill

- 'I am an optimist. But I'm an optimist who takes his raincoat.'
  British Prime Minister Harold Wilson

- 'I'm an excellent housekeeper. Every time I get a divorce, I keep the house.'
  Zsa Zsa Gabor

- 'A hippie is someone who looks like Tarzan, walks like Jane and smells like Cheetah.'
  Ronald Reagan

- 'I cannot sing, dance or act; what else would I be but a talk-show host.'
  US talk-show host David Letterman

- 'What's another word for thesaurus?'
  Steven Wright

- 'Keep your eyes wide open before marriage, and half-shut afterwards.'
  Benjamin Franklin

THE THINGS PEOPLE SAY

* 'We spent a lot of time talking about Africa, as we should. Africa is a nation that suffers from incredible disease.'
  George W Bush

* 'When the inventor of the drawing board messed things up … what did he go back to?'
  Bob Monkhouse

* 'It's funny the way most people love the dead. Once you are dead, you are made for life.'
  Genius guitar player Jimi Hendrix

* 'Coming on to pitch is Mike Moore, who is six foot one and 212 years old.'
  Sportscaster Herb Score

* 'Those who dance are considered insane by those who cannot hear the music.'
  Comic George Carlin

* 'I could take Sean Connery in a fight... I could definitely take him.'
  Harrison Ford

* 'Man – a figment of God's imagination.'
  Mark Twain

THE THINGS PEOPLE SAY

- 'I'm a 4-wheel-drive pickup type of guy. So is my wife.'
  Baseball player Mike Greenwell

- 'We don't want the television script good. We want it Tuesday.'
  TV writer Dennis Norden

- 'We didn't think about its proper use. We just wanted something to be weird, and the umlaut is very visual. It's German and strong, and that Nazi Germany mentality – "the future belongs to us" – intrigued me.'
  US rocker Nikki Sixx, explaining the use of umlauts over the 'o' and 'u' of 'Mötley Crüe'

- 'I know what I believe. I will continue to articulate what I believe and what I believe – I believe what I believe is right.'
  George W Bush

- 'What's a geriatric? A German footballer scoring three goals.'
  Bob Monkhouse

- 'Good enough for the homeless but not for an international striker.'
  Footballer Pierre Van Hooijdonk, on his rejection of a £7,000-a-week pay rise offer at Celtic

——— **THE THINGS PEOPLE SAY** ———

* 'History will be kind to me for I intend to write it.'
  Winston Churchill

* 'When I am dead, I hope it may be said: "His sins
  were scarlet but his books were read."'
  Writer Hilaire Belloc

* 'Shoot a few scenes out of focus. I want to win the
  foreign film award.'
  Film-maker Billy Wilder

* 'Television: A medium. So called because it's neither
  rare nor well done.'
  US comic Ernie Kovacs

* 'You're not a real manager unless you've been sacked.'
  Football manager Malcolm Allison

* 'I wish to be cremated. One-tenth of my ashes shall
  be given to my agent, as written in our contract.'
  Groucho Marx

* 'I hate to advocate drugs, alcohol, violence, or insanity
  to anyone, but they've always worked for me.'
  Author Hunter S Thompson

* 'I wanted a name that would put us first in the phone
  directory or second if you count ABBA...'
  ABC singer Martin Fry

THE THINGS PEOPLE SAY

- 'Build a man a fire, and he'll be warm for a day. Set a man on fire, and he'll be warm for the rest of his life.'
  British author Terry Pratchett

- 'In Russia we only had two TV channels. Channel One was propaganda. Channel Two consisted of a KGB officer telling you: Turn back at once to Channel One.'
  Russian comic Yakov Smirnoff

- 'People think we make $3 million and $4 million a year. They don't realize that most of us only make $500,000.'
  Baseball player Pete Incaviglia

- 'You miss 100 per cent of the shots you never take.'
  Hockey player Wayne Gretzky

- 'You can tell German wine from vinegar by the label.'
  Mark Twain

- 'Christmas at my house is always at least six or seven times more pleasant than anywhere else. We start drinking early. And while everyone else is seeing only one Santa Claus, we'll be seeing six or seven.'
  W C Fields

- 'On another night, they'd have won 2–2.'
  Football pundit Ron Atkinson

THE THINGS PEOPLE SAY

- 'I resign. I wouldn't want to belong to any club that would have me as a member.'
  Groucho Marx

- 'I agree the lad's pace can be deceptive. He's much slower than you think.'
  Liverpool manager Bill Shankly on footballer Roy Evans

- 'So little time and so little to do.'
  US pianist and actor Oscar Levant

- 'They say such nice things about people at their funerals that it makes me sad that I'm going to miss mine by just a few days.'
  Writer Garrison Keilor

- 'Beware of the man who denounces women writers; his penis is tiny and he cannot spell.'
  US writer and feminist Erica Jong

- 'Life's tragedy is that we get old too soon and wise too late.'
  Benjamin Franklin

- 'When did I realize I was God? Well, I was praying and I suddenly realized I was talking to myself.'
  British actor Peter O'Toole

THE THINGS PEOPLE SAY

* 'This is not a novel to be tossed aside lightly. It should be thrown with great force.'
  Dorothy Parker

* 'In Hollywood, if you don't have happiness you send out for it.'
  Actor Rex Reed

* 'There's only one person who hugs the mothers and the widows, the wives and the kids upon the death of their loved one. Others hug but having committed the troops, I've got an additional responsibility to hug and that's me and I know what it's like.'
  George W Bush

* 'You know when you put a stick in water and it looks bent? That's why I never take baths.'
  US comic Stephen Wright

* 'Ah, the patter of little feet around the house. There's nothing like having a midget for a butler.'
  W C Fields

* 'What the world needs is more geniuses with humility, there are so few of us left.'
  US pianist and actor Oscar Levant

THE THINGS PEOPLE SAY

- 'We've all passed a lot of water since then.'
  Producer Sam Goldwyn

- 'I don't want any yes-men around me. I want everyone to tell me the truth – even if it costs him his job.'
  Producer Samuel Goldwyn

- 'Outside a dog, a book is a man's best friend. Inside a dog, it's too dark to read.'
  Groucho Marx

- 'There are two sides to every question: my side and the wrong side.'
  US pianist and actor Oscar Levant

- 'The only imaginative fiction being written today is income tax returns.'
  Pulitzer Prize-winning author Herman Wouk

- 'You're free. And freedom is beautiful. And, you know, it'll take time to restore chaos and order – order out of chaos. But we will.'
  George W Bush

- 'Someone told me that each equation I included in the book would halve the sales.'
  Stephen Hawking on A Brief History of Time

———— THE THINGS PEOPLE SAY ————

- 'My answer is bring them on.'
  George W Bush, commenting on Iraqi militants attacking US forces

- 'Underneath this flabby exterior is an enormous lack of character.'
  US pianist and actor Oscar Levant

ELVIS

ELVIS

- Elvis's first girlfriend was childhood sweetheart 16-year-old Dixie Locke, a high-school senior who was his first prom date.

- Elvis was born at 4.36 a.m. on 8 January 1935 at the home of his parents, Gladys and Vernon Presley, in Old Bailey Road, East Tupelo, Mississippi.

- He weighed 5lb (2kg) at birth and was the second of twins. His older brother, Jesse Aaron, was stillborn at 4 a.m.

- In October 1945, at age ten, Elvis won second prize in a talent contest, singing the tearjerker 'Old Shep' at the Mississippi-Alabama Fair and Dairy Show in Tupelo.

- Elvis's mother bought him his first guitar, costing $7.75, at a Tupelo hardware store as a present for his 11th birthday.

- At his first public appearance, with the L C Humes High School band in April 1963, his name was misspelled 'Elvis Prestly' on the programme.

- On his first billed appearance, at the Overton Park Shell, Memphis, in the summer of 1964, a newspaper advertisement referred to him as 'Ellis Presley'.

ELVIS

- When Elvis's first record was released he was a semi-illiterate truck driver.

- His first commercial recording session took place in the Sun Records studio in Memphis on 5 July 1954. He taped 'Harbour Lights', and after a break, recorded 'That's All Right (Mama)' and 'Blue Moon of Kentucky' with Scotty Moore and Bill Black.

- Scotty Moore and disc jockey Bob Neal were Elvis's managers before he signed with self-styled 'Colonel' Tom Parker, a former dog catcher and carnival barker, on 15 March 1956.

- Parker, an illegal immigrant from the Netherlands in 1929, who claimed to have been born in Virginia, went on to shamefully mishandle Elvis's career – taking a 50 per cent cut of all Elvis's earnings, as well as lucrative fees for granting contracts. He made more money than his client.

- After his conscription in the army, mainly served in Germany, Elvis returned to the United States on 5 March 1960, and was honourably discharged at Fort Dix.

- Since his death Elvis is said to have been spotted by scores of witnesses both in the United States and other countries.

ELVIS

* Elvis recorded more than 650 songs – 18 of his singles reached number one in the charts. With a three-octave voice, his hits covered a range of styles, including country, gospel, rock 'n' roll, rhythm and blues, and pop.

* In 1957, at age 22, Elvis bought Graceland. It was a 23-room mansion ten miles (16 km) south of Memphis, which, with various outbuildings, stood in 13.8 acres of land. It overlooked Route 51, which was later renamed Elvis Presley Boulevard. He paid $100,000 cash for the property.

* Major Bill Smith, a record producer who met Elvis in 1956, says he talked to Elvis after his supposed death and received two remarkable cassettes in the mail, allegedly sent by the King. A police voice identification expert from Houston compared one of the tapes with an Elvis interview from 1962 and found a staggering 35 instances where the voice patterns matched.

* The biggest Elvis hit, 'Heartbreak Hotel', was written in just 22 minutes by retired dishwasher repairman Tommy Durden and Nashville songwriter Mae Boren Axton.

* Elvis had his longest run in the Top 100 singles chart with 'All Shook Up', which lasted an incredible 30 weeks – with eight straight weeks at number one.

ELVIS

- Elvis produced a staggering 45 gold records, each one selling over a million copies. No artist had ever achieved such sales, until Elvis proved it could be done.

- Gail Brewer Giorgio, author of *Is Elvis Alive?* released an hour-long cassette of an alleged conversation with Elvis, recorded four years after his death. Elvis talks of travelling around Europe, his need for privacy and his wish to resume his career – all in the familiar, low, slightly slurred drawl.

- Elvis and Priscilla divorced on 11 October 1973. He had several girlfriends afterwards. The last was Ginger Aiden, who found him sprawled on the bathroom floor at 2.30 p.m. on 18 August 1977. She said they had planned to marry on Christmas Day. Elvis had already ordered a £27,600 ring.

- Partly because of his wild spending, and partly because 'Colonel' Parker took such a huge slice of his income, Elvis had only £2.75 million when he died. His estate has made more since his death than he made when he was alive.

- Elvis's first screen kiss came in his second movie, *Loving You*, when actress Jana Lund made screen history by being the first woman to kiss Elvis on film. It was also his first colour movie.

--------- **ELVIS** ---------

- For Elvis, *Loving You* was a family affair, as both his mother and father appeared on camera in the production.

- Elvis was touchy about his height and secretly wore lifts in his shoes to make him appear taller.

- Elvis's favourite actress was Shelley Fabares, who appeared in three of his films.

- If he wanted to book seats or travel incognito, Elvis frequently used the names Dr John Carpenter or John Burrows Jnr.

- Elvis was a big animal-lover and his many pets at Graceland included cats, dogs, ducks, fish, ponies, peacocks, a parrot and a chimpanzee.

- Priscilla Ann Beaulieu was just 14, a grey-eyed, 5 ft 3 (1.5 m) schoolgirl, when Elvis fell in love with her while serving in the army in Germany. Her stepfather was a US Air Force Captain.

- The first music Elvis Aaron Presley ever heard was in his early years at the First Assembly of God Church, in East Tupelo, Mississippi.

ELVIS

* *Love Me Tender* was Elvis's first movie. He played opposite veteran stars Debra Paget and Richard Egan.

* Elvis proposed to Priscilla on Christmas Eve 1966. They married at the Aladdin Hotel in Las Vegas on 1 May 1967. The wedding ring had a three-carat diamond surrounded by 20 other diamonds.

* In 1948, when Elvis was 13, the family packed its belongings in cardboard boxes and paper bags, and moved to Memphis in their 1939 Packard.

* On 14 August 1958 Gladys Presley died of a heart attack, brought on by acute hepatitis, at the Methodist Hospital in Memphis. Elvis was devastated.

* Exactly nine months after the wedding, on 1 February 1968, Lisa Marie Presley was born in Memphis. Had she been a boy, they would have named him John Baron Presley.

* Elvis made 31 movies but desperately wanted more substantial, challenging roles. However, 'Colonel' Parker and the movie moguls saw a source of easy money in his mindless, low-budget films. They used the huge profits to bankroll more important movies, featuring established stars.

ROYALTY

ROYALTY

ROYALTY

- Greenwich Palace was Henry VIII's favourite residence.

- Henry VIII was probably the most athletic monarch, enjoying tennis, archery and wrestling.

- In the 17th century, the Great Hall at Westminster Palace was used as a shopping precinct.

- The first prisoner in the Tower of London, Ranulf Flambard, Bishop of Durham, escaped down a rope smuggled to him in a flagon of wine.

- George III said he didn't like Hampton Court, due to memories of being hit on the ears by his grandfather there as a boy.

- Hot water and clothes were sent to Prince Albert's room every morning after his death. The glass he sipped his last medicine from lay unmoved on the table next to his bed for 40 years.

- Charles II was a keen tennis player and would weigh himself before and after every game to see how much weight he had lost.

- William III and his wife Mary hated Whitehall Palace, as it was bad for William's asthma.

- The Tower of London was once used as a zoo.

ROYALTY

- A cannonball, fired in salute, accidentally crashed into Greenwich Palace. It fell into the very room where Mary I was sitting, but she was unharmed.

- Extensions to Greenwich Palace conflicted with the main road from Deptford to Woolwich, so it was built on either side, with a bridge joining the two halves until the road was diverted.

- Queen Anne is said to have died from a fit of apoplexy, due to overeating, while at an outdoor supper party at Kensington Palace.

- The drains at Windsor Castle were faulty, allegedly causing the death of Prince Albert.

- A man attempted to assassinate Queen Mary I by climbing atop St James's Palace and using a large lens to focus the sun's rays on her walking below. It failed.

- It was quite common for Westminster Palace to flood with mud and fish from the River Thames, and once rowing boats had to be used in the Great Hall.

- Whitehall Palace once contained a chemical laboratory.

- George II died in his water closet at Kensington Palace, deterring later monarchs from living there.

— ROYALTY —

- Henry III kept a quartet of lions in the Tower of London. They were called Fanny, Miss Fanny, Miss Howe and Miss Fanny Howe.

- James I introduced a swear box to St James's Palace, and all the money was given to the poor.

- King Charles I's dog accompanied him to his execution.

- Queen Anne banned the wearing of spectacles, inappropriate wigs and the smoking of pipes from St James's Palace.

- Queen Victoria referred to Kensington Palace as 'the poor old palace'.

- George II sold tickets to allow the public to watch the King and Queen eat.

- Prince Albert was Queen Victoria's first cousin as well as husband.

- King James VI banned the use of the surname MacGregor.

- At royal banquets, the salt cellar was always the first thing to be laid on the table.

ROYALTY

- Henry III received a polar bear from the King of Norway. It was allowed to hunt for fish in the River Thames on the end of a long rope.

- The first elephant in England was a gift to King Henry III from the King of France.

- William IV considered turning Buckingham Palace into army barracks.

- Charles II had many dogs, and at official meetings of state he preferred playing with them to listening to the discussion.

- Prince Charles and Prince William never travel on the same plane as a precaution against a potential crash.

- The only house in England that the Queen may not enter is the House of Commons, as she is not a commoner.

- When the Duchess of Windsor's jewels were going on the auction block in 1987, Sotheby's sold 24,000 of its pricey catalogues.

- There are 1,783 diamonds on Britain's Imperial State Crown. This includes the 309-carat Star of Africa.

ROYALTY

- 'I want to make certain that I have some plants left to talk to.'
  Prince Charles, opening the Millennium Seed Bank

- 'You were playing your instruments, weren't you? Or do you have tape recorders under your seats?'
  Prince Philip, 'congratulating' a school band on their performance in Australia, in 2002

- 'Most people call their dogs Fergie. I'm kind of proud. You hear it in the park, "Fergie, come here."'
  Sarah Ferguson, on dogs

- 'I talk too much about things of which I have never claimed any special knowledge; just contemplate the horrifying prospect if I were to get my teeth into something even remotely familiar.'
  Prince Philip

- 'A leper colony.'
  Princess Diana, on the Royal Family

- 'Just as we can't blame people for their parents, we can't blame South America for not having been members of the British Empire.'
  Prince Philip, at the British and Latin Chambers of Commerce

- 'I expect a 30-year apprenticeship before I am king.'
  Prince Charles

— ROYALTY —

- 'I declare this thing open – whatever it is.'
  *Prince Philip, at the opening of Vancouver City Hall's
  new annexe*

- 'Sometimes as a bit of twit.'
  *Prince Charles, responding to David Frost's enquiry as to
  how he would describe himself*

- 'Like all the best families, we have our share of
  eccentricities, of impetuous and wayward youngsters
  and of family disagreements.'
  The Queen

- 'Deaf? If you are near there, no wonder you are deaf.'
  *Prince Philip, to deaf people, in reference to a nearby school's
  steel band, playing in his honour*

- 'I have never drunk and never wanted to. I can never
  understand how anyone can get past the taste.'
  Princess Anne, on alcohol

- 'I'm glad we've been bombed. It makes me feel I can
  look the East End in the face.'
  The Queen Mother

- 'I now complete the process of helping my father to
  expose himself.'
  Prince Charles, unveiling a sculpture of Prince Philip

ROYALTY

- 'If a cricketer, for instance, suddenly decided to go into a school and batter a lot of people to death with a cricket bat, which he could do very easily, are you going to ban cricket bats?'
Prince Philip, responding to calls to ban firearms after the Dunblane massacre

- 'Being a princess isn't all it's cracked up to be.'
Princess Diana

- 'A few years ago everybody was saying, "We must have more leisure, everybody's working too much." Now that everybody's got more leisure, they're complaining they're unemployed. They don't seem to be able to make up their minds what they want, do they?'
Prince Philip, on the recession

- 'Your work is the rent you pay for the room you occupy on earth.'
The Queen Mother

- 'The problem with London is the tourists. They cause the congestion. If we could just stop tourism, then we could stop the congestion.'
Prince Philip, on London's congestion charge

- 'What a po-faced lot these Dutch are.'
Prince Philip, on a visit to Holland

ROYALTY

- 'If I'm deciding on whom I want to live with for 50 years, well, that's the last decision on which I would want my head to be ruled by my heart.'
  Prince Charles, speaking in 1972

- 'I don't think a prostitute is more moral than a wife, but they are doing the same thing.'
  Prince Philip

- 'I don't even know how to use a parking meter, let alone a phone box.'
  Princess Diana

- 'I sometimes wonder if two-thirds of the globe is covered in red carpet.'
  Prince Charles

- 'I'm doing pretty well considering. You know, in the past, when anyone left the Royal Family they had you beheaded.'
  Sarah Ferguson

- 'I myself prefer my New Zealand eggs for breakfast.'
  The Queen

- 'You can't have been here that long, you haven't got a potbelly.'
  Prince Philip, to a Briton residing in Hungary

ROYALTY

- 'If you have a sense of duty, and I like to think I have, service means that you give yourself to people, particularly if they want you, and sometimes if they don't.'
Prince Charles

- 'Are you Indian or Pakistani? I can never tell the difference between you chaps.'
Prince Philip, at a Washington Embassy reception for Commonwealth members

- 'I'm as thick as a plank.'
Princess Diana

- 'I suppose, I'll now be known as Charlie's Aunt.'
Princess Margaret, after the birth of Prince Charles

- 'Dig that crazy rhythm.'
Prince Charles, trying to get down with the kids at a Prince's Trust shelter

- 'The thing I might do best is be a long-distance truck driver.'
Princess Anne

- 'I couldn't believe it the other day when I picked up a British newspaper and read that 82 per cent of men would rather sleep with a goat than me.'
Sarah Ferguson

ROYALTY

* 'If it has got four legs and it is not a chair, if it has two wings and it flies but is not an aeroplane, and if it swims and it is not a submarine, the Cantonese will eat it.'
Prince Philip, commenting on Chinese eating habits to a WWF conference in 1986

* 'All money nowadays seems to be produced with a natural homing instinct for the Treasury.'
Prince Philip

* 'People think that at the end of the day a man is the only answer. Actually, a fulfilling job is better for me.'
Princess Diana

* 'I'm no angel, but I'm no Bo-Beep either.'
Princess Margaret, after the birth of Prince Charles

* 'The Queen is most anxious to enlist everyone in checking this mad, wicked folly of "Women's Rights". It is a subject which makes the Queen so furious that she cannot contain herself.'
Queen Victoria

* 'Awkward, cantankerous, cynical, bloody-minded, at times intrusive, at times inaccurate and at times deeply unfair and harmful to individuals and to institutions.'
Prince Charles, on the press

ROYALTY

- 'Aren't most of you descended from pirates?'
  Prince Philip, to a wealthy resident of the Cayman Islands

- 'You are a pest, by the very nature of that camera in your hand.'
  Princess Anne

- 'An ugly baby is a very nasty object – and the prettiest is frightful.'
  Queen Victoria

- 'Are you still throwing spears at other tribes?'
  Prince Philip, to an Aborigine elder, on a royal visit to Australia

- 'The important thing is not what they think of me, but what I think of them.'
  Queen Victoria

- 'It's like swimming in undiluted sewage'
  Prince Charles, emerging from the sea in Melbourne.
  His remarks didn't earn him any brownie points with the Australians and the press went mad

- 'I never see any home cooking – all I get is fancy stuff.'
  Prince Philip

- 'We've never had a holiday. A week or two at Balmoral, or ten days at Sandringham is the nearest we get.'
  Princess Anne

ROYALTY

* 'I must confess that I am interested in leisure in the same way that a poor man is interested in money.'
  Prince Philip

* 'I'm the heir apparent to the heir presumptive.'
  Princess Margaret

* 'Ghastly.'
  Prince Philip, on Beijing, China, in 1986

* 'Unless one is there, it's embarrassing. Like hearing the Lord's Prayer while playing canasta.'
  The Queen Mother, speaking of the National Anthem

* 'Dontopedology is the science of opening your mouth and putting your foot in it.'
  Prince Philip

* 'Everybody grows but me.'
  Queen Victoria

* 'If I hear one more joke about being hit in the face with a carnation by a Bolshevik fascist lady, I don't know what I'll do. I'm very glad it's given pleasure to everybody. It's what I'm here for.'
  Prince Charles, referring to an incident in Latvia when a 16-year-old schoolgirl slapped him in the face with a bunch of carnations

ROYALTY

* 'My children are not royal; they just happen to have the Queen for their aunt.'
Princess Margaret

* 'How do you keep the natives off the booze long enough to get them to pass the test?'
Prince Philip, quizzing a Scottish driving instructor

* 'Great events make me quiet and calm; it is only trifles that irritate my nerves.'
Queen Victoria

* 'The biggest waste of water in the country is when you spend half a pint and flush two gallons.'
Prince Philip

* 'Make a friend of your mind. Free your mind, and your bottom will follow.'
Sarah Ferguson, giving slimming advice

* 'It looks as if it was put in by an Indian.'
Prince Philip, pointing at an old-fashioned fuse box while on a tour of a factory near Edinburgh in 1993

* 'The Queen is the only person who can put on a tiara with one hand, while walking downstairs.'
Princess Margaret

ROYALTY

- 'You never know, it could be somebody important.'
  *Queen Elizabeth II, advising an embarrassed young woman
  to answer her mobile phone which rang while they were
  in conversation*

- 'I feel sure that no girl would go to the altar if she
  knew all.'
  Queen Victoria

- 'Who is Llewellyn?'
  *Prince Charles, questioning the name on a banner at his
  investiture in Wales. Llewellyn was the previous Prince of Wales.*

- 'I rather doubt whether anyone has ever been
  genuinely shocked by anything I have said.'
  Prince Philip

- 'We live in what virtually amounts to a museum,
  which does not happen to a lot of people.'
  Prince Philip

- 'I would venture to warn against too great intimacy
  with artists as it is very seductive and a little dangerous.'
  Queen Victoria

- 'You managed not to get eaten then.'
  *Prince Philip, to a student who had just visited
  Papua New Guinea*

ROYALTY

- 'Manchester, that's not such a nice place.'
  Queen Elizabeth II

- Saul, the first Hebrew king, was selected by the prophet Samuel to be king simply because he was very tall.

- Tsar Peter the Great made Russian peasants dig the foundations of St Petersburg with their bare hands.

- Mary Stuart became Queen of Scotland when she was only six days old.

- Every queen named Jane has either been murdered, imprisoned, gone mad, died young or been dethroned.

- Queen Elizabeth II was an 18-year-old mechanic in the English military during World War II.

- King Edward VII was so enthusiastic about his shooting that he arranged for all of the 180 or so clocks on the Sandringham Estate to be set half-an-hour early to allow him more time for his sport. Anyone having business with the King needed to ensure they kept their appointment to 'Sandringham Time'. George V maintained this same tradition throughout his reign. However, when Edward VIII took the throne in 1936, he arranged for all of the clocks to be reset and kept in line with those in the rest of his kingdom.

ROYALTY
---

* Queen Elizabeth I regarded herself as a paragon of cleanliness. She declared that she bathed once every three months, whether she needed it or not.

* Each king in a deck of playing cards represents a great king from history. Spades – King David, Clubs – Alexander the Great, Hearts – Charlemagne, and Diamonds – Julius Caesar.

* *The Madness of King George III* was released in America under the title *The Madness of King George*, because it was believed that American moviegoers would believe it to be a sequel and would not go to see it because they had never seen The Madness of King George I and II.

* King George I of England could not speak English. He was born and raised in Germany, and never learned to speak English even though he was king from 1714 to 1727. The King left the running of the country to his ministers, thereby creating the first government cabinet.

* Queen Anne had a transvestite cousin, Lord Cornbury, whom she assigned to be governor of New York and New Jersey. The colonists were not amused.

* Anne Boleyn, Queen Elizabeth I's mother, had 6 fingers on one hand.

ROYALTY

- In the 14th century, King Edward II was deposed in favour of his son, Edward III, and later killed. In order not to mark his body, and hide evidence of murder, a deer horn was inserted into his rectum and a red-hot poker placed inside that. His ghostly screams are said still to be heard in the castle.

- Queen Anne (1665–1714) outlived all 17 of her children.

- Sir Walter Raleigh financed his trip to America to cultivate tobacco by betting Queen Elizabeth I that he could weigh the weight of smoke. He did so by placing 2 identical cigars on opposite sides of a scale, lighting 1 and making sure no ashes fell. The difference in the weight after the cigar was finished was the weight of smoke and Raleigh was on his way to America.

- Prince Harry and Prince William are uncircumcised.

- King Alfonso of Spain (1886–1931) was so tone-deaf that he had one man in his employ known as the 'Anthem Man', whose duty it was to tell the King to stand up whenever the Spanish national anthem was played because the Monarch couldn't recognize it.

- The Spanish kingdom of Castile once had a reigning queen who had been a nun. She was Doña Urraca of

— ROYALTY —

the house of Navarre, daughter of Alfonso the VI of
Leon and Castile, and reigned from 1109 to 1126.
Eventually she married and had a son, who took the
throne when she died.

- King Louis the XIV, also known as the Sun King, was
  almost certainly not the son of Louis the XIII, but the
  son of the Danish nobleman Josiah Rantzau, who
  served in France as a general and marechal of France.
  He had to leave France when the boy grew up
  because Louis was his spitting image.

- Pepin the Short, King of the Franks (751–768 AD)
  was 4ft 6in tall. His wife was known as Bertha of the
  Big Foot.

- In her entire lifetime Queen Isabella of Spain
  (1451–1504) bathed twice.

- When Elizabeth I of Russia died in 1762, 15,000
  dresses were found in her closets. She used to
  change what she was wearing two or even three
  times an evening.

- Czar Paul I of Russia banished soldiers to Siberia for
  marching out of step.

- Catherine the Great of Russia, known as 'The
  Enlightened Despot', relaxed by being tickled.

ROYALTY

- King Louis XV was the first person to use a lift; in 1743 his 'flying chair' carried him between the floors of the Versailles Palace.

- The reign of Czar Nicholas II of Russia ended in tragedy in 1918, when he and his family were murdered, but it had started badly as well. At his coronation, presents were given to all those who attended. But a rumour started that there weren't enough to go around and, in the stampede that followed, hundreds of women and children were killed.

- Queen Supayalat of Burma ordered about 100 of her husband's relatives to be clubbed to death to ensure he had no contenders for the throne.

- While performing her duties as queen, Cleopatra sometimes wore a fake beard.

- After Sir Walter Raleigh introduced tobacco into England in the early 17th century, King James I wrote a booklet against smoking.

- Queen Elizabeth II was *Time* magazine's 'Man of The Year' in 1952.

- King Charles VII, who was assassinated in 1167, was the first Swedish king with the name of Charles. Charles I, II, III, IV, V and VI never existed. No one

— ROYALTY —

knows why. To add to the mystery, almost 300 years went by before there was a Charles VIII (1448–57).

- If the arm of King Henry I had been 42in long, the unit of measure of a 'foot' today would be 14in. But his arm happened to be 36in long and he decreed that the 'standard' foot should be one-third that length: 12in.

- Queen Lydia Liliuokalani was the last reigning monarch of the Hawaiian Islands. She was also the only Queen the United States ever had.

- Queen Victoria used marijuana to help relieve menstrual cramp pain.

- When Queen Elizabeth I died, she owned over 3,000 gowns.

- Prince Philip, the Duke of Edinburgh, names his dogs after orchestral conductors.

7

INSULTS

INSULTS

- 'He is racist, he's homophobic, he's xenophobic and he's a sexist. He's the perfect Republican candidate.'
  Liberal political commentator Bill Press, speaking about Pat Buchanan

- 'Am reserving two tickets for you for my premiere. Come and bring a friend – if you have one.'
  George Bernard Shaw to Winston Churchill

- 'Impossible to be present for the first performance. Will attend second – if there is one.'
  Winston Churchill, in reply to George Bernard Shaw

- 'You can't see as well as these f★★★ing flowers – and they're f★★★ing plastic.'
  Tennis player John McEnroe, speaking to a line judge

- 'You're like a pay toilet, aren't you? You don't give a shit for nothing.'
  Producer Howard Hughes to actor Robert Mitchum

- 'Who picks your clothes – Stevie Wonder?'
  US comic Don Rickles to talk-show host David Letterman

- 'He has never been known to use a word that might send a reader to the dictionary.'
  William Faulkner, speaking about Ernest Hemingway

INSULTS

- 'Poor Faulkner. Does he really think big emotions come from big words?'
  Ernest Hemingway's response to William Faulkner

- 'If I were married to you, I'd put poison in your coffee.'
  Lady Astor to Winston Churchill

- 'If you were my wife, I'd drink it.'
  Winston Churchill, in reply to Lady Astor

- 'Sir, you're drunk!'
  Lady Astor to Winston Churchill

- 'Yes, madam, I am drunk. But in the morning I will be sober and you will still be ugly.'
  Winston Churchill, replying to Lady Astor

- 'Joe Frazier is so ugly, he should donate his face to the US Bureau of Wildlife.'
  Muhammad Ali's response to Joe Frazier

- 'He got a reputation as a great actor by just thinking hard about the next line.'
  Director King Vidor, speaking about Gary Cooper

- 'He's phoney, using his blackness to get his way.'
  Joe Frazier, speaking about Muhammad Ali

INSULTS

- 'The only reason he had a child is so that he can meet babysitters.'
  US talk-show host David Letterman, speaking about Warren Beatty

- 'Do you mind if I sit back a little? Because your breath is very bad.'
  Donald Trump to interviewer Larry King

- 'He's the type of man who will end up dying in his own arms.'
  Actress Mamie Van Doren, speaking about Warren Beatty

- 'He couldn't adlib a fart after a baked-bean dinner.'
  US talk-show host Johnny Carson, speaking about Chevy Chase

- 'He acts like he's got a Mixmaster up his ass and doesn't want anyone to know it.'
  Marlon Brando, speaking about Montgomery Clift

- 'His ears made him look like a taxicab with both doors open.'
  Producer Howard Hughes, speaking about Clark Gable

- 'Steve Martin has basically one joke and he's it.'
  Musician Dave Felton

— INSULTS —

- 'Now there sits a man with an open mind. You can feel the draught from here.'
  Groucho Marx, speaking about his brother Chico

- 'Do you mind if I smoke?'
  Oscar Wilde to actress Sarah Bernhardt

- 'I don't care if you burn.'
  Sarah Bernhardt, in reply to Oscar Wilde

- 'Most of the time he sounds like he has a mouth full of wet toilet paper.'
  Actor Rex Reed, speaking about Marlon Brando

- 'I've got three words for him: Am. A. Teur.'
  Former hell-raising actor Charlie Sheen, speaking about current hell-raising actor Colin Farrell

- 'He sings like he's throwing up.'
  Musician Andrew O'Connor, speaking about Bryan Ferry

- 'Well at least he has finally found his true love. What a pity he can't marry himself.'
  Frank Sinatra, speaking about Robert Redford

- 'Bambi with testosterone.'
  Film critic Owen Gleiberman, speaking about Prince

INSULTS

* 'There were three things that Chico was always on –
  a phone, a horse or a broad.'
  Groucho Marx

* 'Arnold Schwarzenegger looks like a condom full
  of walnuts.'
  TV critic and journalist Clive James

* 'McEnroe was as charming as always, which means
  that he was as charming as a dead mouse in a loaf
  of bread.'
  Clive James

* 'Michael Jackson's album was only called *Bad* because
  there wasn't enough room on the sleeve for 'Pathetic'.
  US songwriter Prince

* 'I love his work but I couldn't warm to him even if I
  was cremated next to him.'
  Keith Richards, speaking about Chuck Berry

* 'Boy George is all England needs – another queen
  who can't dress.'
  US comedienne Joan Rivers

* 'Michael Jackson was a poor black boy who grew up
  to be a rich white woman.'
  Author Molly Ivins

INSULTS

- 'He has turned almost alarmingly blond – he's gone past platinum, he must be plutonium; his hair is co-ordinated with his teeth.'
  Film critic Pauline Kael, speaking about Robert Redford

- 'He has so many fish hooks in his nose, he looks like a piece of bait.'
  Sports commentator Bob Costas, speaking about basketball star Dennis Rodman

- 'He has the vocal modulation of a railway-station announcer, the expressive power of a fencepost and the charisma of a week-old head of lettuce.'
  Film critic Fintan O'Toole, speaking about Quentin Tarantino

- 'I think Mick Jagger would be astounded and amazed if he realized to how many people he is not a sex symbol but a mother image.'
  David Bowie

- 'Elvis transcends his talent to the point of dispensing with it altogether.'
  Rock music critic Greil Marcus, speaking about Elvis Presley

- 'Pamela Lee said her name is tattooed on her husband's penis. Which explains why she changed her name from Anderson to Lee.'
  US talk-show host Conan O'Brien, speaking about ex-Mötley Crüe drummer Tommy Lee

INSULTS

- 'He sounds like he's got a brick dangling from his willy, and a food-mixer making purée of his tonsils.'
  Musician Paul Lester, speaking about Jon Bon Jovi

- 'Presley sounded like Jayne Mansfield looked – blowsy and loud and low.'
  Columnist Julie Burchill, speaking about Elvis Presley

- 'He looks like a dwarf who's been dipped in a bucket of pubic hair.'
  British musician Boy George, speaking about Prince

- 'Sleeping with George Michael would be like having sex with a groundhog.'
  Boy George

- 'If ignorance ever goes to $40 a barrel, I want drilling rights on George Bush's head.'
  Columnist and author Jim Hightower

- 'A pin-stripin' polo-playin' umbrella-totin' Ivy-Leaguer, born with a silver spoon so far in his mouth that you couldn't get it out with a crowbar.'
  Former Alabama Attorney General Bill Baxley, speaking about George Bush

- 'He's a Boy Scout with a hormone imbalance.'
  Political analyst Kevin Phillips, speaking about George Bush

————————— **INSULTS** —————————

- 'He can't help it – he was born with a silver foot in his mouth.'
  Former Texas Governor Ann Richards, speaking about George Bush

- 'He would kill his own mother just so that he could use her skin to make a drum to beat his own praises.'
  Society figure and wit Margot Asquith, speaking about Winston Churchill

- 'Bill Clinton's foreign policy experience is pretty much confined to having had breakfast once at the International House of Pancakes.'
  Republican Pat Buchanan

- 'He is a shifty-eyed goddamn liar… He's one of the few in the history of this country to run for high office talking out of both sides of his mouth at the same time, and lying out of both sides.'
  Harry Truman, speaking about Richard Nixon

- 'Clinton is a man who thinks international affairs means dating a girl from out of town.'
  Best-selling author Tom Clancy

- 'Avoid all needle drugs – the only dope worth shooting is Richard Nixon.'
  Abbie Hoffman, 1960s counter-culture icon

INSULTS

- 'He doesn't die his hair – he's just prematurely orange.'
  Gerald Ford, speaking about Ronald Reagan

- 'He is so dumb, he can't fart and chew gum at the same time.'
  Lyndon Baines Johnson, speaking about Gerald Ford

- 'Nixon's motto was: If two wrongs don't make a right, try three.'
  Editor and writer Norman Cousins, speaking about Richard Nixon

- 'When he does smile, he looks as if he's just evicted a widow.'
  Pulitzer Prize-winning columnist Mike Royko on former presidential candidate Bob Dole

- 'Dan Quayle is more stupid than Ronald Reagan put together.'
  The Simpsons creator Matt Groening

- 'That's not writing, that's typing.'
  US author Truman Capote, commenting on Jack Kerouac's style

- 'He inherited some good instincts from his Quaker forebears, but by diligent hard work, he overcame them.'
  Author James Reston, speaking about Richard Nixon

INSULTS

- 'I may not know much, but I know chicken shit from chicken salad.'
  Lyndon Baines Johnson, commenting on a speech by Richard Nixon

- 'President Clinton apparently gets so much action that every couple of weeks they have to spray WD-40 on his zipper.'
  US talk-show host David Letterman

- 'If life were fair, Dan Quayle would be making a living asking, "Do you want fries with that?"'
  British actor and comedian John Cleese

- 'He doesn't dye his hair, he bleaches his face.'
  US talk-show host Johnny Carson, speaking about Ronald Reagan

- 'The stupid person's idea of the clever person.'
  Irish writer Elizabeth Bowen, speaking about Aldous Huxley

- 'The only time he opens his mouth is to change feet.'
  Golf commentator David Feherty, speaking about Nick Faldo

- 'I think Nancy does most of his talking; you'll notice that she never drinks water when Ronnie speaks.'
  US actor and comedian Robin Williams, speaking about Ronald Reagan

INSULTS

- 'Washington could not tell a lie; Nixon could not tell the truth; Reagan cannot tell the difference.'
  US comic Mort Sahl

- 'Once he makes up his mind, he's full of indecision.'
  US pianist and actor Oscar Levant, speaking about Dwight D Eisenhower

- 'The world is rid of him, but the deadly slime of his touch remains.'
  English painter John Constable, commenting on the death of Lord Byron

- 'He was a great friend of mine. Well, as much as you could be a friend of his, unless you were a 14-year-old nymphet.'
  US author Truman Capote, speaking about William Faulkner

- 'The last time I was in Spain I got through six Jeffrey Archer novels. I must remember to take enough toilet paper next time.'
  Comic Bob Monkhouse

- 'Nothing but old fags and cabbage-stumps of quotations from the Bible and the rest, stewed in the juice of deliberate, journalistic dirty-mindedness.'
  D H Lawrence, speaking about James Joyce

INSULTS

- 'Once you've put one of his books down, you simply can't pick it up again.'
  Mark Twain, speaking about Henry James

- 'What other culture could have produced someone like Hemingway and not seen the joke?'
  Author and columnist Gore Vidal

- 'Dr Donne's verses are like the peace of God; they pass all understanding.'
  James I

- 'There are two ways of disliking poetry; one way is to dislike it, the other is to read Pope.'
  Oscar Wilde, speaking about Alexander Pope

- 'That insolent little ruffian, that crapulous lout. When he quitted a sofa, he left behind him a smear.'
  Poet Norman Cameron, speaking about Dylan Thomas

- 'Reading him is like wading through glue.'
  Lord Alfred Tennyson, speaking about Ben Jonson

- 'They told me that Gladstone read Homer for fun, which I thought served him right.'
  Winston Churchill

INSULTS

- 'Elizabeth Taylor has more chins than the Chinese telephone directory.'
  Joan Rivers

- 'I have more talent in my smallest fart than you have in your entire body.'
  Walter Matthau to Barbra Streisand

- 'He has a face like a warthog that has been stung by a wasp.'
  Golf commentator David Feherty, speaking about Colin Montgomerie

- 'The only person who ever left the Iron Curtain wearing it.'
  US actor and pianist Oscar Levant, speaking about Zsa Zsa Gabor

- 'She ran the whole gamut of emotions from A to B.'
  Dorothy Parker, speaking about Katharine Hepburn

- 'You can calculate Zsa Zsa Gabor's age by the rings on her fingers.'
  Bob Hope

- 'The plain truth is, that he was a most intolerable ruffian, a disgrace to human nature, and a blot of blood and grease upon the history of England.'
  Charles Dickens, speaking about Henry VIII

INSULTS

- 'He writes his plays for the ages – the ages between five and twelve.'
  US author George Nathan, speaking about George Bernard Shaw

- 'Sarah Brightman couldn't act scared on the New York subway at 4 o'clock in the morning.'
  Film-maker Joel Segal, speaking about theatre actress Sarah Brightman

- 'Zsa Zsa Gabor has been married so many times, she has rice marks on her face.'
  US comic and actor Henry Youngman

- 'She has breasts of granite and a mind like a Gruyère cheese.'
  Film-maker Billy Wilder, speaking about Marilyn Monroe

- 'Martina was so far in the closet, she was in danger of being a garment bag.'
  Lesbian author Rita Mae Brown, speaking about tennis star Martina Navratilova

- 'Joan always cries a lot. Her tear ducts must be close to her bladder.'
  Bette Davis, speaking about Joan Crawford

- 'She speaks five languages and can't act in any of them.'
  John Gielgud, speaking about Ingrid Bergman

INSULTS

- 'She looks like she combs her hair with an eggbeater.'
  Columnist Louella Parsons, speaking about Joan Collins

- 'A woman whose face looked as if it had been made of sugar and someone had licked it.'
  George Bernard Shaw, speaking about dancer Isadora Duncan

- 'Hah! I always knew Frank would end up in bed with a boy!'
  Actress Ava Gardner, speaking about Mia Farrow's marriage to her ex-husband Frank Sinatra

- 'Elizabeth Taylor's so fat, she puts mayonnaise on aspirin.'
  US comic Joan Rivers

- 'The only genius with an IQ of 60.'
  Author and columnist Gore Vidal, speaking about Andy Warhol

- 'She's a vacuum with nipples.'
  Film-maker Otto Preminger, speaking about Marilyn Monroe

- 'Nowadays a parlour maid as ignorant as Queen Victoria was when she came to the throne would be classed as mentally defective.'
  George Bernard Shaw, speaking about Queen Victoria

- 'Dramatic art in her opinion is knowing how to fill a sweater.'
  Bette Davis, speaking about Jayne Mansfield

INSULTS

* 'It's a new low for actresses when you have to wonder what's between her ears instead of her legs.'
  Katharine Hepburn, speaking about Sharon Stone

* 'The closest thing to Roseanne Barr's singing the national anthem was my cat being neutered.'
  US talk-show host Johnny Carson

* 'When it comes to acting, Joan Rivers has the range of a wart.'
  Author Stewart Klein

* 'She is closer to organized prostitution than anything else.'
  Singer Morrissey, speaking about Madonna

* 'Comparing Madonna with Marilyn Monroe is like comparing Raquel Welch to the back of a bus.'
  Boy George

* 'A cross between an aardvark and an albino rat.'
  Film critic John Simon, speaking about Barbra Streisand

* 'I didn't know her well, but after watching her in action I didn't want to know her well.'
  Joan Crawford, speaking about Judy Garland

* 'Her voice sounded like an eagle being goosed.'
  Author Ralph Novak, speaking about Yoko Ono

INSULTS

* 'If I found her floating in my pool, I'd punish my dog.'
  US comic Joan Rivers, speaking about Yoko Ono

* 'A senescent bimbo with a lust for home furnishings.'
  Author and social critic Barbara Ehrenreich, speaking about Nancy Reagan

* 'In her last days, she resembled a spoiled pear.'
  Author and columnist Gore Vidal, speaking about US experimental writer Gertrude Stein

* 'She looks like something that would eat its young.'
  Dorothy Parker, speaking about actress Dame Edith Evans

* 'Virginia Woolf's writing is no more than glamorous knitting. I believe she must have a pattern somewhere.'
  Poet Dame Edith Sitwell, speaking about Virginia Woolf

* 'She looked like a huge ball of fur on two well-developed legs.'
  Novelist Nancy Mitford, speaking about Princess Margaret

* 'A fungus of pendulous shape.'
  Writer Alice James, speaking about George Eliot

* 'Every word she writes is a lie, including "and" and "the".'
  US writer and critic Mary McCarthy, speaking about US playwright and memoirist Lillian Hellman

INSULTS

- 'I am fairly unrepentant about her poetry. I really think that three quarters of it is gibberish. However, I must crush down these thoughts, otherwise the dove of peace will shit on me.'
  Noel Coward, speaking about poet Dame Edith Sitwell

HISTORY

HISTORY

- In America and England, witches were hanged not burnt.

- The celebration of May Day was forbidden in the time of Oliver Cromwell.

- John Hawkins began the slave trade by shipping Africans to the West Indies in the 1560s.

- St Columba and his followers first saw the Loch Ness monster in ad 565.

- The Ku Klux Klan was originally founded in the 1860s.

- The first truly humanlike creatures on earth were called *Homo habilis* or 'handyman'.

- To celebrate the battle of Trafalgar, a naval battle was fought on the Serpentine Lake at Hyde Park.

- The fork did not appear until the 16th century, and fork-and-knife pairs were not in general use in Britain until the 17th century.

- The first country to introduce paper money was China in 812, but it wasn't until 1661 that a bank in Sweden issued banknotes.

HISTORY

- Residential, economic, or educational qualification gave half a million Englishmen more than one vote in England in 1885. A university graduate who also owned a business in the City of London voted three times – once at his home, once for his university, and once in the City.

- Soap was considered a frivolous luxury of the British aristocracy from the early 1700s until 1862, and there was a tax on those who used it in England.

- The loudest sound that could be made in 1600 was that of a pipe organ.

- The pharaohs of ancient Egypt wore garments made with thin threads of beaten gold, with some fabrics having up to 500 gold threads per inch (2.54 cm) of cloth.

- Cockney rhyming slang began in London around the 1850s as a statement of independence felt by those who prided themselves on having been born within the sound of Bow Bells.

- Greenwich Mean Time only became universally accepted as the standard time throughout Britain with the growth of the railways in the late 19th century. It was felt that all train timetables should be standardized, so GMT was adopted.

HISTORY

- In ancient Greece, courtesans wore sandals with nails studded into the sole so that their footprints would leave the message 'Follow me'.

- The first discovery of a South African diamond was made by children playing on a beach.

- Australia gave women the vote in 1901.

- The distinctive flat-topped caps worn by the fish porters at Billingsgate market in London are said to be modelled on those worn by the English archers at the Battle of Agincourt.

- More than 100 years ago, the felt-hat-makers of England used mercury to stabilize wool, with many eventually becoming poisoned by the fumes – as demonstrated by the Mad Hatter in Lewis Carroll's *Alice's Adventures in Wonderland*.

- In 1937, the emergency 999 telephone service was established in London. More than 13,000 genuine calls were made in the first month.

- The oldest city in Britain is Ripon, which received its original charter in 886.

- During the 16th century, platform shoes called 'chopines' became popular in Europe, with some

HISTORY

chopines over 20 inches (50 cm) tall. In the 1400s, a popular form of shoes called 'crakows' sported extremely long toes, some over 20 inches (50 cm). The length was an indication of the social status of the person wearing them.

- In 1060, a coin was minted in England shaped like a clover. The user could break off any of the four leaves and use them as separate pieces of currency.

- In 1752, 11 days were dropped from the year when the switch from the Julian calendar to the Gregorian calendar was made. The 25 December date was effectively moved 11 days backwards. Some Christian church sects, called old calendarists, still celebrate Christmas on 7 January.

- The first contraceptive diaphragms, centuries ago, were citrus rinds.

- Obsidian balls, or occasionally brass balls, were placed in the eye sockets of Egyptian mummies.

- During the French Reign of Terror from 1793 to 1794, 500,000 people were arrested and 17,000 of them were publicly executed at the guillotine.

- Tangshan, in China, suffered the deadliest earthquake of the 20th century on 28 July 1976. One quarter of

---
HISTORY
---

the population was killed or seriously injured and an estimated 242,000 people killed.

- The population of the entire world in 5000 BC was five million.

- In World War II it cost the Allies about $22,500 to kill one enemy soldier.

- Cambridge University was established in 1209.

SCIENCE AND NATURE

---------- **SCIENCE AND NATURE** ----------

- Every power tool on the market has passed 20 safety tests.

- An energy-saving washing machine can save you enough money to buy your washing powder for six months.

- RAM stands for Random Access Memory.

- Pocket calculators first appeared in the 1970s.

- IBM is nicknamed 'Big Blue'.

- The earliest type of robot was a water clock invented in Egypt in 250 BC.

- The compact disc was developed in the 1970s.

- The first miniature TV sets appeared in the 1980s.

- Helium is the element with the lowest boiling point.

- Work on the first Channel tunnel started in 1877.

- Japanese cedars have bright green leaves in summer and turn purple and bronze in winter.

- The refrigerator was first successfully developed in the 1860s.

SCIENCE AND NATURE

- Gorse and broom belong to the pea family.

- If we were to upturn the Millennium Dome at Greenwich, it would take 3.8 billion half-litres of beer to fill it up.

- Halley's Comet will next appear in 2061.

- Wheeled vehicles were first invented in about 3000 BC.

- Edwin Beard Budding invented the lawnmower in 1830.

- All Model T Fords were black.

- The Mercalli scale measures the intensity of an earthquake.

- The Romans bought the sycamore tree to Britain.

- The wood at the centre of the tree stem is called heartwood.

- The kerosene fungus can live in jet fuel tanks, so if there is a minute amount of water in the tank, the fungus can use the fuel as food.

- The kowhai is the national flower of New Zealand.

SCIENCE AND NATURE

- The cedar is the national tree of Lebanon.

- Lavender takes it name from the Latin lavare, meaning to wash, because of its use in toilet preparations.

- Water lilies were a symbol of immortality in ancient times.

- Two objects have struck the earth with enough force to destroy a whole city. Each object, one in 1908 and again in 1947, struck regions of Siberia. Not one human being was hurt either time.

- Stitching through a piece of sandpaper is an effective way to sharpen a sewing machine needle.

- More than 45,000 pieces of plastic debris float on every square mile of ocean.

- An ounce (about 28 g) of platinum can be stretched to 10,000 ft (3,048 m).

- With 980-plus species, bats make up more than 23 per cent of all known mammals by species.

- Nourishment, capable of sustaining life for a short time, can be gained by chewing on leather.

- A dog can understand between 35 to 40 commands.

──────── **SCIENCE AND NATURE** ────────

- The 1906 San Francisco earthquake was the equivalent of 12,000 Hiroshima nuclear bombs.

- The minimum safe distance between a wood-burning stove and flammable objects is 3 ft (0.9 m).

- More than half of the world's animal groups are found only in the sea.

- A 'hairbreadth away' is 1/48 in (0.05 cm).

- Cows can smell odours 6 miles (10 km) away.

- The average accumulation of barnacles on the hull of a ship over six months can produce enough drag to force the vessel to burn 40 per cent more fuel than normal when cruising.

- The world's chicken population is more than double the human population, while the world cattle population outnumbers the population of China.

- A car uses 1.6 oz (0.05 litres) of petrol idling for one minute. Half an ounce (0.015 litres) is used to start the average car.

- A quality, fully faceted brilliant diamond has at least 58 facets.

--------------- SCIENCE AND NATURE ---------------

- The average lead pencil will draw a line 35 miles (56 km) long or write approximately 50,000 English words.

- Horses can sleep standing up.

- The sun is estimated to be 20 to 21 cosmic years old.

- A 10-gallon (UK/US?) (45 litre) hat holds less than a gallon (4.5 litres) of liquid.

- The sun's warming rays travel through 93 million miles (149,664,900km) of space to reach Earth.

- Only one polished diamond in a thousand weighs more than a carat.

- The average raindrop falls at seven mph (11 kph).

- Other than humans, the pigs family are the only animals that can get sunburn.

- A bolt of lightning travels at speeds of up to 100 million fps (30,480,000 m/s), or 72 million mph (115,869,600 kph).

- Dirty snow melts faster than white snow because it's darker and absorbs more heat.

SCIENCE AND NATURE

- The cargo bay of a space shuttle is large enough to hold one humpback whale, and still have room for 1,000 herrings. That's the equivalent of filling it with 250,000 4-oz chocolate bars.

- Forest fires move faster uphill than downhill.

- There are a thousand times more living things in the sea than there are on land.

- An employee of the Alabama Department of Transportation installed spyware on his boss's computer and proved that the boss spent ten per cent of his time working, 20 per cent of time checking stocks and 70 per cent of the time playing solitaire. The employee was fired, but the boss kept his job.

- Physicists have already performed a simple type of teleportation, transferring the quantum characteristics of one atom on to another atom at a different location.

- A German supermarket chain has introduced a new way of allowing customers to pay using just their fingerprints.

- The annual growth of WWW traffic is 314,000 per cent.

- James Dyson has invented a vacuum cleaner that can order its own spare parts.

HISTORY

- The 'save' icon on Microsoft Word shows a floppy disk, with the shutter on backwards.

- Thirty-two per cent of singles polled think they will meet their future mate online.

- Scientists have performed a surgical operation on a single living cell, using a needle that is just a few millionths of a metre wide.

- As much as 80 per cent of microwaves from mobile phones are said to be absorbed by your head.

- Thomas Edison designed a helicopter that would work with gunpowder. It exploded and also blew up his factory.

- An x-ray security scanner that sees through people's clothes has been deployed at Heathrow Airport.

- The last time an astronaut walked on the moon was in 1979.

- The time spent deleting SPAM costs United States businesses £11.2 billion annually.

- A remote tribe in the Brazilian jungle are now online after a charity gave them five battery-powered computers.

SCIENCE AND NATURE

* The cruise liner *Queen Elizabeth II* burns a gallon of diesel for each six inches that it moves.

* The Church of England has appointed its first web pastor to oversee a new parish that will exist only on the net.

* The light from your computer monitor streams at you at almost 186,000 miles a second.

* 35 billion emails are sent each day throughout the world.

* Insurance company Esure announced plans to use voice stress analysis technology to weed out fraudulent claims.

* The screwdriver was invented before the screw.

* Scientists in Australia have developed software that allows people to log on to PCs by laughing.

* The first meal eaten on the moon by Neil Armstrong and Buzz Aldrin was cold roast turkey and trimmings.

* The newest trend in the Netherlands is having tiny jewels implanted directly into the eye.

SCIENCE AND NATURE

* Researchers have found that doctors who spend at least three hours a week playing video games make about 37 per cent fewer mistakes in laparoscopic surgery than surgeons who didn't play video games.

* The first domain name ever registered was Symbolics.com.

* Every single 'all-a' domain name, from a.com to aaaaaaaaaaaaaaaaaaaaaaaaaaaaaaaaaaaaaaaaaaaaaaaaaaaaaaaaa.com (63 as), has been registered.

* Every single possible 3-character .com domain (over 50,000) has long since been registered!

* Bill Gates was once an Apple employee.

* The highest publicly reported amount of money paid for a domain name is £3.9 million, paid for business.com.

* A single individual, Dr Lieven P Van Neste, owns over 200,000 domain names.

* Every five seconds a computer is infected with a virus.

* The first personal computer was called the Altair and was made by a company called MITS in 1974. It came in a kit and had to be assembled by the user.

SCIENCE AND NATURE

- IBM introduced their first personal computer in 1981.

- The basis of the Macintosh computer was Apple's Lisa, which was released in 1983. This was the first system to utilize a GUI or Graphical User Interface. The first Macintosh was released in 1984.

- The name 'Intel' stems from the company's former name, 'Integrated Electronics'.

- Over 23 per cent of all photocopier faults worldwide are caused by people sitting on them and photocopying their bottoms.

- The town of Halfway, Oregon, temporarily changed its name to half.com as a publicity stunt for the website of the same name.

- Scandinavia leads the world in internet access according to the UN communications agency.

- Hornby has invented a way of connecting a Scalextric track to a PC so people can race each other on the internet.

- Readers of the technical innovation website T3.co.uk have voted the widget as the greatest technological invention in 40 years.

SCIENCE AND NATURE

- The first scheme in the UK which allows drivers to pay for parking by mobile phone was launched in Scotland.

- The telescope on Mount Palomar, California, can see a distance of 7,038,835,200,000,000 million miles.

- PlayStation2 game *WWE SmackDown: Here Comes The Pain* features female competitors trying to rip each other's clothes off.

- Britney Spears, Harry Potter and *The Matrix* topped the list of the most frequently searched subjects in 2003 on Google.

- A Belgian couple got married by SMS because text messaging played such a big part in their relationship.

- In February 2002, Friends Reunited was in the top-ten most visited websites in the UK.

- In April 2003, the total number of registered Friends Reunited members was 8.6 million.

- Twenty-seven per cent of all web transactions are abandoned at the payment screen.

- Four out of five visitors never come back to a website.

SCIENCE AND NATURE

- Space on a big company's homepage is worth about 1,300 times as much as land in the business districts of Tokyo.

- The typewriter was invented before the fountain pen.

- Monster truck engines are custom-built, alcohol-injected and usually cost around $35,000. They burn 2–2.5 gallons of methanol per run (approx. 250ft).

- 1,314 phone calls are misplaced by telecom services every minute.

- According to research, Britons collectively make 132 million mobile-phone calls a day.

- A plane that flies without fuel by riding on a ground-based laser beam has been successfully tested by scientists.

- Airbags are deployed at a rate of 200mph.

- Two very popular and common objects have the same function, but one has thousands of moving parts, while the other has absolutely no moving parts – an hourglass and a sundial.

- Russian scientists have developed a new drug that prolongs drunkenness and enhances intoxication.

SCIENCE AND NATURE

- The fish reel was invented around 300 AD.

- An ounce of gold can be stretched into a wire 50 miles long.

- Spam filters that catch the word 'cialis' will not allow many work-related emails through because that word is embedded inside the word 'specialist'.

- Orange and DaimlerChrysler UK joined forces to launch the UK's first car that comes with an integrated handsfree phone system.

- There are 150,000,000 mobile phones in use in the United States, more than one for every two human beings in the country.

- A Boeing 767 airliner is made of 3,100,000 separate parts.

- Replying more than 100 times to the same piece of spam e-mail will overwhelm the sender's system and interfere with their ability to send any more spam.

- A person sneezing was the first thing Thomas Edison filmed with his movie camera.

- A German company has built the world's first washing machine that talks and recognizes spoken commands.

RELIGION

RELIGION

- The Bible does not say there were three wise men, or magi; it only says there were three gifts. It is believed there were anywhere between 2 and 9 magi.

- The youngest pope was 11 years old.

- Pope Innocent X was known as 'Innocent the Honest' because he admitted fathering his love children while he was the supreme leader of the Catholic Church.

- Jesus was described as 'King of the Jews' as a deliberate insult to the Jewish authorities on the part of Pilate, the governor of Judea.

- 'Allah Akbar, Allah Akbar, La Allah Il Allah, La Allah Il Allah U Mohammed Rassul Allah' is heard by more people than any other sound of the human voice. This is the prayer recited by muezzins from each of the four corners of the prayer tower as Muslims all over the world face towards Mecca and kneel at sunset. It means 'God is great. There is no God but God, and Mohammed is the prophet of God'.

- The Gospel of Mary (Mary Magdalene) was discovered in 1896 by Dr Carl Reinhardt. Due to a series of unfortunate events, a translation wasn't published until 1955, when it appeared first in German. It first appeared in English along with the texts from the Nag Hammadi Library in 1977. It is

RELIGION

missing several pages, but enough survives to draw the conclusion that at least one sect of early Christianity held Mary Magdalene in high esteem as a visionary, apostle and leader.

- King Henry I charged a tax to ecclesiastics who abandoned celibacy. The practice began in 1129.

- St Boniface is the saint that one should pray to in cases of sodomy.

- As specified by the Christian Church, the canonical hours are Matins, Lauds, Prime, Terce, Sext, None, Vespers and Compline.

- It was not until 1969 that the Roman Catholic Church quietly removed all references to Mary Magdalene as a penitent sinner and harlot, and began to refer to her instead as a disciple, although this has been little publicized.

- The two robbers crucified next to Jesus were named Dismas and Gestas, though these names are not in the Bible.

- The four gospels, Matthew, Mark, Luke and John, selected for inclusion in the New Testament, are examples of books that did not carry the names of their actual authors. The present names were assigned

RELIGION

long after these four books were written. In spite of what the gospel authors say, biblical scholars are now almost unanimously agreed that none of the gospel authors was either a disciple of Jesus or an eyewitness to his ministry. In reality, there is no evidence of these gospels' existence until the last quarter of the 2nd century, between 170 and 180 AD.

- 'Hagiology' is the branch of literature dealing with the lives and legends of saints.

- Alexander VI, known as 'the most notorious pope in all of history', often left his daughter, Lucrezia, in charge of the papacy on his frequent trips away from Rome. His papacy was marked by 'nepotism, greed and unbridled sensuality'.

- The shortest verse in the Bible consists of two words: 'Jesus wept' (John 11:35).

- The seven archangels are Michael, Gabriel, Raphael, Uriel, Chamuel, Jophiel and Zadkiel.

- Early Christians used red-coloured eggs to symbolize the Resurrection.

- In 312 AD, Emperor Constantine made Christianity the official Roman religion, and the result was the Roman Catholic Church, which is a mixture of about

RELIGION

one-third Christianity, one-third Judaism, including the holy days and priesthood, and one-third paganism, with its superstitions, fetishes and charms such as holy water, candles and images.

- Pope Innocent IV (1243–54) wasn't! He used torture to extract confessions.

- In 325 AD, Constantine called a meeting of Christian bishops at Nicaea to decide what a Christian was, and what Christians should believe. He changed the time of the Resurrection to coincide with the festival celebrating the death and resurrection of the pagan god Attis. This celebration was held annually from 22 to 25 March. Christians adapted the actual date, 25 March, as the anniversary of the passion.

- At least six popes have been excommunicated or condemned as heretics, including one who was excommunicated twice and two who excommunicated one another.

- In the first 12 centuries of existence, the Church was disturbed some 25 times by rival claimants of the papacy. The resulting strife was always an occasion of scandal, sometimes of violence and bloodshed.

- The longest name in the Bible is Mahershalalbaz (Isaiah 8:1).

RELIGION

- The Hindu holy day begins at sunrise, the Jewish holy day starts at sunset, and the Christian holy day at midnight.

- Salt is mentioned more than 30 times in the Bible.

- The letters inscribed in the Pope's mitre are 'VICARIUS FILII DEI', which is the Latin for 'VICAR OF THE SON OF GOD'. In Roman numerals, the letters of this title which have assigned value add up to 666. For VICARIUS: V = 5, I = 1, C = 100, I + 1, U (or V) = 5; for FILII: I = 1, L = 50, I = 1, I = 1; for DEI: D = 500, I = 1; totalling 666 the traditional number of the Devil. (Apocalypse 13:16 says, 'Here is wisdom. He who has understanding, let him calculate the number of the beast, for it is the number of a man; and its number is six hundred and sixty-six.')

- In the 10th century, it was ruled that a cleric who experienced a wet dream would have to sing seven prescribed penitential psalms right after the fact, and in the morning he needed to sing 30 more.

- The Assumption of Mary into heaven, which was not mentioned in the Bible, did not become Catholic dogma until being formally declared by Pope Pius XII in 1950. This states that Mary's uncorrupt body was carried straight to heaven after her death.

─────────── **RELIGION** ───────────

- Early Catholic doctrine declared that women did not have souls. Adam gave a rib to create Eve, it was claimed, but did not give a part of his soul. This belief has never been officially changed.

- In 1854, it was decided, on a majority vote of cardinals, that Mary had been immaculately conceived. The Immaculate Conception, never mentioned in the Bible, means that Mary, whose conception was brought about the normal way, was conceived without original sin or its stain.

- All the teaching concerning Mary as Mother of God, Queen of Heaven, Refuge of Sinners, Gate of Heaven, Mother of Mercies, Spouse of the Holy Ghost, etc is not mentioned in the Bible.

- The first translation of the English Bible was initiated by John Wycliffe and completed by John Purvey in 1388.

- The Four Horsemen of the Apocalypse, named in the Book of Revelation, are Conquest, Slaughter, Famine and Death.

- For 40 years (in the 14th century), there were simultaneously up to three different infallible popes. A division occurred in the Church of Rome, and the two factions vied for superiority. One faction officially elected Pope Urban VI as the head of the Church,

RELIGION

who was succeeded by Boniface IX in 1389 and later Pope Gregory XII. The other party elected Pope Clement VII, called historically the 'Anti-Pope', who was succeeded by Pope Benedictine XIII in 1394 as the head of the Church. Then, in 1409, a third party of reactionaries, who now claimed to represent the true Church, elected Pope Alexander V as head of the Roman hierarchy. Now there were three infallible popes. In June 1409, Pope Alexander V officially excommunicated the other two popes, and gradually the incident was resolved.

- On 6 April 1830, in a small log cabin, 6 men including Joseph Smith and his brother Hyrum, founded and publicly signed the charter for the Church of Jesus Christ of Latter-day Saints.

- In 1844, Joseph and Hyrum Smith were led with two other men to Carthage Jail in Quincy, Illinois, on trumped-up charges. There, the jail was stormed by an angry mob of 150–200 men and Joseph and Hyrum were killed in the mêlée.

- The Mormons (led by Brigham Young) were forced to flee the confines of the United States to the Salt Lake Valley, which at the time was part of Mexico. There, they were free to live their religion as they saw fit without the constant persecution at the hands of mobocracy.

RELIGION

* The Church of Scientology was founded in 1953 in Washington DC, by US science-fiction writer L Ron Hubbard.

* Two bumper stickers seen in America:
  'Lord, help me be the kind of person my dog thinks I am.'
  'Jesus is coming! Look busy!'

* Religion is the sigh of the oppressed creature, the heart of a heartless world… It is the opium of the people.
  Karl Marx

* Our religion is made so as to wipe out vices; it covers them up, nourishes them, incites them.
  Montaigne

* Thanks to God, I am still an atheist.
  Louis Buñuel

* We have in England a particular bashfulness in everything that regards religion.
  Joseph Addison

* The attitude that regards entanglement with religion as something akin to entanglement with an infectious disease must be confronted broadly and directly.
  William J Bennett

RELIGION

- Things have come to a pretty pass when religion is allowed to invade the sphere of private life.
  William Lamb

- An atheist is a man who has no invisible means of support.
  John Buchan

- A Protestant, if he wants aid or advice on any matter, can only go to his solicitor.
  Benjamin Disraeli

- The two dangers which beset the Church of England are good music and bad preaching.
  Lord Hugh Cecil

- I am always most religious on a sunshiny day.
  Lord Byron

- A lady, if undressed at church, looks silly; one cannot be devout in dishabille.
  George Farquhar

- What, after all, is a halo? It's only one more thing to keep clean.
  Christopher Fry

- Pray, good people, be civil. I am a Protestant whore.
  Nell Gwyn

—— RELIGION ——

* Roman Emperor Nero sentenced St Peter to crucifixion.

* The Church of the Holy Sepulchre marks the spot where Joseph of Arimathea buried Jesus.

* In the Black Forest area in Germany, religious families lay an extra place at the Christmas table for the Virgin Mary.

* Jesus gave St Peter his name. It means 'the rock'.

* The carol 'Good King Wenceslas' commemorates the martyr who is patron saint of Bohemia.

* The name 'Beelzebub' means 'lord of the flies'.

* St Jude is the patron saint of hopeless causes.

* New Zealand has had women priests since the 1960s.

* The ancient Norse associated mistletoe with their goddess of love, leading to the tradition of kissing under the mistletoe.

* In Italy, they do not use Christmas trees; instead they decorate small, pyramid-shaped wooden stands with fruit.

RELIGION

- In Islamic myth, Israfil is the angel who will sound the trumpet announcing the end of the world.

- It is forbidden to take photographs at a Quaker wedding.

- Orthodox Judaism forbids the practice of cremation.

- In Armenia, the traditional Christmas Eve meal consists of fried fish, lettuce and spinach.

- The Lord's Prayer appears twice in the Bible – in Matthew VI and Luke XI.

- Studies of the Dead Sea scrolls indicate that the passage in the Bible known as the Sermon on the Mount is actually an ancient Essene prayer dating back hundreds of years before the birth of Christ.

- Two chapters in the Bible, 2 Kings and Isaiah 37, are alike almost word for word.

- A kelpie was a water spirit of Scottish folklore, reputed to cause drownings.

- A Hindi bride wears a red sari.

- Christendom did not begin to date its history from the birth of Christ until 500 years after his death. The

RELIGION

system was introduced in 550 by Dionysius Exigus, a monk in Rome.

- The 27 books of the Bible's New Testament are believed to have been written circa ad 100, about 70 to 90 years after the death of Jesus.

CUSTOMS AND TRADITIONS

CUSTOMS AND TRADITIONS

- In ancient Egypt, priests plucked every hair from their bodies, including their eyebrows and eyelashes.

- In olden days in Britain, a green wedding dress was thought to be unlucky unless the bride was Irish. The expression, 'green gown' implied promiscuity, as the green staining of a woman's clothing was the result of rolling about in grassy fields with a lover.

- When a man died in ancient Egypt, the females in his family would smear their heads and faces with mud, and wander through the city beating themselves and tearing off their clothes.

- In ancient Egypt, when a woman's husband was convicted of a crime, she and her children were punished as well, usually being enslaved.

- In ancient Rome, there was a superstitious custom of nailing owls over doors, with their wings outspread, to deflect storms.

- A couple living together for two years in Russia is considered married. This is called a citizen marriage.

- In Pakistan, it is rude to show the soles of your feet or point a foot when you are sitting on the floor.

———— CUSTOMS AND TRADITIONS ————

- In medieval times, church bells were often consecrated to ward off evil spirits. Because thunderstorms were attributed to the work of demons, the bells would be rung in an attempt to stop the storms.

- In Russia, buying carnations or roses is a prerequisite for a first date and must be given in odd numbers, as flowers given in even numbers are reserved for funerals.

- In China, it is unwise to give a clock as a gift, as to the older Chinese generation a clock is a symbol of bad luck.

- In Jordan, when a host asks a visitor to stay for dinner it is customary to refuse twice before accepting. Unless the host insists a couple of times, seconds of any dish offered should also be refused and even then accepted only with a slight air of reluctance.

- Thai women only wear black for funerals and periods of mourning.

- Polish hospitality calls for ample food being offered, and woe is the guest who declines; yet the guest who grabs food without being encouraged disgraces himself. This is referred to as the host being a 'nukac' – 'the one who urges.'

CUSTOMS AND TRADITIONS

- In Russia, yellow flowers are a sign of grieving or separation.

- In Russia, women appreciate receiving cosmetics as a gift, as they are scarce in almost all Eastern European countries.

- Until the 1950s, Tibetans disposed of their dead by taking the body up a hill, hacking it into little pieces, and feeding the remains to the birds.

- In Scotland, it is believed that if someone walks any distance between two redheaded girls, it is a sign that he or she will soon be wealthy.

- In Russia, when a friend is leaving on a trip, it is common for this person and a close friend or spouse to sit in silence on the traveller's packed suitcases for a few minutes prior to departing. It is believed that this moment of togetherness will cause the traveller to have a safe journey.

- Overturned shoes (soles up) are considered very bad luck and even omens of death in Greece. If you accidentally take them off and they land soles up, turn them over immediately and say 'skorda' (garlic) and spit once or twice.

CUSTOMS AND TRADITIONS

- In the highlands of Chiapas, Mexico, weaving skills are treasured, and a colourful, well-made shawl worn by an unmarried woman advises potential husbands of its wearer's dexterity.

- In Japan it is considered polite to initially refuse someone's offer of help. The Japanese may also initially refuse your offer, even if they really want or need it. Traditionally, an offer is made three times.

- In the United States, Navajo culture discourages doctors from discussing end-of-life directives and negative prognoses for fear that talking about grim subjects may trigger them.

- Some restaurants in Kyoto, Japan, have a custom called 'Ichigensan okotowari', which means that you must be introduced by someone to be welcomed. This enables the restaurant to give its warmest hospitality and services to all its customers. Business cards are preferred to credit cards – most establishments will only accept cash.

- It is a common practice in China for people to spit or blow their noses (without a handkerchief) on a street or sidewalk. This is not considered rude, whereas blowing one's nose in a handkerchief and returning it to one's pocket is considered vulgar.

—— CUSTOMS AND TRADITIONS ——

- A hot cross bun kept from one Good Friday to the next was considered a lucky charm; it was not supposed to grow mouldy and was used as a charm against shipwreck. Good Friday bread, when hung over the chimney piece, was supposed to guarantee that all bread baked after that would be perfect.

- In Zambia, handshaking with the left hand supporting the right is common, while direct eye contact with members of the opposite sex avoided, as it may suggest romantic overtures.

- In South America, it would be rude not to ask a man about his wife and children. In most Arab countries, it would be rude to do so.

- Ancient Romans respected land boundary laws to such an extent that farmers who moved boundary stones, even if by accident, were executed, and then the guilty party's oxen were sacrificed to Jove.

- The 'fingers circle' gesture is the British sign for 'ok', but in Brazil and Germany, the gesture is considered vulgar or obscene. The gesture is also considered impolite in Greece and Russia, while in Japan it means 'money'. In Southern France, the fingers-circle sign signifies 'worthless' or 'zero'.

—— CUSTOMS AND TRADITIONS ——

- In Sweden, when leaving someone's home, the coat must not be put on until you reach the doorway, To do so earlier suggests an eagerness to leave. When entering or departing a Russian home, it is considered very bad form to shake hands across the threshold.

- In Tibet, it's good manners to stick out your tongue at your guests.

- In Western culture spitting is rude, but it is common as a Russian gesture to ward off bad luck or to express the hope for continued good fortune. A Russian individual will spit three times over his or her left shoulder.

- In Thailand, the left hand is considered unclean, so should not be used when eating. Also, pointing with one finger is considered rude and is only done when pointing to objects or animals, never humans.

- Mourning clothes in India are often brown, which symbolizes withered leaves.

- When members of the Western African Wodaabe tribe greet each other, they may not look each other directly in the eyes. Also, during daylight hours, a man cannot hold his wife's hand in public, call her by name, or speak to her in a personal way.

———— CUSTOMS AND TRADITIONS ————

- The Japanese have many rules concerning chopsticks. Improper use includes wandering the chopsticks over several foods without decision ('mayoibashi') and licking the ends of chopsticks ('neburibashi'), which is considered unforgivable. Similarly, chopsticks must never be used to point at somebody or be left standing up out of the food.

- In Japan, almost every weekday morning, free tissues are handed to bus and rail commuters by workers of the companies who print messages and advertisements on them. This is because most public bathrooms do not have paper towels or toilet paper.

- Among the Danakil tribesmen of Ethiopia, when a male dies, his grave is marked with a stone for every man he has killed.

- In France and Belgium, snapping the fingers of both hands has a vulgar meaning.

- An old Ethiopian tradition requires the jewellery of a bride to be removed after her wedding, with its likeness then tattooed on her skin.

- In Germany, shaking hands with the other hand in a pocket is considered impolite.

——— CUSTOMS AND TRADITIONS ———

- Natives of the Turkish village of Kuskoy communicate through whistling, allowing them to communicate over distances of up to one mile (1.6 km).

- Before eating, Japanese people say 'itadakimasu', meaning 'I receive this food', an expression of thanks to whoever worked to prepare the food in the meal.

- In Clarendon, Texas, lawyers must accept eggs, chickens or other produce, as well as money, as forms of payment of legal fees.

- In Egypt, social engagements usually begin very late, with dinner not served until 10.30 p.m. or later. When invited to dine, it is customary to take a gift of flowers or chocolates, though the giving and receiving of gifts should be done with both hands or with the right hand – never with the left.

- In India, it is perfectly proper for men to wear pyjamas in public. They are accepted as standard daytime wearing apparel.

- In Mali, a man will shake hands with a woman only if she offers her hand first. The handshake is often done with the left hand touching the other person's elbow as well.

CUSTOMS AND TRADITIONS

* In Greece, it is a wedding tradition to write the names of all single female friends and relatives of the bride on the sole of her shoe. After the wedding, the shoe is examined, and those whose names have worn off are said to be the next in line for marriage.

* An American custom, when moving to a new home, is that the cat should be put in through the window, not the door, so that the animal will not leave.

* A wedding custom in early Yorkshire involved a plate holding a piece of wedding cake being thrown out of the window as the bride returned to her parental home after the wedding. If the plate broke, she would enjoy a happy marital future; if the plate remained intact, her future was bleak.

* From earliest times, body piercings were a superstitious practice, with the holes produced thought to release demons from the body.

* It was once the custom for French brides to step on an egg before crossing the threshold of their new homes.

* Hundreds of years ago people travelling by stagecoach in Britain often sent a servant ahead to make arrangements for their arrival. The servant would give the service providers money 'to ensure promptness', which was shortened by initials to 'tip'. Today a tip is

—— CUSTOMS AND TRADITIONS ——

more of a thank-you after good service than a bribe to get good service.

- In Anglo Saxon times, brides were often kidnapped before a wedding and brawls during the service were common. For this reason a bride stood to the groom's left at a wedding so that his sword hand would be free. This also explains why the best man stands with the groom: the tribe's best warrior was there to help the groom defend the bride.

- In Japan, frogs are the symbols of good luck.

- In Japan, the dragonfly symbolizes good luck, courage, and manliness. Japanese warriors customarily wore the dragonfly emblem in battle.

- During the Middle Ages a dinner party consisting of 13 people was the worst of omens, as it foretold of the impending death of one in the group. This number was associated with the Last Supper, and also with a witch's coven, as both had 13 members.

- An old folk custom for selecting a husband from several suitors involved taking onions and writing each suitor's name individually on each. All the onions were put in a cool, dark storeroom, with the first to to grow sprouts determining which man the undecided maiden should marry.

—— CUSTOMS AND TRADITIONS ——

* For a time, it was the custom to use eggs as a form of currency in France. Once a year, poverty-stricken clerics and students trudged through the streets of Paris, carrying an egg basket, and collected what they could.

* A hundred years ago, it was the custom of sailors to put a tattoo of a pig on one foot and a rooster on the other, to prevent drowning.

* Bad weather on the way to the wedding is thought to be an omen of an unhappy marriage. Some cultures, however, consider rain a good omen. Cloudy skies and wind are believed to cause stormy marriages, while snow is associated with fertility and wealth.

* In Britain, a horseshoe was thought to be a guardian against all evil forces, as inhabitants of the spirit world were supposed to flee from the sight of cold iron.

* To see how many children a newlywed couple will have, the Finns count the number of grains of rice in the bride's hair. Czechs send off the newlyweds under a barrage of peas. Italians throw sugared almonds. An African tradition is to throw corn kernels to signify fertility.

* In central Australia, it was once the custom for balding Aranda Aborigines to wear wigs made of emu feathers.

CUSTOMS AND TRADITIONS

- According to old farmers' traditions, to test your love, you and your lover should each place an acorn in water. If they swim together, your love is true; if they drift apart, so will you.

- Kissing one's fingertips is a common gesture throughout Europe and Latin America countries, declaring 'Ah, beautiful!' The gesture originates from the ancient Greeks and Romans who, when entering and leaving the temple, threw a kiss towards sacred objects such as statues and altars.

- During ancient times, egg-shaped stones were placed at the corners of a field, or by a fruit tree, to ensure a good crop. Symbolically, anything egg-shaped represented fertility.

- In 1829, New England rum was considered to be excellent for washing hair and keeping it healthy, while brandy was supposed to strengthen the roots.

- In Iceland, tipping at a restaurant is considered an insult.

- A conventional sign of virginity in Tudor England was a high exposed bosom and a sleeve full to the wrists.

- In Britain, witches were once said to disguise themselves as cats, so many people refused to talk near a cat for fear that a witch would learn their secrets.

CUSTOMS AND TRADITIONS

- According to old farmers' traditions, the best time of the day to select a new pair of shoes is in the afternoon, when the exercise of the day has stretched the muscles to their largest extent.

- Kettledrums were once used as currency on the island of Aler in Indonesia.

- Ladies in Europe took to wearing lightning rods on their hats and trailing a ground wire – a fad that began after Benjamin Franklin published instructions on how to make them in his almanac.

- In Greek legend, malicious creatures called kallikantzaroi sometimes play troublesome pranks at Christmas time. To get rid of them, you would burn either salt or an old shoe, as the stench would drive them off. Other effective methods included hanging a pig's jawbone by the door and keeping a large fire so they couldn't sneak down the chimney.

- The widespread superstition that green is an unlucky colour dates from a centuries-old tradition that only fairies living at the bottom of the garden had the right to wear green, and would deal harshly with anyone else found wearing the colour.

- Until the 19th century, solid blocks of tea were used as money in Siberia.

CUSTOMS AND TRADITIONS

- Ancient Greeks considered the philtrum, the indentation in the middle area between the nose and the upper lip, to be one of the body's most erogenous zones.

- In Victorian London, the Lord Mayor's Show always finished with a banquet that began with turtle soup.

- Iridescent beetle shells were the source of the earliest eye glitter ever used – devised by the ancient Egyptians.

- In ancient Rome, wealthy Romans always drank from goblets made of quartz crystal, as they believed the transparent mineral was a safeguard against their enemies. Legend had it that a cup carved from the transparent mineral would not hold poison.

- The San Blas Indian women of Panama consider giant noses a mark of great beauty, so they paint black lines down the centre of their noses to make them appear longer.

- It was once customary to use pieces of bread to erase lead pencil before rubber erasers came into use.

- Leather money was used in Russia up until the 17th century, as was tea money in China.

——— CUSTOMS AND TRADITIONS ———

* Turkana tribesmen, who live on the barren soils of the Great Rift Valley in Kenya, add iron to their diet by drinking cows' blood – they puncture a cow's jugular vein with a sharp arrow and catch the spurting liquid in a clay jug. The cows, though bled frequently, suffer no ill effects.

* Until the 1920s babies in Finland were often delivered in saunas. The heat was thought to help combat infection, and the warm atmosphere was considered pleasing to the infant. The Finns also considered a sauna to be a holy place.

* In America, a tip at a family restaurant should be 15 per cent of the bill without tax, while a ten per cent tip is sufficient for a buffet, but you should never leave less than a quarter, even if you only have a cup of coffee.

* In Japan, white is associated with death.

LAWS –
OLD AND NEW

LAWS - OLD AND NEW

- In Bahrain, a male doctor may legally examine a woman's genitals, but is prohibited from looking directly at them. He may only see their reflection in a mirror.

- Muslims are banned from looking at the genitals of a corpse. This also applies to undertakers; the organs of the deceased must be covered with a piece of wood or brick at all times.

- The penalty for masturbation in Indonesia is decapitation.

- In Hong Kong, a betrayed wife is legally allowed to kill her adulterous husband, but may only do so with her bare hands. The husband's lover may be killed in any manner desired.

- In Cali, Colombia, a woman may only have sex with her husband, and the first time this happens her mother must be in the room to witness the act.

- In New Hampshire, you may not tap your feet, nod your head, or in any way keep time to the music in a tavern, restaurant, or cafe.

- In Santa Cruz, Bolivia, it is illegal for a man to have sex with a woman and her daughter at the same time.

—————— LAWS - OLD AND NEW——————

- In Maryland, it is illegal to sell condoms from vending machines, with one exception: places where alcoholic beverages are sold for consumption on the premises.

- In Maine, you will be charged a fine if you still have your Christmas decorations up after 14 January.

- It is illegal to 'annoy a bird' in any city park of Honolulu, Hawaii.

- In Massachusetts, taxi drivers are prohibited from making love in the front seat of their taxi during their shifts.

- In Hawaii, all residents may be fined as a result of not owning a boat.

- In Arizona, you may not have more than two dildos in a house.

- In Florida, you are not allowed to break more than three dishes per day, or chip the edges of more than four cups and/or saucers.

- All bees entering Kentucky shall be accompanied by certificates of health, stating that the apiary from which the bees came was free from contagious or infectious disease.

—————— LAWS - OLD AND NEW——————

- In Iowa, kisses may last for no more than five minutes.

- In Michigan, there is a ten per cent bounty for each rat's head brought into a town office.

- In New Jersey, you cannot pump your own gas. All gas stations are full service, and full service only.

- In Arizona, when being attacked by a criminal or burglar, you may only protect yourself with the same weapon as your attacker.

- In Louisiana, biting someone with your natural teeth is 'simple assault', while biting someone with your false teeth is 'aggravated assault'.

- In Alaska, while it is legal to shoot bears, waking a sleeping bear for the purpose of taking a photograph is prohibited.

- In Fort Madison, Iowa, the fire department is required to practise fire fighting for 15 minutes before attending a fire.

- In Connecticut, no one may use a white cane unless they are blind.

- In Californian animal shelters, lizards and snakes are treated under the same guidelines as cats and dogs.

LAWS - OLD AND NEW

- In Arizona, cutting down a cactus carries a possible 25 year prison sentence.

- In Nebraska, if a child burps during church, his parents may be arrested.

- In Indiana, you are not allowed to carry a cocktail from the bar to a table. The waiter or waitress has to do it.

- In New Jersey, all motorists must honk before passing another car, cyclist, skater, and even a skateboarder.

- In New Jersey, it is illegal to wear a bullet-proof vest while committing a murder.

- In Massachusetts, no gorilla is allowed in the back seat of any car.

- In New York, while riding in an elevator you must talk to no one, and fold your hands while looking towards the door.

- In Denmark, if a horse carriage is trying to pass a car and the horse becomes uneasy, the car is required to pull over. If necessary, to calm the horse down, you are required to cover the car up.

- In Massachusetts, snoring is prohibited unless all bedroom windows are closed and securely locked.

LAWS - OLD AND NEW

- In Florida, women can be fined for falling asleep under a hair dryer, as can salon owners.

- In Indiana, you may not back into a parking spot because it prevents police officers from seeing the licence plate.

- In Massachusetts, it is illegal to go to bed without first having a full bath.

- In New Mexico, state officials ordered 400 words of 'sexually explicit material' to be cut from Romeo and Juliet.

- In Nevada, it is still 'legal' to hang someone for shooting your dog on your property.

- In Montana, it is illegal for married women to go fishing alone on Sundays, and illegal for unmarried women to fish alone at all.

- In Massachusetts, it is unlawful to injure a football goal post. Doing so is punishable by a $200 fine.

- In Louisiana, it is illegal to gargle in public places.

- In Alabama, it is illegal for a driver to be blindfolded while operating a vehicle.

LAWS - OLD AND NEW

- In Indiana, baths may not be taken between the months of October and March.

- In Alabama, bogies may not be flicked into the wind.

- In Alabama, it is illegal to impersonate any type of minister, of any religion.

- In Alabama, putting salt on a rail-road track may be punishable by death.

- In Indiana, no one may catch a fish with their bare hands.

- In Georgia, it is illegal to use profanity in front of a dead body lying in a funeral home or in a coroner's office.

- In Kentucky, it is illegal to fish with a bow and arrow.

- In Arizona, it is unlawful to refuse a person a glass of water.

- In New York, a fine of $25 can be levied for flirting. This old law specifically prohibits men from turning round on any city street and looking 'at a woman in that way'. A second conviction for a crime of this magnitude calls for the violating male to be forced to

LAWS - OLD AND NEW

wear a 'pair of horse-blinders', wherever and whenever he goes outside for a stroll.

* In Kansas, pedestrians crossing the highways at night must wear tail-lights.

* In Massachusetts, bullets may not be used as currency.

* In Connecticut, in order for a pickle to officially be considered a pickle, it must bounce.

* In Florida, if an elephant is left tied to a parking meter, the parking fee has to be paid just as it would for a vehicle.

* In Massachusetts, it is illegal to allow someone to use stilts while working on the construction of a building.

* In Florida, it is illegal to skateboard without a licence.

* In Alabama, it is illegal to wear a fake moustache that causes laughter in church.

* In Colorado, car dealers may not show cars on a Sunday.

* In New Jersey, it is against the law to 'frown' at a police officer.

LAWS - OLD AND NEW

- In Indiana, it is illegal for a liquor store to sell cold soft drinks.

- In Minnesota, citizens may not enter Wisconsin with a chicken on their head.

- In Montana, it is a misdemeanour to show movies that depict acts of felonious crime.

- In Kansas, if two trains meet on the same track, neither shall proceed until the other has passed.

- In Georgia, signs are required to be written in English.

- If any person charges for a puppet show, wire dancing or tumbling act in the state of Indiana they will be fined $3 under the Act to Prevent Certain Immoral Practices.

- In California, animals are banned from mating publicly within 1,500 ft (457 m) of a bar, school, or place of worship.

- In Michigan, it is legal for a robber to file a lawsuit, if he or she got hurt in your house.

- In Indiana, a $3 fine per pack will be imposed on anyone playing cards, under the Act for the Prevention of Gaming.

LAWS - OLD AND NEW

- In Illinois, you may be convicted of a Class 4 felony offence, punishable by up to three years in state prison, for the crime of 'eavesdropping' on your own conversation.

- In Louisiana, it is illegal to rob a bank and then shoot at the bank teller with a water pistol.

- In Nebraska, it is illegal for a mother to give her daughter a perm without a state licence.

- In Indiana, a man over the age of 18 may be arrested for statutory rape if the passenger in his car is not wearing her socks and shoes, and is under the age of 17.

- In Fairbanks, Alaska, it is illegal to feed alcoholic beverages to a moose.

- In Michigan, any person over the age of 12 may have a licence for a hand-gun as long as he or she has not been convicted of a felony.

- In Iowa, a man with a moustache may never kiss a woman in public.

- In Arizona, any misdemeanour committed while wearing a red mask is considered a felony. This goes back to the days of the Wild West.

LAWS - OLD AND NEW

- In Georgia, you have the right to commit simple battery if provoked by 'fighting' words.

- In Indiana, anyone the age of 14 or older who profanely curses, damns or swears by the name of God, Jesus Christ or the Holy Ghost, shall be fined between $1 and $3 for each offence, with a maximum fine of $10 per day.

- In Idaho, you may not fish on a camel's back.

- In Massachusetts, affiliation with the Communist Party is illegal.

- In Montana, it is illegal to have a sheep in the cab of your truck without a chaperone.

- In Kentucky, it is illegal to fish in the Ohio River without an Indiana Fishing Licence.

- In Florida, it is illegal to block any travelled wagon road.

- In New York, a person may not walk around on Sundays with an ice-cream cone in his or her pocket.

- In Michigan, a woman isn't allowed to cut her own hair without her husband's permission.

———— LAWS - OLD AND NEW————

* In Massachusetts, tomatoes may not be used in the production of clam chowder.

* In Connecticut, you can be stopped by the police for cycling over 65 mph (105 kph).

* In New York, it is against the law to throw a ball at someone's head for fun.

* In California, it is a misdemeanour to shoot at any kind of game from a moving vehicle, unless the target is a whale.

* In Indiana, drinks on the house are illegal.

* In Ireland, wearing a Halloween costume could result in up to one year in prison.

* In Georgia, members of the state assembly cannot be ticketed for speeding while the state assembly is in session.

* In Alaska, moose may not be viewed from a plane.

* In Indiana, hotel sheets must be exactly 99 inches (251 cm) long and 81 inches (206 cm) wide.

* In Nebraska, it is illegal to go whale fishing.

LAWS - OLD AND NEW

- In New Jersey, you may not slurp your soup.

- In Massachusetts, public boxing matches are outlawed.

- In Arizona, donkeys cannot sleep in bathtubs.

- In Maine, shotguns are required to be taken to church in the event of a Native American attack.

- In Nevada, it is illegal to drive a camel on the highway.

- In New Hampshire, you cannot sell the clothes you are wearing to pay off a gambling debt.

- In Iowa, one-armed piano players must perform free of charge.

- In Spearfish, South Dakota, if three or more American Indians are walking down the street together, they can be considered a war party and fired upon.

- In Montana, seven or more American Indians are considered a raiding or war party, and it is legal to shoot them.

- In Arkansas, alligators may not be kept in bathtubs.

- In New York, a licence must be purchased before hanging clothes on a clothes-line.

LAWS - OLD AND NEW

- In Mississippi, horses are not to be housed within 50 ft (15 m) of any road.

- In Florida, the penalty for horse theft is death by hanging.

- In Indiana, moustaches are illegal if the bearer has a tendency to habitually kiss other humans.

- In Maine, you may not step out of a plane in flight.

- In South Carolina, merchandise may not be sold within a half mile (0.8 km) of a church, unless fruit is being sold.

- In Massachusetts, it is illegal to drive Texan, Mexican, Cherokee or other American Indian cattle on a public road.

- In Alabama, incestuous marriages are legal.

- In Montana, it is a felony for a wife to open her husband's mail.

- In Idaho, riding a merry-go-round on Sundays is considered a crime.

- In Colorado, it is illegal to ride a horse while under the influence.

LAWS - OLD AND NEW

- In Massachusetts, mourners may eat no more than three sandwiches during a wake.

- In California, sunshine is guaranteed to the masses.

- In Hawaii, coins are not allowed to be placed in a person's ears.

- In New Hampshire, it is illegal to pick up seaweed off the beach.

- In Minnesota, all men driving motorcycles must wear shirts.

- In 17th century Japan, no citizen was allowed to leave the country on penalty of death. Anyone caught coming or going without permission was executed on the spot.

- In Minnesota, all bathtubs must have feet.

- In Indiana, smoking in the state legislature building is banned, except when the legislature is in session.

- In New Jersey, spray paint may not be sold without a posted sign warning juveniles of the penalty for creating graffiti.

- In Alabama, dominoes may not be played on Sunday.

—————— LAWS - OLD AND NEW ——————

- Jaguar images and costumes were outlawed by the Catholic Church in the 17th century because of their association with Indian religion, militia and politics.

- In Iowa, it is illegal to sell or distribute drugs or narcotics without having first obtained the appropriate Iowa drug tax stamp.

- In Florida, having sexual relations with a porcupine is illegal.

- It is against the law for a monster to enter the corporate limits of Urbana, Illinois.

- In Norway, you may not spay your female dog or cat. However, you may neuter the males of the species.

- The minimum age for marriage of Italian girls was raised by law to 12 years in 1892.

- In 17th century Massachusetts, smoking was legal only at a distance of five miles (8 km) from any town.

- In ancient Cambodia, it was illegal to insult a rice plant.

- In 1845, Boston banned bathing unless you had a doctor's prescription.

——— LAWS - OLD AND NEW ———

- In the 1630s, a decree in Japan forbade the building of any large ocean-worthy ships, to deter defection.

- It was illegal for women to wear buttons in 15th century Florence.

- During the 15th century, special laws ensured only the nobility could use a handkerchief.

- In Canada, if a debt is higher than 25 cents, it is illegal to pay it with pennies.

- In the latter part of the 1300s, dress code laws in Florence, Italy, stipulated precisely the depth of a woman's décolletage.

- In Florida, it is illegal to release more than ten lighter-than-air balloons at a time. This is to protect marine creatures that often mistake balloons for food and can suffer intestinal injuries if they eat the balloons.

- In Massachusetts, it is illegal to keep a mule on the second floor of a building not in a city, unless there are two exits.

- It is unlawful to lend your vacuum cleaner to your next-door neighbour in Denver, Colorado.

LAWS - OLD AND NEW

- The Germans considered Casablanca (1942) a propaganda film and made it illegal to show in German theatres during World War II. Even after the war, only a censored version was allowed to be shown in Germany, with all references to Nazis removed.

- On Sundays in New Hampshire, citizens may not relieve themselves while looking up.

- It is illegal to drink beer out of a bucket while sitting on a kerb in St Louis, Missouri.

- In London, you will face a 24-hour detainment if you are caught sticking gum under a seat on the upper deck of a bus.

- In Natoma, Kansas, it's illegal to throw knives at men wearing striped suits.

- In Florida, it is illegal to litter intentionally with plastic fishing gear or lines.

- A law in Illinois prohibits barbers from using their fingers to apply shaving cream to a patron's face.

- In Atwoodville, Connecticut, it is illegal to play Scrabble while waiting for a politician to speak.

- It is against the law to pawn your dentures in Las Vegas.

LAWS – OLD AND NEW

- Connecticut and Rhode Island never ratified the 18th Amendment: Prohibition.

- It is against the law to pawn your dentures in Las Vegas. Twenty-two inches (56 cm) is the minimum legal length for commercial sale of California halibut.

- The penalty for conviction of smuggling in Bangladesh is death.

- During the fourth century in Sparta, Greece, if you were male and over 20 years of age, you were required by law to eat 2lb (0.9kg) of meat a day, as it was supposed to make a person brave.

- The sale of chewing gum is outlawed in Singapore because it is a means of 'tainting an environment free of dirt'.

- In Germany and Argentina, a screwing gesture at your head, meaning 'You're crazy', is illegal when driving.

- No store is allowed to sell a toothbrush on the Sabbath in Providence, Rhode Island. Yet these same stores are allowed to sell toothpaste and mouthwash on Sundays.

- Candy made from pieces of barrel cactus is illegal in the United States, to protect the species.

———— LAWS - OLD AND NEW ————

- Dancing to the 'Star-Spangled Banner' is against the law in several American states.

- In Kentucky, it is against the law to throw eggs at a public speaker.

- In London, it is illegal to drive a car without sitting in the front seat.

- No two-cycle engines are allowed in Singapore. The licence fee for a new car is small, about £2.50, but as the vehicle grows older, the fee increases. When the car reaches eight years old, it is no longer allowed on the streets. These strict laws have virtually wiped out air pollution in the country.

- The state of Vera Cruz, in Mexico, outlaws priests as citizens.

- In colonial America, tobacco was acceptable legal tender in several southern colonies, and in Virginia, taxes were paid in tobacco.

- For hundreds of years, the Chinese zealously guarded the secret of sericulture; imperial law decreed death by torture to those who disclosed how to make silk.

- In Milan, Italy, there is a law that requires a smile on the face of all citizens at all times. Exemptions include

———— LAWS - OLD AND NEW ————

time spent visiting patients in hospitals or attending funerals. Otherwise, a person may be fined £55 if they are seen in public without a smile on their face.

- No patent can ever be taken out on a gambling machine in the United States.

- In St Catalina, unlike the rest of Southern California, the number of cars on the island is strictly limited. The waiting time for a car permit is eight to ten years, so most residents drive electric-powered golf carts.

- Under Norwegian law, a polar bear may be shot only if deemed a menace.

- Oxford University requires all members upon admission to the Bodleian Library to read aloud a pledge that includes an agreement to not 'kindle therein any fire or flame'. Regulations also prohibit readers bringing sheep into the library.

- In New Mexico, it is against the law to ship horned toads out of the state.

- In New York State, it is illegal to shoot a rabbit from a moving trolley car.

- In North Dakota, it is legal to shoot an American Indian on horseback, provided you are in a covered wagon.

LAWS - OLD AND NEW

- Texas is the only state that permits residents to cast absentee ballots from space. The first to exercise this right was astronaut David Wolf, who cast his vote for Houston mayor via e-mail from the Russian space station Mir in November 1997.

- Pennsylvania law mandates that each year all counties provide veterans' graves with flags, most of which are distributed before Memorial Day.

- In Pacific Grove, California, it is a misdemeanour to kill a butterfly.

- The states of Vermont, Alaska, Hawaii and Maine do not allow billboards.

- In Pennsylvania, ministers are forbidden from performing marriages when either the bride or groom is drunk.

- Until about 150 years ago, church-going was required by law in Britain.

- In Riverside, California, it is illegal to kiss, unless both people wipe their lips with rose-water.

- In San Salvador, El Salvador, drunk drivers can be punished by death before a firing squad.

LAWS - OLD AND NEW

* In Sandusky, Ohio, anyone older than age 14 looking for goodies at Halloween is breaking the law.

* Scandinavian law forbids television advertising of foods to children.

* Officials of ancient Greece decreed that mollusc shells be used as ballots, because once a vote was scratched on the shell, it couldn't be erased or altered.

* In some smaller towns in the state of Arizona, it is illegal to wear suspenders.

* Christmas carolling is banned at two major malls in Pensacola, Florida, as shoppers and shopkeepers complained that the carollers were too loud and took up too much space.

* In Somalia, it has been decreed illegal to carry old chewing gum stuck on the tip of your nose.

* In Arizona, a hunting licence is required by law to hunt rattlesnakes, but not to own them as pets.

* Women are banned by royal decree from using hotel swimming pools in Jeddah, Saudi Arabia.

* There is a law in South Pittsburg, Tennessee, 'The Cornbread Capitol of the World', concerning the

LAWS - OLD AND NEW

cooking of this southern staple. It declares: 'Cornbread isn't cornbread unless it be made correctly. Therefore, all cornbread must be hereby made in nothing other than a cast-iron skillet. Those found in violation of this ordinance are to be fined one dollar.'

* It is illegal to marry the spouse of a grandparent in Maine, Maryland, South Carolina and Washington DC.

* In Winnetka, Illinois, while you are in a theatre it is against the law to remove your shoes if your feet smell bad.

* In the United States, federal law states that children's TV shows may contain only ten minutes of advertising per hour, and on weekends the limit is ten-and-a-half minutes.

* In the state of Queensland, Australia, it is still constitutional law that all pubs must have a railing outside for patrons to tie up their horse.

* In Hazelton, Pennsylvania, it is illegal to sip a carbonated drink while lecturing students in a school auditorium.

* It is against the law to yell out 'Snake!' within the city limits of Flowery Branch, Georgia.

LAWS - OLD AND NEW

- In New York City it is illegal to make your living through the skinning of horses or cows, the growing of ragweed, or the burning of bones.

- Until 1893, lynching was legal in the United States. The first anti-lynching law was passed in Georgia, but it only made the violation punishable by four years in prison.

- In Britain, the law was changed in 1789 to make hanging the method of execution, instead of burning.

- Licensed London taxis are required by law to carry a bale of hay at all times, dating from the days of the horse-drawn cab. The relevant law has never been revoked.

- The Kentucky Supreme Court has ruled that the prosecution must throw its files wide open to the defence if the accused is suffering from amnesia.

- In 1547, British law was amended to end the practice of boiling people to death as punishment for criminal behaviour.

- In the US, in 1832, a law was passed requiring all American citizens to spend one day each year fasting and praying. People ignored the law, and no effort was made to enforce the legislation.

LAWS - OLD AND NEW

- The US Supreme Court once ruled federal income tax unconstitutional. It was first imposed during the Civil War as a temporary revenue-raising measure.

- In 1908, a law was passed in New York City making it illegal for women to smoke in public.

- In Greenwich, UK, during the 1800s it was unlawful to impersonate a retired person on a pension.

- LSD was legal in California until 1967.

- According to US law, a patent may not be granted on a useless invention or on a machine that will not operate. Even if an invention is novel or new, a patent may not be obtained if the invention would have been obvious to a person having ordinary skill in the same area at the time of the invention.

- In 1984, the Minnesota State Legislature ordered that all gender-specific language, which referred only to one gender, usually men, be removed from the state laws. After two years of work, the rewritten laws were adopted. The word 'his' was changed 10,000 times and 'he' was changed 6,000 times.

- It was only in 1968 that the state of Tennessee abolished its anti-evolution law and accepted the doctrine of evolution.

LAWS - OLD AND NEW

- It was only after John F Kennedy was assassinated that Congress enacted a law making it a federal crime to kill, kidnap, or assault the president, vice-president or president-elect.

- Murdering a travelling musician was not a serious crime in Britain during the Middle Ages.

- Private cars were forbidden on the island of Bermuda until 1948, explaining why there are still so many bicycles there.

- Married women were forbidden by law to watch, let alone compete, in the ancient Olympics, the penalty being death. The Greeks believed that the presence of wives in Olympia would defile Greece's oldest religious shrine there, although young girls were allowed in. Women who broke the rule were thrown from a nearby cliff.

- In Gwinnett County, Georgia, it is illegal for residents to keep rabbits as pets, with rabbits restricted to farm areas and homes with at least three acres (1.2 hectares) of land. However, the law was amended in 1993 to allow Vietnamese pot-bellied pigs after a woman with a pet pig pleaded for the exemption.

- It was only in 1968 that the state of Tennessee abolished its anti-evolution law and accepted the

LAWS - OLD AND NEW

doctrine of evolution. The design of a US coin cannot be changed more than once in 25 years without special legislation by Congress.

- It was only in 1968 that the state of Tennessee abolished its anti-evolution law and accepted the doctrine of evolution. During World War II, US ice-cream manufacturers were restricted by law to produce only 20 different flavours of ice-cream.

- E-signatures have the same legal standing as handwritten signatures.

- The first state minimum wage law in the United States went into effect in Massachusetts in 1913. It would be another 25 years before the law went into effect nationally providing a minimum wage of 25 cents an hour.

- In December 1997, the state of Nevada became the first state to pass legislation categorising Y2K data disasters as 'acts of God' – protecting the state from lawsuits that may potentially be brought against it by residents in the year 2000.

- In Scotland, all people of nobility are free from arrest for debt, as they are the king's hereditary counsellors. They cannot be outlawed in any civil action, and no attachment lies against their persons.

LAWS - OLD AND NEW

- In Britain, a Witchcraft Act of the early 1700s identified black cats as dangerous animals to be shunned.

- Circus showman P T Barnum created a spectacle when he hitched an elephant to a plough beside the train tracks to announce that his circus had come to town. Barnum attracted many newsmen and the public, but it soon became illegal in North Carolina to plough a field with an elephant. The law still remains to this day.

- In Britain, in 1571, a man could be fined for not wearing a wool cap.

- In France, Napoleon instituted a scale of fines for sex offences, which included 35 francs for a man guilty of lifting a woman's skirt to the knee and 70 francs if he lifted it to the thigh.

- In the 1940s, California law made it illegal to serve alcohol to a homosexual or someone dressed as a member of the opposite sex. Drag queens avoided the latter restriction by attaching pieces of paper to their dresses that read 'I'm a boy'. The courts accepted the argument that anyone wearing such a notice was technically dressed as a man, not a woman.

- During the Renaissance period, laws were passed that prescribed which fashions could not be worn by the

LAWS - OLD AND NEW

lower classes, so as to keep social distinctions intact. Queen Elizabeth I of England would not allow the ruff to be worn by commoners; in Florence, women of the lower class were not allowed to use buttons of certain shapes and materials.

- During the reign of Catherine I of Russia, the rules for parties stipulated that no man was to get drunk before 9 o'clock and ladies were not to get drunk at any hour.

- It was against the law to tie a male horse next to a female horse on Main Street in Wetaskiwin, Canada, in 1917.

- Centuries ago, in London, someone drinking at a tavern had the legal right to demand to see the wine cellar to verify that the wine hadn't been watered down. Refusal by the taverner could result in severe penalties, including time in prison.

- The California Board of Equalization has ruled that bartenders cannot be held responsible for misjudging the age of midgets.

- Barbie dolls are considered anti-Islamic and importing them to Iran is prohibited. However, in the late 1990s dozens of shops in Tehran displayed original all-American Barbie dolls, some wearing only a swimsuit.

LAWS - OLD AND NEW

A 3-ft-tall (0.9 m) Barbie bride model sold for as much as £390 in a country where the average monthly salary was £55.

- Due to heavy traffic congestion, Julius Caesar banned all wheeled vehicles from Rome during daylight hours.

- The Recruitment Code of the US Navy states that anyone 'bearing an obscene and indecent' tattoo will be rejected.

- Before 1933, the dime was legal as payment only in transactions of $10 or less. In that year, Congress made the dime legal tender for all transactions.

- The US Government will not allow portraits of living persons to appear on stamps.

SPORTS AND GAMES

--------- SPORTS AND GAMES ---------

- Horse-racing regulations state that no racehorse's name may contain more than 18 letters. Names that are too long would be cumbersome on racing sheets.

- Statistics show that the favourite wins less than 30 per cent of all horse races.

- The most landed-on square in Monopoly is Trafalgar Square.

- To prevent some numbers from occurring more frequently than others, dice used in crap games in Las Vegas are manufactured to a tolerance of 0.0002 inches (0.0005 cm), less than 1/17 the thickness of a human hair.

- In 1950, at the Las Vegas Desert Inn, an anonymous sailor made 27 straight wins with the dice at craps. The odds against such a feat are 12,467,890 to 1. The dice today are enshrined in the hotel on a velvet pillow under glass.

- In Japan, the deadly martial art called 'tessenjutsu' is based solely on the use of a fan.

- The Nike 'swoosh' logo was designed by University of Oregon student Carolyn Davidson in 1964. She was paid $35 dollars.

SPORTS AND GAMES

- Monopoly is the best-selling board game in the world, licensed or sold in 80 countries and produced in 26 languages.

- An estimated £600,000 is lost at racetracks each year by people who lose or carelessly throw away winning tickets.

- More cheating takes place in private, friendly gambling games than in all other gambling games combined.

- The children's game Rock, Paper, Scissors is also popular in Japan, where it is called Janken. The game is also played by some children using their feet, with closed feet equalling stone (gu), spread legs equalling paper (pa) and one foot behind the other equalling scissors (choki).

- There are 170,000,000,000,000,000,000,000,000 ways to play the ten opening moves in a game of chess.

- Alec Brown invented a miniature snooker cue the size of a fountain pen for tricky shots, but it was outlawed because of its size in 1938.

- A twice-retaken penalty kick for Notts County at Portsmouth in 1973 was missed by all three takers – Don Masson, Brian Stubbs and Kevin Randall.

------- **SPORTS AND GAMES** -------

* On a bingo card of 90 numbers, there are approximately 44 million ways to make B-I-N-G-O.

* Scrabble is found in one out of every three American homes.

* Model soldiers date back 4,000 years to ancient Egypt.

* The highest known score for a single word in competition Scrabble is 392. In 1982, Dr Saladin Khoshnaw achieved this score for the word 'caziques', which means an Indian chief.

* Since the Lego Group began manufacturing blocks in 1949, more than 189 billion pieces in 2,000 different shapes have been produced. This is enough for about 30 Lego pieces for every living person on earth.

* The longest recorded Monopoly game was 1,680 hours – more than 70 days.

* Damon Hill worked as a motorcycle despatch rider from 1982–85.

* Full seeding at Wimbledon began in 1927.

* There was a total prize-money fund of £10 for the British Golf Open in 1863.

SPORTS AND GAMES

- US boxer Sugar Ray Leonard won titles at five different weights.

- About 50 competitors in the 1999 Dakar Rally were held up and robbed at gunpoint after the end of the 12th stage.

- Ladies used blue cricket balls during Edwardian times in case they became over-excited at the prospect of red ones.

- The sin bin was introduced in rugby league in 1983.

- The only golf course on the island of Tonga has 15 holes, and there's no penalty if a monkey steals your golf ball.

- A US motor racing fan sent more than half a million emails to Fox Entertainment because they'd shown a baseball game instead of a race.

- A gambler won £25,000 by staking £100 on Manchester City to beat Spurs at odds of 250/1 when they were losing 3–0 and down to ten men at half-time.

- Before football referees started using whistles in 1878, they used to rely on waving a handkerchief.

SPORTS AND GAMES

- An experiment at Manchester United showed that David Beckham ran an average 8.8 miles per game – more than any other player in the team.

- If you add up the letters in all the names of the cards in the deck (Ace, two), the total number of letters is 52, the same as the number of cards in the deck.

- Rio Ferdinand was not happy when teammates put yoghurt on his new £200,000 Bentley.

- When the Ancient Greeks played cards, aces were known as 'dogs'.

- Football is the most attended or watched sport in the world.

- Belgian football team FC Wijtschale conceded 58 goals in just two games.

- In the 1988 Calgary Olympics, Eddie 'the Eagle' Edwards finished 58th (last) in the 70m jump and 55th (last) in the 90m.

- The New York Jets were unable to find hotel rooms for a game in Indianapolis because they had all been booked up by people attending Gencon, a gaming convention.

SPORTS AND GAMES

- Arsenal stars have been told to stop giving other players their football tops.

- There is a regulation size half-court where employees can play basketball inside the Matterhorn at Disneyland.

- One of baseball pitcher Nolan Ryan's jockstraps recently sold at auction for £13,000.

- The study of David Beckham is part of a 12-week 'football culture' module for a University Degree course at Staffordshire University.

- A female photographer has been banned from flying with the Romanian soccer team because of superstitions that women could bring bad luck.

- A man from Medellin in Colombia has changed his name to Deportivo Independiente Medellin, after his favourite football team.

- Rio Ferdinand was given a parking ticket because his car was too wide for the space. Britain's most expensive footballer fell foul of three wardens when he tried to park his Aston Martin on King Street, in Manchester.

- Another word for volleyball is minonette.

——————— SPORTS AND GAMES ———————

- Chelsea stars are to get a new training-ground aid – a bank of sunbeds.

- The first golf rule booklet was published in Scotland in 1754.

- Tennis pro Evonne Goolagong's last name means 'kangaroo's nose' in Australia's aboriginal language.

- A stringent Real medical revealed that David Beckham has one leg shorter than the other. However, a boot insert to eradicate the problem proved too uncomfortable, so he stopped using it.

- Billiards great Henry Lewis once sank 46 balls in a row.

- Golf great Billy Casper turned pro during the Korean War while serving in the Navy. Casper was assigned to operate and build golf driving ranges for the Navy in the San Diego area.

- Norwich City were urged to wear red underpants to help them win a game when they were bottom of the league.

- David Beckham has his wife Victoria's name in Hindi – albeit misspelled – tattooed on his arm. She has 'DB' tattooed on her wrist.

SPORTS AND GAMES

* If you lined up all the slinkys ever made in a row, they could wrap around the Earth 126 times.

* Not all golf balls have 360 dimples. Some have as many as 420. There are also many different kinds of dimple patterns.

* In July 1934, Babe Ruth paid a fan $20 dollars for the return of the baseball he hit for his 700th career home run.

* In 1969, a brief battle broke out between Honduras and El Salvador. Although tensions were already high between the two, the reason for the war was El Salvador's victory over Honduras in the World Cup football playoffs. Gunfire was exchanged for about 30 minutes before reason prevailed.

* David Beckham says he is not a beer drinker, and prefers a nice glass of wine or Pepsi.

* Horseracing is one of the most dangerous sports. Between two and three jockeys are killed each year. That's about how many baseball players have died in baseball's entire professional history.

* Michael Owen has joked that he likes wearing tights in the privacy of his own home.

SPORTS AND GAMES

* America's national sport of baseball was mentioned in a novel by Jane Austen.

* Gene Sarazen, a golfer from several generations ago, set the record for the fastest golf drive: 120mph.

* Michael Sangster, who played tennis in the 1960s, once clocked a serve at 154mph.

* In 1964, for the 10th time in his major-league baseball career, Mickey Mantle hit home runs from both the left and right sides of the plate in the same game – setting a new record.

* David Beckham and his pop star wife Victoria are said to be worth a combined £50 million.

* The late Pope John Paul II was named an 'Honorary Harlem Globetrotter' in 2000.

* More money is spent on gardening than any other hobby.

* In a TV poll at the end of 2003, David Beckham was voted the fifth most popular 'Spaniard'. Experts said people had not understood the question properly.

* Goran Ivanisevic's father crashed his £2 million yacht, not long after a friend wrote off his £100,000 Porsche.

———— SPORTS AND GAMES ————

- A north-west cricket club held a minute's silence to remember a dead club member only to later find out he was still alive.

- Former world chess champion Ruslan Ponomariov has become the first player to be disqualified at a major event after his mobile phone rang during a game.

- The pitches that baseball player Babe Ruth hit for his last-ever home run and that Joe DiMaggio hit for his first-ever home run were thrown by the same man.

- The national sport of Nauru, a small Pacific island, is lassoing flying birds.

- Between 1985-91 Boris Becker only once failed to reach the Wimbledon men's singles final, in 1987.

- Eight competitors took part in the 1860 British Golf Open.

- The two courses at Emirates Golf Club in Dubai need two million gallons (9,092,000 litres) of water each day during the summer to keep them in condition.

- Charlotte Brew was the first woman to ride in the Grand National.

- Fifteen teams entered the first FA Cup competition.

SPORTS AND GAMES

- A mouse stopped play in the 1962 Edgbaston Test between England and Pakistan.

- A French infantry captain named Mingaud invented the leather tip of a snooker cue in 1807.

- FIFA referee Ken Aston thought up the idea of red and yellow cards.

- The Azteca, Etrusco, Questra and Tricolore are all types of football which have been used for World Cup Final tournaments.

- England cricketer J W H T Douglas also won the 1908 Olympic middleweight boxing gold medal.

- The 1979/80 Bangalore Test Match between India and Pakistan was halted due to the invasion of a swarm of bees.

- Manchester United's mascot Fred the Red had his nose broken during the squad's overzealous celebration of the 1996 Premiership.

- The original FA Cup was stolen 1895 and never recovered.

- Singapore hosted a RoboCup in 1998, involving teams of robot footballers.

LANGUAGE AND LITERATURE

LANGUAGE AND LITERATURE

- The word 'palace' comes from the name of one of the hills in the ancient city of Rome – the Palatine Hill.

- *The Times* was nicknamed 'The Thunderer'.

- Britain's oldest Sunday newspaper is the *Observer*.

- The word 'education' is based on the Latin 'educo', which means 'to draw out'.

- James Bond author Ian Fleming also wrote the children's novel *Chitty Chitty Bang Bang*.

- Mary Ann Evans is the real name of George Eliot.

- American poet Emily Dickinson was a recluse by the age of 30, dressing only in white and carrying on friendships through correspondence.

- Margaret Mitchell wrote her only novel *Gone with the Wind* as she was bored while recuperating from a sprained ankle.

- The word 'taxi' is spelled the same in English, German, French, Swedish and Portuguese.

- Danielle Steel is a descendant of the Löwenbrau brewery family and ran a PR firm called Supergirls before becoming a novelist.

———— LANGUAGE AND LITERATURE ————

- Agatha Christie created a mystery herself by disappearing for a fortnight in 1926, only to be discovered at a Harrogate hotel.

- Etymology is the study of the history of words.

- Lewis Carroll was a mathematics professor at Oxford University.

- D H Lawrence's novel *Lady Chatterley's Lover* was the subject of an obscenity trial in Britain in 1959.

- The Soviet Union banned Sir Arthur Conan Doyle's *The Adventures of Sherlock Holmes* because of the book's references to occultism and spiritualism.

- The classic tale of *Little Red Riding Hood* was banned in the town of Empire, California, as the book cover showed a bottle of wine in Little Red Riding Hood's basket. The local school board was afraid that the story encouraged the drinking of alcohol.

- Conchology is the study of shells.

- Hans Christian Andersen's *Wonder Stories* was banned from children's reading lists in Illinois, with the book stamped 'For Adult Readers' to make it 'impossible for children to obtain smut.'

LANGUAGE AND LITERATURE

- The Indian epic poem the *Mahabharata* is eight times longer than the Greek epic poems *The Iliad* and *The Odyssey* combined.

- Scarlett O'Hara, Margaret Mitchell's *Gone with the Wind* heroine, was originally given the name Pansy.

- There are more than 40,000 characters in Chinese script.

- In Latin, the term 'lego' means 'I put together' or 'I assemble'.

- The phrase 'in the limelight' originates from chemist Robert Hare discovering that a blowpipe flame acting upon a block of calcium oxide (lime) produces a brilliant white light that could be used to illuminate theatre stages.

- Winnie, from A A Milne's story *Winnie the Pooh*, was named after a bear at the London Zoo. The animal had been born in Canada but was brought to London in 1914 as the mascot of a Canadian regiment.

- A 'keeper' is the loop on a belt that holds the loose end.

- There are three sets of letters on the standard typewriter and computer keyboards, which are in alphabetical order reading left to right. They are f-g-h, j-k-l, and o-p.

——— **LANGUAGE AND LITERATURE** ———

* *The Boston Nation*, a newspaper published in Ohio during the mid-19th century, had pages 7 1/2 feet (2 m) long and 5 1/2 feet (1.6 m) wide. It required two people to hold the paper in a proper reading position.

* The original title of Jane Austen's novel *Pride and Prejudice* was 'First Impression'.

* Lord Alfred Tennyson wrote a 6,000-word epic poem when he was 12 years old.

* A 'vamp' is the upper front top of a shoe.

* Created by author Astrid Lindgren, the children's book character Pippi Longstocking's full name is Pippilolta Provisionia Gaberdina Dandeliona Ephraimsdaughter Longstocking.

* Jacqueline Susann's best-selling novel *Valley of the Dolls* was originally titled 'They Don't Build Statues to Businessmen'.

* The expression 'knuckle down' originated with marbles – players put knuckles to the ground for their best shots.

* Due to a suggestive illustration that might encourage children to break dishes so they don't have to dry them, Shel Silverstein's children's book *A Light in the Attic* was banned in the US.

LANGUAGE AND LITERATURE

- Fagin, the sinister villain in Charles Dickens' *Oliver Twist*, was also the name of Dickens' best friend, Bob Fagin.

- All the proceeds earned from James M Barrie's book *Peter Pan* were bequeathed to the Great Ormond Street Hospital for Sick Children in London.

- Almost half the newspapers in the world are published in the United States and Canada.

- Anyone writing a letter to the *New York Times* has one chance in 21 of having the letter published. Letter writers to the *Washington Post* do significantly better, with one letter out of eight finding its way to print.

- In *Gulliver's Travels*, Jonathan Swift described the two moons of Mars, Phobos and Deimos, giving their exact size and speeds of rotation. He did this more than a hundred years before either moon was discovered.

- The French Academy took 297 years, from 1635 to 1932, to write a grammar book of 263 pages. When finally published, it contained 50 typographical errors.

- The hero in Robert Burns' poem 'Tam O'Shanter' gave name to the flat Scottish wool cap with a pompom at its centre.

LANGUAGE AND LITERATURE

- According to experts, the fungi that feed on old paper may be mildly hallucinogenic. Writing in the British medical journal *The Lancet*, one of Britain's leading mycologists (fungus experts) Dr R J Hay said that the 'fungal hallucinogens' in old books could lead to an 'enhancement of enlightenment' in readers. 'The source of inspiration for many great literary figures may have been nothing more than a quick sniff of mouldy books,' wrote Hay.

- The first advertisement printed in English in 1477 offered a prayer book. The advert was published by William Caxton on his press in Westminster Abbey. No price was mentioned, only that the book was 'good chepe'.

- Of all the professionals in the United States, journalists are credited with having the largest vocabulary – approximately 20,000 words.

- Huckleberry Finn's remedy for warts was swinging a dead cat in a graveyard at night.

- On average, clergymen, lawyers, and doctors each have 15,000 words in their vocabulary. Skilled workers who haven't had a college education know between 5,000 and 7,000 words, and farm labourers know about 1,600.

———— LANGUAGE AND LITERATURE ————

- The Procrastinators' Club of America sends news to its members under the mast-head 'Last Month's Newsletter'.

- The piece that protrudes from the top end of an umbrella is called a 'ferrule'. The word 'ferrule' is also used to describe the piece of metal that holds a rubber eraser on a pencil.

- The little bits of paper left over when holes are punched in data cards or tape are called 'chad'.

- 'Brontology' is the study of thunder.

- Victor Hugo wrote *The Hunchback of Notre Dame* in just six months and, it is said, with a single bottle of ink.

- *Harriet the Spy* by Louise Fitzhugh, has been banned in parts of the US for teaching children to lie, spy, talk back and curse.

- More than 63 million *Star Trek* books, in more than 15 languages, are in print; 13 are sold every minute in the United States.

- The smallest book in the Library of Congress is *Old King Cole*. It is 1/25 of an inch (0.6 cm) by 1/25 of an inch (0.6 cm). The pages can only be turned with the use of a needle.

———— **LANGUAGE AND LITERATURE** ————

- There are over 375 organisations around the world devoted to Sherlock Holmes. The largest, the Japan Sherlock Holmes Club has over 1,200 members.

- The largest book in the Library of Congress is John James Audubon's *Birds of America*, containing life-size illustrations of birds. The book is 39.37 inches (1 m) high.

- 'Absterse' is a little-used verb meaning 'to clean'.

- Dr Seuss wrote *Green Eggs and Ham* after his editor dared him to write a book using fewer than 50 different words.

- The first issue of *Life* magazine – dated 23 November 1936 and featuring the work of photographer Margaret Bourke-White – sold for ten cents.

- In 1955, a book was returned to Cambridge University Library – 288 years overdue.

- Victor Hugo was inspired to write *The Hunchback of Notre Dame* following a visit to Notre Dame Cathedral, where he discovered a cryptic inscription – the Greek word for 'fate' carved deep into a stone wall in the tower. As he pondered the origins and meaning of the message, a story began to take shape in his mind.

———— **LANGUAGE AND LITERATURE** ————

- American poet Emily Dickinson wrote more than 900 poems, of which only four were published during her lifetime.

- Robert Louis Stevenson said he had envisioned the entire story of *The Strange Case of Dr Jekyll and Mr Hyde* in a dream and simply recorded it the way he saw it. Stevenson claimed to be able to dream plots for his stories at will.

- The Dr Seuss book *Yertle the Turtle* was based on Adolf Hitler, while Marvin K. Mooney's, *Will You Please Go Away Now?* featured a character, based on former president Richard M Nixon, that is constantly asked to go away.

- Rudyard Kipling would only write when he had black ink in his pen.

- In America, *The Diary of Anne Frank* has been banned due to being too depressing for children.

- Shakespeare invented the phrase 'laugh it off' and the words 'bedroom' and 'puke'.

- Between 1986 and 1996, Brazilian author Jose Carlos Ryoki de Alpoim Inoue had 1,058 novels published.

———— LANGUAGE AND LITERATURE ————

- The first *Encyclopaedia Britannica* was published in 1768.

- Norwegian playwright Henrik Ibsen had a pet scorpion that he used to keep on his desk for inspiration.

- Barbara Bush's book about her English springer spaniel, *Millie's Book*, was on the best-seller list for 29 weeks. Millie was the most popular 'First Dog' in history.

- Charles Dickens always used to touch things three times for luck.

- Charles Dickens earned no more money from his many books than he did from giving lectures.

- Before he settled on the name Mark Twain, writer Samuel Clemens published work under the names Thomas Jefferson Snodgrass, Sergeant Fathom and W Apaminondas Adrastus Blab.

- Lewis Carroll wrote most of his books standing up.

- In the 1631 publication of the Bible, a printer accidentally omitted the word 'not' from the seventh commandment, encouraging readers to commit adultery.

- The very first book about plastic surgery was written in 1597.

LANGUAGE AND LITERATURE

- Russian writer Konstantin Mikhailov had 325 pseudonyms.

- Dr Samuel Johnson wrote the story *Rasselas* in one week so he could earn the money to pay for his mother's funeral.

- Lord Byron had an affair with his half-sister and made her pregnant.

- Ben Johnson had his heel bone stolen by the Dean of Westminster when his grave was disturbed in 1849. It later turned up again in a junk shop in 1938.

- Lord Alfred Tennyson once had a pony called Fanny, which used to pull his wife along in a wheelchair.

- Marcel Proust once had a pet swordfish.

- Kemo Sabe means 'soggy shrub' in Navajo.

- The word 'honcho' comes from a Japanese word meaning 'squad leader' and first came into usage in the English language during the American occupation of Japan following World War II.

- 'Rhythms' is the longest English word without the normal vowels a, e, i, o or u.

LANGUAGE AND LITERATURE

- 'Ough' can be pronounced in eight different ways. The following sentence contains them all: 'A rough-coated, dough-faced ploughman strode through the streets of Scarborough, coughing and hiccoughing thoughtfully.'

- 'Second string', meaning 'replacement or backup', comes from the Middle Ages. An archer always carried a second string in case the one on his bow broke.

- The 'O' when used as a prefix in Irish surnames means 'descendant of'.

- The plastic things on the end of shoelaces are called aglets.

- The ridges on the sides of coins are called reeding or milling.

- The right side of a boat was called the starboard side because the astronavigators used to stand out on the plank (which was on the right side) to get an unobstructed view of the stars. The left side was known as the port side because that was the side where you put in on at the port.

- The term 'devil's advocate' comes from the Roman Catholic Church. When deciding if someone should be made a saint, a devil's advocate is always appointed to give an alternative view.

LANGUAGE AND LITERATURE

* The term 'dog days' has nothing to do with dogs. It dates back to Roman times when it was believed that Sirius, the Dog Star, added its heat to that of the Sun from 3 July to 11 August, creating exceptionally high temperatures. The Romans called the period *dies caniculares*, or 'days of the dog'.

* The white part of your fingernail is called the lunula.

* Oddly, no term existed for 'homosexuality' in Ancient Greece – there were only a variety of expressions referring to specific homosexual roles. Experts find this baffling as the old Greek culture regarded male/male love in the highest regard. According to several linguists, the word 'homosexual' was not coined until 1869 by the Hungarian physician Karoly Maria Benkert.

* The word 'set' has the highest number of separate definitions in the English language (192 definitions according to the Oxford English Dictionary).

* The word 'coach' is derived from the village of Kocs, Hungary, where coaches were invented and first used.

* The word 'karate' means 'empty hand'.

* The word 'samba' means 'to rub navels together'.

LANGUAGE AND LITERATURE

- 'Long in the tooth' meaning 'old' was originally used to describe horses. As horses age, their gums recede, giving the impression that their teeth are growing. The longer the teeth look, the older the horse.

- No word in the English language rhymes with month, orange, silver or purple.

- The word 'quisling' meaning 'traitor' comes from the name of Major Vidkun Quisling, a Norwegian who collaborated with the Germans during their occupation of Norway.

- Theodore Roosevelt was the only US President to deliver an inaugural address without using the word 'I'. Abraham Lincoln, Franklin D Roosevelt and Dwight D Eisenhower tied for second place, using 'I' only once in their inaugural addresses.

- The world's largest alphabet is Cambodian, with 74 letters.

- The ZIP in Zip code stands for 'Zoning Improvement Plan'.

- The side of a hammer is a cheek.

- There are roughly 6,500 spoken languages in the world today. However, about 2,000 of those languages

——— **LANGUAGE AND LITERATURE** ———

have fewer than 1,000 speakers. The most widely spoken language in the world is Mandarin Chinese. There are 885,000,000 people who speak that language.

- When two words are combined to form a single word (e.g. motor + hotel = motel, breakfast + lunch = brunch), the new word is called a 'portmanteau'.

- The symbol # is called an octothorpe.

- The Paomnnehal Pweor Of The Hmuan Mnid. Aoccdrnig to a rscheearch at Cmabrigde Uinervtisy, it deosn't mttaer in waht oredr the ltteers in a wrod are, the olny iprmoatnt tihng is taht the frist and lsat ltteer be in the rghit pclae. The rset can be a taotl mses and you can sitll raed it wouthit porbelm. Tihs is bcuseae the huamn mnid deos not raed ervey lteter by istlef, but the wrod as a wlohe.

- There is a word in the English language with only one vowel, which occurs six times: indivisibility.

- The seven-letter word 'therein' contains ten words without rearranging any of its letters: the, there, he, in, rein, her, here, ere, therein, herein.

- The Old English word for 'sneeze' is 'fneosan'.

- A speleologist studies caves.

LANGUAGE AND LITERATURE

- A bibliophile is a collector of rare books. A bibliopole is a seller of rare books.

- A magic potion or charm thought to arouse sexual love, especially towards a specific person, is known as a 'philter'.

- A poem written to celebrate a wedding is called an epithalamium.

- Anagrams amused the Ancient Greeks, Romans and Hebrews, and were popular during the Middle Ages.

- Twelve or more cows are known as a 'flink'.

- 'Aromatherapy' is a term coined by French chemist René Maurice Gattefossé in the 1920s to describe the practice of using essential oils taken from plants, flowers, roots, seeds, etc in healing.

- A group of frogs is called an army.

- A group of rhinos is called a crash.

- A group of kangaroos is called a mob.

- A group of ravens is called a murder.

- A group of officers is called a mess.

LANGUAGE AND LITERATURE

- A group of larks is called an exaltation.

- A group of owls is called a parliament.

- Cannibalism, eating human flesh, is also called anthropophagy.

- DNA stands for Deoxyribonucleicacid.

- In 1945, a computer at Harvard malfunctioned. When Grace Hopper, who was working on the computer, investigated, she found a moth in one of the circuits and removed it. Ever since, when something goes wrong with a computer, it is said to have a 'bug' in it.

- The study of insects is called entomology.

- The study of word origins is called etymology.

- The term 'flying on cloud 9' originates from military flights. Cloud types are classified as numbers with 'cloud 9' being a very tall thunderstorm. Jets have to climb to an extremely high altitude in order to fly over 'cloud 9'.

- The shortest complete sentence in the English language is 'Go'.

- The 'dot' over the letter 'i' is called a 'tittle'.

LANGUAGE AND LITERATURE

- The longest one-syllable word in the English language is 'screeched'.

- There are only four words in the English language that end in 'dous': tremendous, horrendous, stupendous and hazardous.

- Men can read smaller print than women.

- The only 15-letter word that can be spelled without repeating a letter is 'uncopyrightable'.

- 'Underground' is the only word in the English language to begin and end with 'und'.

- The longest word in the English language, according to the *Oxford English Dictionary*, is: pneumonoultramicroscopicsilicovolcanoconiosis.

FOOD AND DRINK

FOOD AND DRINK

- Americans buy 2.7 billion packages of breakfast cereal each year. If laid end to end, the empty boxes would stretch to the moon and back.

- The largest pumpkin pie ever made was over 5ft in diameter and weighed over 350lb.

- Smarties were launched as Chocolate Beans in 1937 by Rowntree of York. They were originally priced at 2d. (less than 1p). They were renamed Smarties and packed in the familiar tube one year later. A tube now sells for about 35p.

- More than ten million turkeys are eaten in Britain every Christmas – with nine out of ten people having it for dinner.

- The ONLY cure for a hangover is to drink alcohol. The most effective is champagne because it gets into the blood stream fastest. Warning: only one drink is needed to do the trick.

- In the 13th century, Europeans baptized children with beer.

- Weekend beer drinkers in Dublin consume 9,800 pints an hour between 5.30 p.m. Friday and 3 a.m. on Monday.

FOOD AND DRINK

- The cereal industry uses 816 million pounds of sugar per year, enough to coat each and every American with more than three pounds of sugar. The cereal with the highest amount of sugar per serving is Smacks, which is 53 per cent sugar.

- The largest egg ever had five yolks and was 31cm around the long axis.

- In the 1820s, a temperance movement tried to ban coffee and nearly succeeded.

- Charles Lindbergh took only four sandwiches with him on his famous transatlantic flight.

- At one time, pumpkins were recommended for the removal of freckles and curing snakebites.

- When production of Smarties resumed after World War II, they were made with plain chocolate because of the shortage of milk.

- Henry VIII was the first British king to eat turkey at Christmas but Edward VII made it fashionable.

- Acorns were used as a coffee substitute during the American Civil War.

FOOD AND DRINK

- Boiled eggs are the most popular way to eat eggs in Britain, followed by scrambled and fried.

- Chocolate was used as medicine during the 18th century. It was believed that chocolate could cure a stomach ache.

- Twenty-five per cent of the fish you eat are raised on fish farms.

- Each year, Americans use enough foam peanuts to fill ten 85-storey buildings.

- Laws forbidding the sale of fizzy drinks on Sunday prompted William Garwood to invent the ice-cream sundae in Illinois, in 1875.

- McDonald's and Burger King sugar-coat their fries so they will turn golden brown.

- The world's deadliest mushroom is the *Amanita phalloides*, the Death Cap. The five different poisons contained in the mushroom cause diarrhoea and vomiting within six to 12 hours of ingestion. This is followed by damage to the liver, kidneys and central nervous system – and finally, in the majority of cases, coma and death.

——— FOOD AND DRINK———

- In an authentic Chinese meal, the last course is soup because it allows the roast duck entrée to 'swim' towards digestion.

- When potatoes first appeared in Europe in the 17th century, it was thought that they were disgusting, and they were blamed for starting outbreaks of leprosy and syphilis. As late as 1720 in America, eating potatoes was believed to shorten a person's life.

- Since Hindus don't eat beef, the McDonald's in New Delhi makes its burgers with mutton.

- Liquorice can raise your blood pressure.

- The largest item on any menu in the world is roast camel, sometimes served at Bedouin wedding feasts. The camel is stuffed with a sheep's carcass, which is stuffed with chickens, which are stuffed with fish, which are stuffed with eggs.

- The world's most expensive coffee, at $130 a pound, is called Kopi Luwak. It is in the droppings of a type of marsupial that eats only the very best coffee beans. Plantation workers track them and scoop their precious droppings.

- Large doses of coffee can be lethal. Ten grams, or 100 cups over four hours, can kill the average human.

―――――― **FOOD AND DRINK** ――――――

* Lime Jell-o gives off the same brain waves as adult males.

* When Heinz ketchup leaves the bottle, it travels at a rate of 25 mph.

* A survey of international travellers revealed that the best restaurants in the world are in Paris. Second place was awarded to Rome, and third place went to Hong Kong.

* There are more than 30,000 diets on public record.

* There are 18 different animal shapes in the Animal Crackers cookie zoo.

* A lion was the symbol for Dr Pepper's earliest ad campaign, used with the slogan 'King of Beverages'.

* From 1941 until 1950, violet was part of the colour mixture for M&M's plain chocolates, but was replaced by tan.

* The pumpkin has been known to develop roots whose total length reached 82,000 ft (24,994 m) – more than 15 miles (24 km).

* Chocolate manufacturers use 40 per cent of the world's almonds and 20 per cent of the world's peanuts.

─────────── **FOOD AND DRINK** ───────────

- In 1938, a comic strip was used to advertise Pepsi-Cola. It was titled 'Pepsi and Pete'.

- Of about 350 million cans of chicken noodle soup are sold annually in the United States, 60 per cent are purchased during the cold and flu season. January is the top-selling month of the year.

- Official guidelines allow whole pepper to be sold with up to 1 per cent of the volume made up of rodent droppings.

- Centuries ago, men were told that the evil effects of coffee would make them sterile; women were cautioned to avoid caffeine unless they wanted to be barren.

- 'Okonomiyaki' is considered to be Japan's answer to pizza. It consists of a pot-pourri of grilled vegetables, noodles, and meat or seafood, placed between two pancake-like layers of fried batter.

- In 1954, US food company General Mills introduced Trix breakfast cereal. The new cereal, a huge hit with kids, was 46.6 per cent sugar.

- Olive oil is made only from green olives. Nearly the entire production of green olives grown in Italy is converted into olive oil.

FOOD AND DRINK

- 'Colonial goose' is the name Australians give to stuffed mutton.

- 'Poached egg' means 'egg-in-a-bag' from the French word 'poche'. When an egg is poached, the white of the egg forms a pocket around the yolk, hence the name.

- In Alaska's Matanuska Valley, the long hours of sunlight are used by some farmers to grow giant vegetables. One such farmer grew a 100lb (45kg) cabbage.

- 'Grunt' and 'slump' are two names that refer to a fruit dessert with a biscuit topping.

- 'Sherbet' is Australian slang for beer.

- 'Baby-cut' carrots aren't baby carrots. They're actually full-sized ones peeled and ground down to size.

- The US magazine *Cook's Illustrated* conducted blind-taste testings of vanillas and was surprised to find that, in baked goods, expensive, aromatic vanillas performed almost exactly the same as the cheaper brands of real vanilla. The differences virtually disappeared during cooking.

- On the Italian Riviera in Viareggio, there is a culinary tradition that a good soup must always contain one stone from the sea. This stems from the days when an

FOOD AND DRINK

Italian fisherman's catch was scooped up in nets; fish and stones frequently ended up together in the same cooking pot.

- In 1996, US company Gerber introduced Chicken Alfredo as one of its new flavours of baby food.

- In a traditional French restaurant kitchen, a *Garde Manger* is the person responsible for the preparation of cold foods.

- In ancient China and certain parts of India, mouse flesh was considered a great delicacy.

- Once an orange is squeezed or cut, the vitamin C dissipates quickly. After only eight hours at room temperature or a scant 24 hours in the refrigerator, there is a 20 per cent vitamin C loss.

- You would have to eat 11lb (5kg) of potatoes to put on 1lb (0.45kg) of weight – a potato has no more calories than an apple.

- One of the fattiest fishes is salmon: 4 oz (about 112 g) contains 9 g of fat.

- Oysters were a major part of life in New York in the late 1800s. They were eaten for breakfast, lunch and dinner; they were pickled, stewed, baked, roasted, fried,

FOOD AND DRINK

scalloped and used in soups, patties and puddings. Oystering in New York supported large numbers of families, and oyster theft was a prevalent problem.

* One tablespoon of most brands of ketchup contains 4 g of sugar, 15 calories and 190 g of sodium. There is no fat in ketchup and processed red tomatoes are supposed to be a good source of lycopene, which may reduce the risk of cancer and other diseases.

* In ancient Greece, where the mouse was sacred to Apollo, mice were sometimes devoured by temple priests.

* The chocolate-and-hazelnut spread Nutella is virtually unknown in America.

* The custom of serving a slice of lemon with fish dates back to the Middle Ages. It was believed that if a person accidentally swallowed a fish bone, the lemon juice would dissolve it.

* The darker the olive, the higher the oil content.

* The dessert parfait's name comes from the French word for 'perfect'.

* Only men were allowed to eat at the first self-service restaurant, The Exchange Buffet, in New York in 1885.

FOOD AND DRINK

- The drink Ovaltine was originally named 'Ovomaltine', but it changed due to a clerical error when the manufacturer registered the name.

- Peanut oil is used for underwater cooking in submarines because it does not smoke unless heated above 450°F (232°C).

- It takes a ton of water to make 1lb of refined sugar.

- The first product with a barcode to be scanned at a checkout was a pack of Wrigley's Juicy Fruit chewing gum.

- Lemons have more sugar than oranges.

- Some horticulturists suspect that the banana was the Earth's first fruit. Banana plants have been in cultivation throughout recorded history. One of the first records dates back to Alexander the Great's conquest of India, where he discovered bananas in 327 BC.

- Carrots produce more distilled spirit than potatoes.

- Nutmeg is extremely poisonous if injected intravenously.

- Ninety-five per cent of the USA's entire lemon crop is produced in California and Arizona.

FOOD AND DRINK

- Banana plants are the largest plants on Earth without a woody stem. They are actually giant herbs of the same family as lilies, orchids and palms.

- A common drink among Tibetans is Butter Tea, made out of butter, salt and brick tea.

- A 1kg packet of sugar will contain about 5 million grains of sugar.

- In a Washington study of dieters, one glass of water shut down midnight hunger pangs for almost 100 per cent of the participants.

- The Ancient Greeks called carrots Karoto.

- Lack of water is the main trigger of daytime fatigue.

- Americans consumed more than 20 billion hot dogs in 2000.

- Tobacconists in France used to put a carrot in their bins to keep their tobacco from drying out.

- An egg that is fresh will sink in water, but a stale one won't.

- As bananas ripen, the starch in the fruit turns to sugar. Therefore, the riper the banana the sweeter it will taste.

FOOD AND DRINK
---

* Black pepper is the most popular spice in the world.

* Carrot flowers are also called Birds' Nest, Bees' Nest and the Devil's Plague.

* Britons eat over 22,000 tonnes of chips a week.

* Chewing on gum while cutting onions can help prevent a person from producing tears.

* Americans consumed over 3.1 billion pounds of chocolate in 2001, which is almost half of the total world's production.

* The carrot belongs to the family *Umbelliferae*. The cultivated variety is classified as *Daucus carota, variety sativa*.

* Both of the words in *Daucus carota* mean orange.

* Dandelion root can be roasted and ground as a coffee substitute.

* Germany produces more than 5,000 varieties of beer and has about 1,300 breweries.

* Goat meat contains up to 45 per cent less saturated fat than chicken meat.

FOOD AND DRINK

- Honey is used sometimes for antifreeze mixtures and in the centre of golf balls.

- Macadamia nuts are not sold in their shells because it takes 300lb per square inch of pressure to break the shell.

- Olives which grow on trees were first cultivated 5,000 years ago in Syria.

- A cluster of bananas is called a hand and consists of 10 to 20 fruits known as fingers.

- The word 'banan' is Arabic for finger.

- A 1.5oz milk chocolate bar has only 220 calories.

- A 1.75oz serving of potato chips has 230 calories.

- A recent study indicates that, when men crave food, they tend to crave fat and salt. When women crave food, they tend to desire chocolate.

- American and Russian space flights have always included chocolate.

- American chocolate manufacturers use about 1.5 billion liters of milk, which is only surpassed by the cheese and ice cream industries.

FOOD AND DRINK

- A typical American eats 28 pigs in their lifetime.

- Bananas are one of the few fruits that ripen best off the plant. If left on the plant, the fruit splits open and the pulp has a 'cottony' texture and flavour. Even in tropical growing areas, bananas for domestic consumption are cut green and stored in moist, shady places to ripen slowly.

- The classic Bugs Bunny carrot is the Danvers type.

- It's a myth that Mel Blanc, the voice of Bugs Bunny, was allergic to carrots – he simply didn't like them.

- Aztec emperor Montezuma drank 50 golden goblets of hot chocolate every day. It was thick, dyed red and flavoured with chilli peppers.

- A honeybee must tap 2 million flowers to make 1lb of honey.

- In 1516 Friar Tomas sailed to the Caribbean from Europe bringing banana roots to plant in the rich fertile soil of the tropics, thus first introducing the banana to America. They were not officially introduced to the American public until the 1876 Philadelphia Centennial Exhibition.

FOOD AND DRINK

- Americans spend approximately $25 billion each year on beer.

- Holtville, California dubs itself the 'carrot capital of the world' and has an annual festival, now in its 55th year.

- An etiquette writer of the 1840s advised, 'Ladies may wipe their lips on the tablecloth, but not blow their noses on it.'

- Bananas are perennial crops that are grown and harvested year round. The banana plant does not grow from a seed but rather from a rhizome or bulb. Each fleshy bulb will sprout new shoots year after year.

- Aunt Jemima Pancake Flour, invented in 1889, was the first ready-mix food to be sold commercially.

- Americans spent an estimated $267 billion dining out in 1993.

- There are 100 to 150mg of caffeine in an 8oz cup of brewed coffee, 10mg in a 6oz cup of cocoa, 5 to 10mg in 1oz of bittersweet chocolate, and 5mg in 1oz of milk chocolate.

- California's Frank Epperson invented the Popsicle in 1905 when he was 11 years old.

————————— **FOOD AND DRINK**—————————

- Capsaicin, which makes peppers 'hot' to the human mouth, is best neutralized by casein, the main protein found in milk.

- China's Beijing Duck Restaurant can seat 9,000 people at one time.

- Bananas have no fat, cholesterol or sodium.

- During the Alaskan Klondike gold rush (1897–98), potatoes were practically worth their weight in gold. They were so valued for their vitamin C content that miners traded gold for them.

- The carrot is a member of the parsley family along with celery, parsnip, fennel, dill and coriander.

- During World War II, bakers in the United States were ordered to stop selling sliced bread for the duration of the war on 18 January 1943. Only whole loaves were made available to the public. It was never explained how this action helped the war effort.

- Fortune cookies were invented in 1916 by George Jung, a Los Angeles noodle maker.

- In Eastern Africa, you can buy banana beer, brewed from bananas.

FOOD AND DRINK

---

* Goulash, a beef soup, originated in Hungary in the 19th century.

* To make haggis, the national dish of Scotland, take the heart, liver, lungs and small intestine of a calf or sheep, boil them in the stomach of the animal, season with salt, pepper and onions, add suet and oatmeal.

* Hostess Twinkies were invented in 1931 by James Dewar, manager of Continental Bakeries' Chicago factory. He envisioned the product as a way of using the company's thousands of shortcake pans, which were otherwise employed only during the strawberry season. Originally called 'Little Shortcake Fingers', they were renamed 'Twinkie Fingers', and finally 'Twinkies'.

* Carrot oil is used for flavouring and in perfumery. An extract of carrots was used to colour oleos (margarine) during the fats rationing that took place during World War II.

* In 1860, *Godey's Lady's Book* advised US women to cook tomatoes for at least 3 hours.

* In 1926, when a Los Angeles restaurant owner with the all-American name of Bob Cobb was looking for a way to use up leftovers, he threw together some avocado, celery, tomato, chives, watercress, hard-boiled

————— FOOD AND DRINK —————

eggs, chicken, bacon and Roquefort cheese, and named it after himself: a Cobb salad.

* Rice needs more water to grow than any other crop.

* In Southeast Asia, the banana leaf is used to wrap food, giving it a unique flavour and aroma.

* In 1976, the first eight Jelly Belly® flavours were launched: Orange, Green Apple, Root Beer, Very Cherry, Lemon, Cream Soda, Grape and Liquorice.

* In 1990, Bill Carson of Arrington, Tennessee, grew the largest watermelon at 262lb.

* Astronaut John Glenn ate the first meal in space when he enjoyed pureed apple sauce squeezed from a tube aboard *Friendship* 7 in 1962.

* The Greeks thought that carrots cured venereal disease while the Arab cultures thought it a possible aphrodisiac.

* In the United States, 1lb of potato chips costs 200 times more than 1lb of potatoes.

* Mayonnaise is said to be the invention of the French chef of the Duke de Richelieu in 1756. While the Duke was defeating the British at Port Mahon, his chef was creating a victory feast that included a sauce

---
FOOD AND DRINK
---

made of cream and eggs. When the chef realized that there was no cream in the kitchen, he improvized by substituting olive oil for the cream. A new culinary masterpiece was born, and the chef named it 'Mahonnaise' in honour of the Duke's victory.

* Mushrooms have no chlorophyll so they don't need sunshine to grow and thrive. Some of the earliest commercial mushroom farms were set up in caves in France during the reign of King Louis XIV (1638–1715).

* In Scotland, the Sunday before Michaelmas, 29 September, is called Carrot Sunday.

* India is by far the largest world producer of bananas, growing 16.5 million tonnes in 2002, followed by Brazil, which produced 6.5 million tonnes in 2002. To the Indians, the flower from the banana tree is sacred. During religious and important ceremonies such as weddings, banana flowers are tied around the head, as they believe this will bring good luck.

* Nabisco's Oreos are the world's best-selling brand of cookie at a rate of 6 billion each year. The first Oreo was sold in 1912.

* Americans eat 18 per cent more vegetables today than they did in 1970.

——— FOOD AND DRINK———

- Per capita, the Irish consume more chocolate than Americans, Swedes, Danes, French and Italians.

- Persians first began using coloured eggs to celebrate spring in 3,000 BC and 13th century Macedonians were the first Christians on record to use coloured eggs in Easter celebrations. Crusaders returning from the Middle East spread the custom of colouring eggs, and Europeans began to use them to celebrate Easter and other warm-weather holidays.

- On average, a baby in the United States will eat 15lb of cereal in their first year of life.

- The hottest chilli in the world is the Habanero.

- The Americans know the wild carrot as 'Queen Anne's Lace', 'Rattlesnake Weed' and 'American Carrot'.

- Pine, spruce or other evergreen wood should never be used in barbecues. These woods, when burning or smoking, can add harmful tar and resins to the food. Only hardwoods should be used for smoking and grilling, such as oak, pecan, hickory, maple, cherry, alder, apple or mesquite, depending on the type of meat being cooked.

- Rice is the staple food of more than one-half of the world's population.

FOOD AND DRINK

* In 1995, KFC sold 11 pieces of chicken for every man, woman and child in the US.

* Refried beans aren't really what they seem. Although their name seems like a reasonable translation of the Spanish *frijoles refritos*, the fact is that these beans aren't fried twice. In Spanish, *refritos* literally means 'well-fried', not 're-fried'.

* Americans consumed over 3.1 billion pounds of chocolate in 2001, which is almost half of the total world's production.

* A hard-boiled egg will spin. An uncooked or soft-boiled egg will not.

* Research shows that only 43 per cent of homemade dinners served in the US include vegetables.

* Saffron, made from the dried stamens of cultivated crocus flowers, is the most expensive cooking spice.

* Sliced bread was introduced under the Wonder Bread label in 1930.

16

RUDE FACTS

RUDE FACTS

- On average, everyone farts once per hour.

- Farts are highly flammable.

- Adults produce between 200ml and 2 litres of wind per day.

- The amount you fart is increased by stress, onions, cabbage and beans.

- Vegetarians fart more, but theirs smell less.

- On average, you produce 200g of poo per day.

- Farts are created mostly by E. coli.

- A man became a tourist attraction in the Dominican Republic after admitting himself to hospital with an erection that had lasted six days.

- On average, a fart is composed of about 59 per cent nitrogen, 21 per cent hydrogen, 9 per cent carbon dioxide, 7 per cent methane and 4 per cent oxygen. Less than 1 per cent is what makes them stink.

- The temperature of a fart at time of creation is 98.6°F.

- Farts have been clocked at a speed of 10ft per second.

—— RUDE FACTS ——

- Although they won't admit it, women fart as much as men.

- Termites are the largest producers of farts.

- Bernard Clemmens of London managed to sustain a fart for an officially recorded time of 2 minutes 42 seconds.

- The word 'fart' comes from the Old English 'feortan' (meaning 'to break wind').

- The Romans made condoms from the muscle tissue of warriors they defeated in battle.

- Discovered in the foundations of Dudley Castle near Birmingham, England, were condoms that were made from fish and animal intestines and dated back to 1640.

- Casanova wore condoms made of linen.

- If you farted consistently for six years and nine months, enough gas is produced to create the energy of an atomic bomb.

- Runners sometimes drink urine to replace electrolytes.

- Dinosaur droppings are called coprolites, and are actually fairly common.

RUDE FACTS

* US Navy Seals sometimes urinate in their pants during cold-water training exercises in order to stay warm.

* In Pre-Colonial Peru, the Incas washed their children's hair with urine as a remedy for head lice.

* Urinating on someone or being urinated on for enjoyment is known in fetish parlance as 'water sports'.

* Astronauts cannot burp in space. There is no gravity to separate liquid from gas in their stomachs.

* In Minnesota, the Downtown Minneapolis Neighborhood Association has initiated a campaign to prevent or eliminate public urination, which is considered a 'quality of life' criminal offence in most US cities.

* Laplanders consume a hallucinogenic mushroom called amanita muscaria, also know as Fly Agaric. The mushroom's hallucinogenic compound 'muscanol' is excreted in the urine intact. When the mushroom is in short supply, people who have consumed the mushroom will urinate into a pot. Someone without any mushrooms can then drink the urine and experience the same effects.

——————— RUDE FACTS ———————

- Wolves, bears, apes and other mammals use urine to claim territory, communicate eligibility for mating, body size and other individual characteristics.

- The longest recorded distance for projectile vomiting is 27ft.

- The study of nose picking is called rhinotillexomania.

- In addition to hair and blood, urine is used to test people for illicit drug use.

- In his final book *Civilization and Its Discontents*, Sigmund Freud claimed that civilisation became possible only when ancient peoples resisted the impulse to extinguish their campfires by pissing them out.

- Drinking urine is part of many non-traditional remedies used today, especially in Ayurvedic medicine.

- A party boat filled with 60 men and women capsized in Texas after all the passengers rushed to one side as the boat passed a nudist beach.

- 72.4 per cent of people place their toilet paper on the roll forward (with the loose end over the roll, towards the user).

RUDE FACTS

* The visitors at Yellowstone Park create 270 million gallons of waste per year, and use up to 18 rolls of toilet paper, per toilet, per day!

* One of the most difficult items for sewage workers to handle, as it is insoluble, yet fine enough to pass through most filtration systems, is pubic hair. Every month Thames Water removes over a ton of pubic hair at its water-treatment plants, whereupon it is taken away to a landfill site and buried.

* Ninety-eight per cent of all Americans feel better about themselves when they flush a toilet.

* Scuba divers cannot pass gas at depths of 33ft or below.

* A German who borrowed £5,000 from his mother for a penis extension demanded a refund after it ended up shorter and deformed.

* About a third of all Americans flush the toilet while they're still sitting on it.

* In the USA, more toilets flush at the half-time of the Super Bowl than at any other time of the year.

* A Kimberly-Clark marketing survey on bathroom habits finds that, when it comes to toilet paper, women are 'wadders' and men are 'folders'.

RUDE FACTS

- Twenty-two per cent of American women aged 20 gave birth while in their teens. In Switzerland and Japan, only 2 per cent did so.

- Sex is the safest tranquillizer in the world. It is ten times more effective than valium.

- Sex gets the blood pumping and helps you sweat out booze – and it's good fun.

- Twenty-three per cent of UK employees say they have had sex in the office.

- It is estimated that The Pentagon spent $50 million on Viagra for American troops and retirees in 1999.

- For every 'normal' webpage, there are five porn pages.

- Sex is biochemically no different from eating large quantities of chocolate.

- A man's beard grows fastest when he anticipates sex.

- The French have topped a survey as being the people who have sex the most.

- There are over 3,500 bras hanging behind the bar at Hogs and Heifers, a bar in Manhattan. So many, in fact, that they caused a beam to collapse in the ceiling.

RUDE FACTS

- The average shelf-life of a latex condom is about two years.

- 'Formicophilia' is the fetish for having small insects crawl on your genitals.

- 'Ithyphallophobia' is a morbid fear of seeing, thinking about or having an erect penis.

- Internet auction site eBay has been hit by a new craze in which sellers appear naked in reflections on goods they're selling.

- The word 'gymnasium' comes from the Greek *gymnazein* which means 'to exercise naked'.

- Topless saleswomen are legal in Liverpool – but only in tropical fish stores.

- In India, it is cheaper to have sex with a prostitute than to buy a condom!

- Women who read romance novels have sex twice as often as those who don't.

- 3.9 per cent of women surveyed say they never wear underwear.

—————————— RUDE FACTS ——————————

- An adult sex toy sparked a security scare that closed an Australian airport for nearly an hour.

- Two teenage US soldiers have been arrested for having sex in front of tourists at the Alamo.

- The Earl of Condom was a knighted personal physician to England's King Charles II in the mid-1600s. The Earl was requested to produce a method to protect the King from syphilis.

- A Cambridgeshire village has erected a 5ft-tall statue of dinosaur poo to celebrate its past.

- The world's youngest parents were eight and nine and lived in China in 1910.

- The first couple to be shown in bed together on prime-time television were Fred and Wilma Flintstone.

- Twenty-five per cent of women think money makes a man sexier.

- Some lions mate over 50 times a day.

- Seven per cent of Americans claim they never bathe at all.

RUDE FACTS

* Each day, there are over 120 million acts of sexual intercourse taking place all over the world.

* The most searched term on yahoo.com every year is porn.

* Eight-five per cent of men who die of heart attacks during intercourse are found to have been cheating on their wives.

* Passengers at an Indian airport were shocked when a hardcore porn movie was played on television screens for 20 minutes.

* In Kentucky, 50 per cent of the people who get married for the first time are teenagers.

* Bird droppings are the chief export of Nauru, an island nation in the western Pacific.

* Spotted skunks do handstands before they spray.

* A couple from Germany went to a fertility clinic to find out why – after eight years of marriage – they were still childless. The cause of their trouble conceiving was that they never had sex.

* If a police officer in Coeur d'Alene, Idaho, suspects a couple is having sex inside a vehicle they must honk

RUDE FACTS

their horn three times, and wait two minutes before being allowed to approach the scene.

* In Ames, Iowa, a husband may not take more than three gulps of beer while lying in bed with his wife.

* A law in Alexandria, Minnesota, makes it illegal for a husband to make love to his wife if his breath smells of garlic, onions or sardines.

* A Helena, Montana law states that a woman cannot dance on a saloon table unless her clothing weighs more than 3lb 2oz.

* Hotel owners in Hastings, Nebraska, are required by law to provide a clean, white cotton nightshirt to each guest. According to the law, no couple may have sex unless they are wearing the nightshirts.

* Any couple making out inside a vehicle, and accidentally sounding the horn during their lustful act, may be taken to jail according to a law in Liberty Corner, New Jersey.

* During lunch breaks in Carlsbad, New Mexico, no couple should engage in a sexual act while parked in their vehicle, unless their car has curtains.

—————————— RUDE FACTS ——————————

- In Harrisburg, Pennsylvania, it is illegal to have sex with a truck driver inside a toll booth.

- Hotels in Sioux Falls, South Dakota, are required by law to furnish their rooms with twin beds only. There should be a minimum of two feet between the beds, and it is illegal for a couple to make love on the floor between the beds.

- In Kingsville, Texas, there is a law against two pigs having sex on the city's airport property.

- A Tremonton, Utah, law states that no woman is allowed to have sex with a man while riding in an ambulance. In addition to normal charges, the woman's name will be published in the local newspaper. The man does not receive any punishment.

- In the state of Washington, there is a law against having sex with a virgin under any circumstances (including the wedding night).

- The only acceptable sexual position in Washington DC is the missionary-style position. Any other sexual position is considered illegal.

AMERICA AND AMERICANS

——— AMERICA AND AMERICANS ———

* Bacteria, including staphylococcus, E. coli, and Klebsiella, are present on 18 per cent of the coins and 7 per cent of the bills in the US.

* One in five Native Americans die in accidents, compared with 1 in 17 of the general American population.

* During the peak of its construction, the building of the Empire State Building proceeded at a pace of four-and-a-half storeys per week.

* A survey of 18- to 24-year-olds from nine nations put the United States last in general geographic knowledge scores. One in seven – about 24 million people – could not find their own country on a world map. And even more alarming, those who participated in the survey were recent high school and college graduates.

* Bat Cave, Duck, Horneytown, Whynot, Welcome, Toast and Frog Pond are all places in the state of North Carolina.

* In the US, more than 50 per cent of the people who, once bitten by venomous snakes go untreated, still survive.

—— AMERICA AND AMERICANS ——

* Louisiana is home to places such as Uncle Sam, Waterproof, Dry Prong and Belcher.

* Due to the Great Depression, it took over 12 years to occupy all the office space in the Empire State Building, earning it the nickname the 'Empty State Building'.

* The average American makes six trips to the bathroom every day.

* Ronald Reagan was the oldest man elected president.

* Until there was a pay rise in 1814, US congressmen were paid $6 per diem when Congress was in session.

* Prior to the adoption of the Twelfth Amendment in 1804, the candidate who ran second in a presidential race automatically became vice-president. Thomas Jefferson became John Adams's vice-president in this way.

* American settlers took six months to reach the west coast by wagon between 1840 and 1850.

* Cut and planed lumber was hard to come by in the New World, and since the Pilgrims didn't intend to return to Europe, they dismantled the *Mayflower* and used its lumber to build a barn.

AMERICA AND AMERICANS

- Residents of Nevada bet an average of £475 a year in gambling casinos.

- By the end of the US Civil War, between one-third and one-half of all US paper currency in circulation was counterfeit, and so the US Secret Service was created under the US Treasury Department. In less than a decade, counterfeiting was sharply reduced.

- The official state musical instrument in South Dakota is the fiddle.

- Nearly a quarter of all United States pet owners take their pets to work.

- In June 2003, 200 American companies participated in the first official 'Take Your Dog to Work Day'.

- In 1791, Washington DC was known as Federal City.

- The official state cooking pot of Utah is the Dutch oven.

- During the American Revolution, inflation was so great that the price of corn rose 10,000 per cent, the price of wheat 14,000 per cent, the price of flour 15,000 per cent, and the price of beef 33,000 per cent.

- Ronald Reagan was the first president to submit a trillion dollar budget to Congress.

AMERICA AND AMERICANS

* Twenty-five per cent of Americans do not know what is meant by the term 'holocaust'.

* The roadrunner is the official bird of New Mexico.

* It is illegal for kids to buy lollipops in Spokane, Washington.

* Approximately 40 per cent of Americans believe they have food allergies, while in reality, less than 1 per cent do. Most involve symptoms caused by food intolerances or other disorders.

* The second National City is Port Angeles, Washington, designated by President Abraham Lincoln. That's where they would move the capital if something happened to Washington DC.

* A record 80 million telephone calls were made in New York City during the blackout on 13-14 July 1977.

* Sixty-two per cent of US dog owners sign letters or cards from themselves and their dogs.

* The state of Maine has at least 28 cities or towns that begin with the word 'North', 23 with the word 'South', 22 with 'West', and 28 with 'East'.

AMERICA AND AMERICANS

* The state motto of Washington is 'Alki', Chinook Indian for 'By and By'.

* During World War II, the US Navy commissioned the world's first floating ice-cream parlour for service in the Pacific theatre. This concrete barge, capable of producing 10 gallons (38 litres) of ice-cream every seven seconds, kept ships well supplied.

* There are places called Boring, Cockeysville, Accident, Secretary and Assawoman Bay in the state of Maryland.

* The state of Pennsylvania can lay claim to the first woman governor, the first zip fastener, the first use of toilet paper and the autogiro, the ancestor to the helicopter.

* Phone calls in the United States plummeted as much as 58 per cent during the reading of the O J Simpson trial verdict in 1995, and workers put their jobs on hold for up to 30 minutes. In contrast, phone-call volume barely budged when President John F Kennedy was assassinated.

* Sculptor Gutzon Borglum spent 14 years sculpting the busts of Presidents George Washington, Thomas Jefferson, Theodore Roosevelt and Abraham Lincoln on Mount Rushmore. When he died, his son continued his work.

AMERICA AND AMERICANS

- In the US there are about 15,000 people in comas.

- The state of Maine was once known as the 'Earmuff Capital of The World' as earmuffs were invented there by Chester Greenwood in 1873.

- President Richard Nixon visited both China and the Soviet Union during his term. He was also the first president to visit all 50 states.

- The US Automobile Association was formed in 1905 for the purpose or providing 'scouts' who could warn motorists of hidden police traps.

- There are three million stutterers in the United States and a similar proportion in every other part of the world.

- There are places called Conception, Peculiar, Frankenstein, Tightwad, Humansville and Enough in Missouri.

- The state of Oregon has one city named Sisters and another called Brothers. Sisters got its name from a nearby trio of peaks in the Cascade Mountains known as the Three Sisters. Brothers was named as a counterpart to Sisters.

- The Declaration of Independence is currently housed

AMERICA AND AMERICANS

in the National Archives, and at one point it was actually repaired with Scotch tape.

* Textbook shortages are so severe in some US public schools that 71 per cent of teachers say they have purchased reading materials with their own money.

* In 1933, a night's stay in a double room at the famous Waldorf-Astoria Hotel in New York City was £10. A single room cost £3.30 and a suite £10.20.

* The state of Minnesota is home to Embarrass, Fertile, Nowthen, Savage and Sleepy Eye.

* Wyoming was the first American state to allow women to vote.

* Forty-nine per cent of Americans don't know that white bread is made from wheat.

* New York City is the sister city of Tokyo.

* There was once an Anti-Tipping Society of America.

* It is illegal to wipe dishes dry in Minneapolis, Minnesota. Dishes should be left to drip dry.

* More than 40 per cent of the women in the United States were in the Girl Scouts organisation. Two-

———— AMERICA AND AMERICANS ————

thirds of the women listed in *Who's Who of Women* were Girl Scouts.

* When Franklin D Roosevelt died on 12 April 1945, Harry Truman became the first US president to take office in the midst of a war.

* The states of Arizona, Indiana and Hawaii have never adopted Daylight Savings Time. Neither has Puerto Rico, the Virgin Islands or American Samoa.

* Crummies, Dwarf, Monkey's Eyebrow, Rabbit Hash, Ordinary, Possum Trot, Oddville, Mud Lick, Hand Shoe and Bugtussle are all places in Kentucky.

* FBI agents were first allowed to carry guns in 1934, 26 years after the agency was established.

* The streets of Victor, Colorado, once a gold-rush town, are paved with low-grade gold.

* The average American's diet today consists of 55 per cent junk food.

* When Andrew Johnson, the first US president to be impeached, died, he asked to be wrapped in an American flag with a copy of the Constitution under his head when he was buried.

AMERICA AND AMERICANS

- Thirty-three per cent of American dog owners admit that they talk to their dogs on the phone or leave messages on an answering machine while away.

- The Hoover Dam is 726 ft (221 m) tall and 660 ft (201 m) thick at its base. Enough rock was excavated in its construction to build the Great Wall of China.

- The town of Fort Atkinson, Iowa, was the site of the only fort ever built by the US government to protect one Indian tribe from another.

- The United States consumes 50 per cent of the world's production of diamonds. However, there is only one diamond mine located in the United States – in Arkansas.

- When he saw his assassin being beaten by his guards, the dying President William McKinley cried out, 'Don't let them hurt him.'

- Philadelphia is a city of big tippers: 18.6 per cent of the bill minus tax is the normal amount given. Second place goes to New York City, with 18.3 per cent. The lowest tipping city in America is Seattle, where the average tip is 17.1 per cent.

- Worms, Colon and Surprise are to be found in the state of Nebraska.

—————— AMERICA AND AMERICANS ——————

- American teenagers bet as much as $1 billion a year, and about 7 per cent of adolescents under 18 may be addicted to gambling.

- Eight per cent of American kissers keep their eyes open, while more than 20 per cent take an occasional peek.

- While serving as a young naval officer in World War II, President Richard M Nixon set up the only hamburger stand in the South Pacific. Nixon's Snack Shack served free burgers and Australian beer to flight crews.

- The Pentagon, in Arlington, Virginia, has twice as many bathrooms as is necessary. When it was built in the 1940s, the state of Virginia still had segregation laws requiring separate toilet facilities for blacks and whites.

- Since 1874, the mints of the United States have been making currency for foreign governments, whose combined orders have at times exceeded the volume of domestic requirements.

- The United States today contains more than 100,000 mounds, earthworks and fortifications that were built by prehistoric races.

- Trident-missile manufacturer Lockheed transmits data from its Sunnyvale, California, headquarters to its Santa Cruz plant 30 miles (48 km) away via carrier pigeon.

AMERICA AND AMERICANS

- Twenty-one per cent of American children eat chocolate every day.

- Almost 90 per cent of Americans label themselves as shy.

- The world's shortest river – the D River in Oregon – is only 121 ft (37 m) long.

- There are places called Manly, Gravity, Diagonal and What Cheer in the state of Iowa.

- A study of New York marathoners a few years ago found that their divorce rate – male and female – was twice the national average.

- Persons that engage in solitary endurance sports are the ones most likely to be compulsive exercisers – for example, joggers, long-distance swimmers, weight lifters, and cross-country skiers. Occasionally, devotees of these activities set unrealistic, ambitious goals and then drive themselves mercilessly to reach them.

- Although the United States has just 5 per cent of the world's population, it has 70 per cent of the world's lawyers.

- President Richard M Nixon suffered from motion sickness and hay fever.

AMERICA AND AMERICANS

- The world's largest Yo-Yo resides in the National Yo-yo Museum in Chico, California. Named 'Big Yo', it is 256lb (116kg), 50 inches (127cm) tall and 31.5 inches (80cm) wide.

- The United States would fit into the continent of Africa three and a half times.

- Odd place names in Maine include Bald Head, Robinhood and Beans Corner Bingo.

- There are 61 towns in the United States with the word 'turkey' in their names – for example, Turkeytown, Alabama, and Turkey Foot, Florida.

- President Abraham Lincoln considered his Gettysburg Address 'a flat failure'.

- There are 40 active volcanoes in Alaska – more than in any other US state.

- There are 293 ways to make change for a dollar.

- Americans consume about 138 billion cups of coffee a year.

- You can fold a piece of US currency forward then backward about 4,000 times before it tears.

———— AMERICA AND AMERICANS ————

- It is illegal to ride a bike into a swimming pool in Baldwin Park, California.

- Americans today consume nearly the same number of calories per day as in 1910, but the weight of the average American has increased substantially due to lack of exercise.

- Americans pay over $30,000 in federal, state and local taxes every second.

- Using satellite-surveying techniques, scientists have determined that Los Angeles, California, is moving east. At a rate estimated to be about one-fifth of an inch (0.5 cm) per year, the city is moving closer to the San Gabriel Mountains.

- One million dollars in $1 bills would weigh approximately one ton. Placed in a pile, the pile would be 360 feet (110 metres) high – as tall as 60 average adults standing on top of each other.

- There are more than 100,000 glaciers in Alaska, and about 75 per cent of all the fresh water in the state is stored as glacial ice.

- In 1980, the Yellow Pages accidentally listed a Texas funeral home under Frozen Foods.

---------- **AMERICA AND AMERICANS** ----------

- 'Uncle Jumbo' was the nickname of President Grover Cleveland.

- There are places called French Lick, Gnaw Bone, Fickle, Plainville, Gas City and Floyd's Knobs in Indiana.

- Americans today use four times as much energy per capita as their grandparents' generation.

- The ten most popular girl's names in America are Emily, Madison, Hannah, Emma, Alexis, Ashley, Abigail, Sarah, Samantha and Olivia.

- The state of West Virginia is home to Crum, War, Pinch, Big Ugly, Left Hand and Lost City.

- The United States had a Society for the Prevention of Cruelty to Animals in 1866, eight years before it had a Society for the Prevention of Cruelty to Children.

- Utah is known as the 'Beehive State'.

- Americans use 50 million tons of paper a year.

- Alaska was bought from Russia for about 2 cents an acre.

- Americans hold more parties in their homes on Super Bowl Sunday than any other day of the year.

—————— AMERICA AND AMERICANS ——————

- Various US cities are named after other countries. You can visit the US city of Peru in the states of Maine, Nebraska and New York.

- About 24 per cent of American adults say they have participated, at some time or another, in illegal gambling.

- There are about 3,000 hot-dog vendors in metropolitan New York.

- There are four places in the United States with the word 'chicken' in their name: Chicken, Alaska; Chicken Bristle, in Illinois and Kentucky; and Chickentown, Pennsylvania.

- Mail to the Havasupai Indian Reservation, in northern Arizona, is delivered by mule. It is the only US Postal Service route of its type in existence today.

- About 60 per cent of all American babies are named after close relatives.

- There is one slot machine in Las Vegas for every eight inhabitants.

- President Richard M Nixon kept a music box in his Oval Office desk that played the tune 'Hail to the Chief'.

AMERICA AND AMERICANS

- About 70 per cent of American households buy yellow mustard every year.

- Richard M Nixon is the only president to have resigned.

- There are over three million lakes in Alaska. The largest, Lake Iliamna, is the size of Connecticut.

- Washington boasts places called Forks, Index and Tumtum.

- An estimated one in five Americans – some 38 million – don't like sex.

- Twelve million Americans do not know that their nation's capital is Washington DC.

- Unlike other US presidents, Jimmy Carter avoided using his initials because 'JC' is usually associated with Jesus Christ.

- It is illegal for dogs to get in the way of people walking in Pateros, Washington.

- Green Bay, Wisconsin, lays claim to being 'The Toilet Paper Capital of The World'. Some other notable Wisconsin capitals include: Belleville – UFO Capital of Wisconsin; Bloomer – Jump Rope Capital of the

AMERICA AND AMERICANS

World; Bonduel – Spelling Capital of Wisconsin;
Boscobel – Turkey Capital of Wisconsin; Hayward –
Muskie Capital of the World; Mercer – Loon Capital
of the World; Monroe – Swiss Cheese Capital of the
World; Mount Horeb – Troll Capital of the World;
Muscoda – Morel Mushroom Capital of Wisconsin;
Potosi – Catfish Capital of Wisconsin; Sheboygan –
Bratwurst Capital of the World; Somerset – Inner
Tubing Capital of the World; Sturgeon Bay –
Shipbuilding Capital of the Great Lakes; and Wausau –
Ginseng Capital of the World.

- The state of California has issued six driver's licences
to Jesus Christ.

- Odd place names in Illinois include Roachtown,
Fishhook, Grand Detour, Kickapoo, Normal
and Oblong.

- Various US cities have been named after popular
European cities. For example, Paris could mean the
city located in any of the states of Arkansas, Florida,
Idaho, Illinois, Kentucky, Massachusetts, Tennessee,
Texas or West Virginia.

- The largest of the 130 national cemeteries in
America is the Calverton National Cemetery, on
Long Island, New York. It conducts more than
7,000 burials each year.

——— **AMERICA AND AMERICANS** ———

- Twenty per cent of Americans don't know that Osama Bin Laden and Saddam Hussein are different people.

- Virginia extends 95 miles (153 km) further west than West Virginia.

- Presidents George Washington and John Adams had to employ protection money, paying off certain pirates in the Mediterranean Sea with a couple of million dollars, while Congress debated the creation of a US navy.

- Texas is home to locations such as Bacon, Looneyville, Wink, Oatmeal and Noodle.

- More than 40 per cent of American households with children have guns.

- Montpelier, Vermont, is the only US state capital without a McDonald's.

- More than 80 languages are spoken in New York. The second most common language spoken, after English, is Spanish.

- The city morgue in the Bronx, New York, has been so busy at times that next of kin take numbers and wait in line for their body-identification call.

AMERICA AND AMERICANS

- In America, 175,000 new laws and two million new regulations are introduced every year, from all levels of government.

- In the United States, courts of law devote about half their time to cases involving cars.

- Four states have active volcanoes: Washington, California, Alaska and Hawaii, with the latter being home to Mauna Loa, the world's largest active volcano. Hawaii itself was formed by the activity of undersea volcanoes.

- In the United States there are two credit cards for every person.

- New York City, named by Americans as the most dangerous, least attractive and rudest city, is also Americans' top choice as the city where they would most like to live or visit on vacation.

- Abraham Lincoln was the first president born outside the original 13 colonies.

- Mount Carmel is one of Chicago's finest graveyards, and is most famous for the graves of Chicago's notorious gangsters of the 1920s - including Al Capone.

AMERICA AND AMERICANS

- Georgia boasts places called Cumming, Hopeulikit and Between.

- The United States produces 19 per cent of the world's trash. The annual contribution includes 20 billion disposable nappies and two billion razors.

- The United States earned the title of having the most cars of any country in the world. With an estimated 135 million cars nation-wide, it is approximated that there is one car for every two Americans.

- It is illegal to enter a public theatre or a tram within four hours of eating garlic in Gary, Indiana.

- There are more Irish in New York City than in Dublin, more Italians in New York City than in Rome, Italy; and more Jews in New York City than in Tel Aviv, Israel.

- Ulysses S Grant was the first president whose parents were both alive when he was inaugurated.

- Myrtle Beach, South Carolina, has the most mini-golf courses per area in the United States.

- In the United States most car journeys are less than 5 miles (8 km).

AMERICA AND AMERICANS

- In the United States the most popular colour for textiles is blue it is one of the least-favourite colours for house paint.

- From the 1830s to 1960s, the Lehigh River, in eastern Pennsylvania, was owned by the Lehigh Coal and Navigation Company, making it the only privately owned river in the United States.

- The United States shreds 7,000 tons (7,112,000 kg) of worn-out currency each year.

- The state of Tennessee boasts locations called Defeated, Static, Nameless, Disco, Difficult, Finger and Life.

- William Henry Harrison was the first US president to die while in office. He also had the shortest term (32 days), falling ill with pneumonia shortly after his inauguration and never recovering.

- In the United States, it is estimated that four million 'junk' telephone calls – phone solicitations by persons or programmed machine – are made every day.

- Grasshopper Glacier, in Montana, was named for the grasshoppers that can still be seen frozen in the ice.

- The average North American will eat 35,000 cookies during their life span.

AMERICA AND AMERICANS

- Before the enactment of the 1978 law that made it mandatory for dog owners in New York City to clean up after their pets, approximately 40 million pounds (around 18 million kilograms) of dog excrement were deposited on the streets every year.

- There are more people in New York City (7.9 million) than there are in the states of Alaska, Vermont, Wyoming, South Dakota, New Hampshire, Nevada, Idaho, Utah, Hawaii, Delaware and New Mexico combined.

- In the US, the penny and the Sacagawea dollar are the only coins currently minted with profiles that face to the right. All other US coins – the half dollar, quarter, dime, and nickel – feature profiles that face to the left.

- Bad Axe, Eden, Jugville, Hell, Pigeon and Paradise are all found in the state of Michigan.

- Hawaii's 'Forbidden Island' of Nihau is owned by a single family named Robinson. On Nihau, there are no phones and no electricity for the population of 250.

- The American Mint once considered producing doughnut-shaped coins.

- At some US malls, security patrols use horses to increase car park security, but at times report a 'Code Brown', meaning one of the horses has made a mess.

AMERICA AND AMERICANS

* Christmas, Frostproof, Niceville, Two Egg and Yellow Water are places in Florida.

* President George Washington was the first person to breed roses in the US. He laid out his own garden at Mount Vernon and filled it with his own selections of roses. One of the varieties was named after his mother and it is still being grown today.

* Hawaii has 150 recognized ecosystems.

* There are more telephones than people in Washington DC.

* There are more television sets in the United States than there are people in Japan.

* President Bill Clinton is allergic to dust, mould, pollen, cats, Christmas trees and dairy products.

* President Rutherford B Hayes' wife, Lucy Webb, was the initial First Lady to graduate from college and did not allow drinking in the White House, earning her the nickname 'Lemonade Lucy'.

* Wall, Farmer, Oral, Potato Creek, Igloo and Hammer are all in the state of South Dakota.

AMERICA AND AMERICANS

- Almost a quarter of the land area of Los Angeles is taken up by cars.

- So confident were some people that alcohol was the cause of virtually all crime that, on the eve of Prohibition, some US towns actually sold their jails.

- It is illegal to push dirt under a rug in Pittsburgh, Pennsylvania.

- There are more art galleries in Scottsdale, Arizona, than either Los Angeles or San Francisco.

- President William Taft was the last president to keep a cow on the White House lawn to supply him with fresh milk.

- Hell's Canyon, on the Snake River in Idaho, is deeper than the Grand Canyon.

- The two most commonly sold items in American grocery stores are breakfast cereals and fizzy drink.

- The state of North Dakota boasts locations called Colgate, Zap, Antler, Concrete and Hoople.

- Reno, Nevada, has the highest rate of alcoholism in the United States; Provo, Utah, has the lowest rate.

AMERICA AND AMERICANS

- The Capitol Records building in Los Angeles, California, is built to resemble a stack of records. A red plane-warning light atop the structure flashes out the word 'Hollywood' in Morse code every 20 seconds.

- In terms of resources used and pollution contributed in a lifetime, one citizen of the United States is the equivalent of about 80 citizens of India.

- If the Nile River were stretched across the United States, it would run just about from New York to Los Angeles.

- A shot of Elvis Presley offering his services as a drug enforcement agent to Nixon is the most requested photo from the US National Archives.

- The state of New Hampshire is home to Hell Hollow, Lost Nation and Sandwich Landing.

- Technically, there are really only 46 states in the United States, as Kentucky, Massachusetts, Pennsylvania and Virginia are commonwealths.

- The ten most popular boys' names in America are Jacob, Michael, Joshua, Matthew, Ethan, Joseph, Andrew, Christopher, Daniel and Nicholas.

AMERICA AND AMERICANS

---

* Fifty-two per cent of Americans think early man coexisted with the dinosaurs.

* There are places in Colorado called Climax, No Name, Hygiene, Dinosaur and Last Chance.

* In the United States, 25,300,500 out of more than 40 million dogs can perform at least one trick: 5,313,105 dogs can sit, 3,795,075 can shake paws, and 379,508 dogs can 'say prayers'.

* The Capitol Building in Washington DC has 365 steps. They represent the days of the year.

* President William McKinley had a pet parrot that he named 'Washington Post'.

* Located in Cochise County, in southern Arizona, the city of Tombstone is probably the most famous and most glamorized mining town in all of North America. According to legend, prospectors Ed Schieffelin and his brother Al were warned not to venture into the Apache-inhabited Mule Mountains because they would only 'find their tombstones'. Thus, with a touch of the macabre, the Schieffelins named their first silver strike claim Tombstone, and it became the name of the town.

AMERICA AND AMERICANS

- Two towns in Vermont claim to be President Chester Arthur's birthplace, but recent research supports his opponents' charges that he was born in Canada, and therefore was not eligible to be president under the US Constitution.

- Maine is the only US state that adjoins only one other state.

- Abraham Lincoln was the first US president to leave no will.

- In the United States, deaf people have safer driving records than hearing people.

- On 10 July 1913, Death Valley had the hottest temperature recorded in the western hemisphere when, in the shade, it reached 134°F (56.6°C).

- In the United States, the number of women living alone has risen 33 per cent to 30 million in the past 15 years.

- Colorado's capital Denver is the largest metro city in a 600-mile radius (966 km) – an area almost the size of Europe.

- Bumpass, Nuttsville, Kermit, Cuckoo, Ben Hur, Threeway and Pocket can all be found in the state of Virginia.

—— AMERICA AND AMERICANS ——

- There is only one city in the United States named 'Beach'. It is found in North Dakota, which is a land-locked state.

- It is illegal for a barber to shave a customer's chest in Omaha, Nebraska.

- There are places in Montana called Square Butt, Hungry Horse, Divide and Rocky Boy.

- Meadowcroft Rock Shelter, in Washington County, Pennsylvania, is the earliest documented place of human habitation in the western hemisphere. Studies done by anthropologist Dr James Adovasio found evidence of early civilisations. Carbon dating revealed the remains were from human habitants living in the area 16,240 years ago.

- Seventy-five per cent of all American women wear a bra that is the wrong size.

- There are locations in Vermont called Satan's Kingdom, Mosquitoville and Notown.

- At the height of the Great Depression in 1932, 12 million people in the US were unemployed.

- Out of the 34,000 gun deaths in the United States each year, fewer than 300 are listed as 'justifiable

AMERICA AND AMERICANS

homicide', the only category that could include shooting a burglar, mugger, or rapist.

- There are places called Wimp, Sucker Flat, Squabbletown, Rough and Ready, Bummerville and Frying Pan in California.

- The New York Stock Exchange had its first million-share trading day in 1886.

- About 66 per cent of magazines found tossed along US roadsides are pornographic.

- After telling the press he was an expert in hand gestures, President George Bush gave the 'V for Victory' sign as he drove past demonstrators in Canberra, Australia. In Australia, holding up two fingers to form a 'V' has the same vulgar meaning as the middle-finger gesture in Britain. The demonstrators were enraged, and they signalled in the same manner back at the US President, who later apologized for his *faux pas*.

- Odd place names in Oregon include Idiotville, Windmaster Corner, Drain and Boring.

- More than 100,000 Americans die annually from adverse reactions to prescription drugs.

AMERICA AND AMERICANS

- At any given time during the day, there is an average of 150,000 people airborne over the United States.

- Michigan was the first US state to have roadside picnic tables.

- Occasionally, hot-dog sales at baseball stadiums exceed the number of spectators, but typically they average 80 per cent of the attendance.

- More than one in nine cars in the United States will be in a collision in any given year.

- There are places called Elephant Butte, Tingle, Truth or Consequences and Texico in New Mexico.

- Potato chips are Americans' favourite snack food. They are devoured at a rate of 1.2 billion pounds (around 540 million kilograms) a year.

- President William McKinley always wore a red carnation in his lapel for good luck.

- Each tour through Natural Bridge Caverns in Texas covers 3/4 mile (1.2 km). An average tour guide will walk almost 560 miles (901 km) in one year while on the job.

AMERICA AND AMERICANS

- Broadway contains 35 theatres with the capacity to seat a combined 42,000 people.

- The state of Oklahoma contains places called Slaughterville, Okay, Cookietown, Happy Land and Bowlegs.

- The population of the American colonies in 1610 was 350.

- Forty-nine per cent of American fathers describe themselves as better parents than their dads.

- There are places in the state of Kansas called Ransom, Buttermilk and Admire.

- With 20.7 divorces out of every 1,000 married people, the United States leads the world in broken marriages. The closest 'rival' is Denmark, with 13.1 divorces per 1,000 marriages.

- Forests cover around 60 per cent of Pennsylvania. Its name means 'Penn's Woods' after its founder, William Penn.

- It has been estimated that at least 33 per cent of blondes in the United States are not natural blondes.

AMERICA AND AMERICANS

- It is illegal for boys to throw snowballs at trees in Mount Pulaski, Illinois.

- Florida averages the greatest number of shark attacks annually – an average of 13.

- Chinatown in San Francisco is the largest Chinese community outside Asia.

- During World War II, Ellis Island in New York was a detention centre for illegal or criminal aliens already in the United States. The Coast Guard also trained recruits there. Following the war, fewer people were detained and the facility was closed in 1954. New Jersey has sovereignty over most of Ellis Island.

- While serving in the army at the age of 13, President Andrew Jackson was captured by the British. When the British officer in charge ordered Jackson to clean his boots, Jackson refused and was struck with a sword, leaving a scar on his face and hand.

- Wisconsin reportedly has the highest proportion of overweight citizens in America.

- During the early days of the Gold Rush in San Francisco, a glass of whisky would cost as much as £3.90.

AMERICA AND AMERICANS

- Odd place names in Arkansas include Bald Knob, Beaver, Fannie, Hooker, Greasy Corner and Flippin'.

- Across the United States, April is the deadliest month for tornadoes.

- Alaska has more caribou than people.

- Yuma, Arizona, has the most sun of any locale in the United States – it averages sunny skies 332 days a year.

- It is estimated that the average person living in North America opens the fridge 22 times daily.

- There are places in the state of Massachusetts called Ware, Mashpee, Cow Yard and Gay Head.

- Police estimated that 10,000 abandoned, orphaned, and runaway children were roaming the streets of New York City in 1852.

- In the US, a train crashes into a passenger vehicle every 90 minutes, despite conspicuous warning systems that include flashing lights, blaring bells, and rail-crossing drop-arm barricades.

- Thomas Jefferson's Vice-President Aaron Burr shot and killed a man in a duel in 1804. Arguing over politics, the men decided on the duel and Burr was

AMERICA AND AMERICANS

charged for murder in New Jersey. However, the state never pursued his conviction on the grounds that 'civilized nations' do not treat duelling deaths as 'common murders'.

- Seventy per cent of those Americans with a high-school education or less would encourage their daughter if she wanted to be Miss America; 41 per cent of college graduates say they would not encourage her.

- Alaska has a sand desert, with dunes over 100 feet (30 metres) high. It is located along the flatland of the Kobuk River in the north-western part of the state.

- Per capita, it is safer to live in New York City than it is to live in Pine Bluff, Arkansas.

- Each year about $200 million worth of US postage stamps go unlicked. They end up in the albums of stamp collectors, of which there are no fewer than 22 million.

- It is illegal for cars to drip oil on the pavement in Green Bay, Wisconsin. There is a $1 fine for each drip.

- Three US presidents have been the sons of clergymen: Chester Arthur, Grover Cleveland and Woodrow Wilson.

AMERICA AND AMERICANS

- Alaska is so vast that if you could see one million acres of the state every day, it would take an entire year to see it all.

- Ohio is home to Home, Knockemstiff, Three Legs Town, Ai and Fly.

- Arizona has official state neckwear – the bolo tie. The necktie consists of a piece of cord fastened with an ornamental bar or clasp.

- While serving in Congress, President Thomas Jefferson introduced a bill that attempted to bar slavery from all future states admitted to the Union, a measure that might later have prevented the US Civil War if it had not been defeated – by a single vote.

- Although Mount Everest, at 29,028 ft (8,848 m), is often called the tallest mountain on earth, Mauna Kea, an inactive volcano on the island of Hawaii, is actually taller. Only 13,796 ft (4,205 m) of Mauna Kea stands above sea level, yet it is 33,465 feet (10,200 metres) tall if measured from the ocean floor to its summit.

- Each year, more than 300,000 American teenagers become afflicted with some form of venereal disease.

- Each year, approximately 250,000 American husbands are physically attacked and beaten by their wives.

AMERICA AND AMERICANS

- Every day in the United States, about a hundred people over the age of 14 commit suicide, a 50 per cent increase in the last decade.

- There are places called Orderville, Plain City and Hurricane in Utah.

- Arizona boasts places called Nothing, Winkleman and Chloride.

- Seventy-three per cent of Americans are willing to wear clothes until the clothes wear out.

- On average, each American consumes 117lb (53kg) of potatoes, 116lb (52kg) of beef, 100lb (45kg) of fresh vegetables, 81lb (37kg) of chicken, 80lb (36kg) of fresh fruit, and 286 eggs per year.

- Pittsburgh, Pennsylvania, is the only one of the nation's largest 50 cities with a higher death rate than birth rate.

- It is illegal to buy ice-cream after 6.00 p.m. in Newark, New Jersey, unless you have a written note from a doctor.

- There are locations in the state of New York called Hicksville, Result and Neversink.

AMERICA AND AMERICANS

- At 282 ft (86 m) below sea level, Badwater, in Death Valley, is the lowest point in the western hemisphere.

- Chicago, Illinois, was nicknamed the 'Windy City' because of the excessive local bragging that accompanied the Columbian Exhibition of 1893. Chicago has actually been rated as only the 16th breeziest city in America.

- Atlanta, Georgia, began as a small train station in 1837 consisting of only a few houses occupied by Western and Atlantic Railroad employees. The last stop on the railroad line, the 'town' was called Terminus. As the importance of the train station grew and the number of employees living in the town increased, Terminus changed its name in 1843, and was known for two years as Marthasville. The name changed to the Atlanta just a few years prior to the US Civil War, in 1845. Atlanta was chosen as the 'female form' of Atlantic to emphasize the city's rail link to the sea.

- There are three times as many households in the United States without telephones as there are without television sets.

- At least 10,000 years old, the creosote bush in California's Mojave Desert is the oldest known living thing in the world.

———— AMERICA AND AMERICANS ————

- John Adams was the first president to live in the White House – then called the Executive Mansion. He and his wife, Abigail, moved into the house in 1800, shortly before it was completed. Construction began in 1792.

- Although lobster is regarded as a delicacy today, early Americans disliked it so much that they fed it to prison inmates several times a week.

- While Jimmy Carter was president, 50 Americans were taken hostage by Iran. They were freed the day Ronald Reagan, his predecessor, was inaugurated.

- Americans spend an estimated £148 billion a year on dining out.

- There are 800,000 dog bites that require medical attention every year. Dog bites rank second behind sexually transmitted diseases as the most costly health problem in the United States. More than 60 per cent of those bitten are children, and 80 per cent of the fatalities are also children.

- Unusual place names in Wisconsin include Spread Eagle, Footville and Ubet.

- Three million cars are abandoned every year in the United States.

——— AMERICA AND AMERICANS ———

* Odd place names in New Jersey include Love Ladies, Cheesequake and Brick.

* From the 1850s to the 1880s, the most common cause of death among cowboys in the American West was being dragged by a horse while caught in the stirrups.

* Barking Sands Beach, on the Hawaiian island of Kauai, is known for its unusual sand that squeaks or 'barks like a dog'. The dry sand grains emit an eerie sound when rubbed with bare feet.

* More Americans have died in car accidents than have died in all the wars ever fought by the United States.

* Seattle is considered the best major US city in which to balance work and family.

* Rutherford B Hayes, James A Garfield, Chester Arthur and Benjamin Harrison – who later became presidents – all attended Abraham Lincoln's inauguration.

* Although President George Washington's wife Martha had four children by a previous marriage, the president left no direct descendant. He never sired a child to continue his family line.

* There are places called Drab, Porkey, Virginville, Moon, Mars and Bird-in-Hand in the state of Pennsylvania.

─────── **AMERICA AND AMERICANS** ───────

- One school bus ride in Texas is a 179 miles (288 km) round trip.

- About 43 million years ago, the Pacific plate took a north-west turn, creating a bend where new upheavals initiated the Hawaiian Ridge. Major islands formed included Kauai, 5.1 million years old; Maui, 1.3 million years old; and Hawaii, a youngster at only 800,000 years old.

- Odd place names in the state of Mississippi include Chunky, Hot Coffee, Sanatorium, Darling and SoSo.

- Of all the potatoes grown in the United States, only 8 per cent are used to make potato chips.

- Sixteen per cent of Americans say they read the Bible every day.

- Borehole seismometry indicates that the land in Oklahoma moves up and down 25 cm throughout the day, corresponding with the tides. Earth tides are generally about one-third the size of ocean tides.

- It is illegal for frogs to croak after 11.00 p.m. in Memphis, Tennessee.

- Richard Nixon has received more votes than any other person in American history. His three

AMERICA AND AMERICANS

Congressional terms, two terms as Vice-President, his narrow defeat by JFK in the 1960 presidential, his run for the California Gubernatorial, his first election to the Presidency in 1968 and his landslide defeat of George McGovern (then the largest in presidential history) makes Nixon the most-voted-for American politician ever.

- More men than women commit suicide in the United States.

- A whirlpool below Niagara Falls iced over for the first time on record, on 25 March 1955. A huge ice jam in Lake Erie caused more than £3.3 million in property damages near Niagara Falls, New York.

- President Rutherford B Hayes was nicknamed 'His Fraudulency' because he allegedly 'stole' the election of 1876.

- Two out of three adults in the United States have haemorrhoids.

- The most dangerous job in the United States is that of sanitation worker. Firemen and policeman are close second and third places, followed by leather tanners in fourth.

——— AMERICA AND AMERICANS ———

- Wyoming boasts odd place names such as Camel Hump, Big Sandy and Muddy Gap.

- Americans spend approximately £13.8 billion each year on beer.

- 'Q' is the only letter in the alphabet that does not appear in the name of any US state.

- Thirty-six per cent of Americans say they would not vote an atheist for presidency.

- One of every 11 boxes of cereal sold in the United States is Cheerios.

- Because of San Francisco's rapid recovery from its devastating 1906 earthquake, the city became known universally as 'The city that knows how'. The phrase was originally credited to President William Howard Taft.

- There are locations in the state of South Carolina called North, Coward, Townville and Southern Shops.

- More than 110,000 marriage licences are issued in Las Vegas each year.

- Unalaska, Eek and Deadhorse are places in Alaska.

- Honolulu means 'sheltered harbour'.

---------- **AMERICA AND AMERICANS** ----------

* The names of some cities in the United States are the names of other US states. These include Nevada and Louisiana in Missouri, California in Maryland, Oregon in Wisconsin, Kansas in Oklahoma, Wyoming in Ohio, Michigan in North Dakota, Delaware in Arkansas, and Indiana in Pennsylvania.

* 'Utah' is from the Navajo word meaning 'upper'.

* Hawaii has the highest percentage of cremations of all other US states, with a 60.6 per cent preference over burial.

* The typical holiday spot for Americans averages 160 miles (257 km) from home.

* There are places in Alabama called Muck City, Burnt Corn and Intercourse.

* California, Arizona, New Mexico, Nevada, Utah, western Colorado and south-western Wyoming comprised the territory taken from Mexico following the Mexican War in 1846.

* Americans consume more than 353 million pounds (about 159 million kilograms) of turkey during National Turkey Lovers' Month in June. By comparison, more than 675 million pounds (about 304 million kilograms) of turkey will be consumed at Thanksgiving.

——— AMERICA AND AMERICANS ———

- Chicago is home to the world's largest population of Poles outside Warsaw.

- President Thomas Jefferson's father was one of the surveyors who laid out the Virginia/North Carolina border.

- Abraham Lincoln was the tallest president of the US at 6 feet 4 inches (1.9 m).

- The New York phone book had 22 'Hitler' names listed before World War II, and none after.

- Every year, Alaska has about 5,000 earthquakes.

- The states of Washington and Montana still execute prisoners by hanging.

- The most common surname in America is Smith, followed by Johnson and Williams.

- It is illegal to read comics while riding in a car in Norman, Oklahoma.

- Fried chicken is the most popular meal ordered in sit-down restaurants in the US. The next in popularity are: roast beef, spaghetti, turkey, baked ham, and fried shrimp.

—— AMERICA AND AMERICANS ——

- One out of every 15 American adults under the age of 45 got his or her first job with McDonald's.

- Someone dies in a fire every 147 minutes in the United States.

- President Benjamin Franklin devised the first wet-suit for divers, as well as a primitive version of today's flippers.

- President Eisenhower, an avid golfer, had a putting green installed on the White House lawn and had squirrels banished from the grounds because they were ruining the green.

- Nearly 70 per cent of American school students say pizza is their favourite entrée, corn their favourite vegetable, and cookies their favourite dessert.

- In North Carolina, in 1980, a library forbade children to read the Holy Bible without parental consent.

- Twenty-five per cent of Americans believe that Sherlock Holmes was a real person.

- In the US, murder is committed most frequently in August and least frequently in February.

AMERICA AND AMERICANS

- Americans collectively eat 100lb (45kg) of chocolate every second.

- There are more female than male millionaires in the United States.

- President Franklin D Roosevelt's three favourite foods were frogs legs, pig knuckles and scrambled eggs.

- Each year 96 billion pounds (about 43 billion kilograms) of food is wasted in the US.

- In Oblong, Illinois, it is punishable by law to make love while hunting or fishing on your wedding day.

- To avoid long encounters with the press, President Ronald Reagan often took reporters' questions with his helicopter roaring in the background.

- On New Year's Day, 1907, President Theodore Roosevelt shook hands with 8,513 people.

- One out of every 11 workers in North Carolina depends on tobacco for their livelihood.

- Nearly ten per cent of American households dress their pets in Halloween costumes.

——— AMERICA AND AMERICANS ———

* In West Virginia, if you run over an animal, you can legally take it home and cook it for dinner.

* Thomas Jefferson wrote his own epitaph without mentioning that he was US President.

* In Florida, it is illegal to sing in a public place while attired in a swimsuit.

* In Connersville, Wisconsin, no man shall shoot off a gun while his female partner is having a sexual orgasm.

* Las Vegas has the most hotel rooms of any city in the world.

* When the diets of inmates of a Virginia juvenile detention centre were changed from typical American junk food to natural foods – cereal without sugar, fruit juice instead of soda, and so on – the number of chronic offenders decreased by 56 per cent and those who were well mannered increased by 71 per cent.

* New Jersey was originally called Albania.

* The US has more bagpipe bands than Scotland does.

* In Dallas, in 1958, fish poured down from a seemingly empty sky. The fish were 3–4 inches (8–10 cm) long and dark grey, with gold specks and red tails. There

—— AMERICA AND AMERICANS ——

were no other types of fish or freshwater creatures with them, rendering it unlikely that a tornado had picked up the contents of a river or lake and dropped them on Dallas.

* Until 1857, any foreign coins made of precious metal were legal tender in the United States.

* When the Prince of Wales went to visit the White House in 1860, so many guests went with him, it is said that President James Buchanan slept in the hallway.

* In 1987, American Airlines saved £23,000 by eliminating one olive from its First Class salads.

* Second Street is the most common street name in the US, but First Street is only the sixth.

* Less than one-third of the meals eaten in America are served to the whole family at once.

* In Nebraska, it is illegal for bar owners to sell beer unless they are simultaneously brewing a kettle of soup.

* First-cousin marriages are legal in Utah, so long as both parties are 65 or older.

* Gerald Ford was the only president to have two women attempt to assassinate him. Both attempts were

——— AMERICA AND AMERICANS ———

in California in September 1975. The first attempt was
on 6 September 1975, by Lynette Fromme, who
thought she could impress Charles Manson by killing
the president. The next attempt was by Sara Jane
Moore, on 22 September 1975. Her motive was
simply that she was bored.

* There are 18 doctors in the US called Dr Doctor, and
  one called Dr Surgeon.

* Three million people in the United States have an
  impairment of the back or limbs that is a direct result
  of an accidental fall.

* It takes 15 to 20 minutes to walk once around
  the Pentagon.

* One American in every 16 will have one of the top
  12 most common surnames.

* The average American family spends £228.63 per
  year on pizza.

* The top of the Empire State Building flexes back and
  forth a few feet in heavy winds, as the building was
  designed so that airships could moor at the top.

* The banjo is America's only native musical instrument.
  It was first developed in the south in the 1790s.

—— AMERICA AND AMERICANS ——

- There is a 6-foot-tall (1.8 m) stone monument dedicated to the cartoon character Popeye in Crystal City, Texas.

- Americans use enough toilet paper in one day to wrap around the world nine times. If it were on one giant roll, you would be unrolling it at the rate of 7,600 mph – roughly Mach 10, ten times the speed of sound.

- In New York City, there are 37 taxi drivers named Amarjit Singh.

- President Nixon was known to his fellow college students as 'Iron Butt'.

- The word 'dimes' was originally pronounced 'deems'.

- There is one psychiatrist or psychologist for every 2,641 Americans.

- The Baby Ruth chocolate bar was named after President Grover Cleveland's baby daughter Ruth.

- Presidents George Washington, John Adams and Thomas Jefferson were all keen marbles players.

- Today, only 33 per cent of Americans exercise regularly, and 66 per cent are overweight.

AMERICA AND AMERICANS

- The most popular magazine in America is *TV Guide*.

- If all the pizza slices Americans eat in one day came from one giant pizza, it would cover more than 11 football fields.

- There is one vending machine for every 55 Americans.

- Bill Clinton is the only president ever to be elected twice without ever receiving 50 per cent of the popular vote. He had 43 per cent in 1992, and 49 per cent in 1996.

- Nine people per day die in America from accidentally drinking, eating or inhaling something other than food.

- One American supermarket chain waxes their cucumbers and apples with floor polish.

- Five hundred Americans freeze to death every year.

- On the outskirts of the small town of Gold Hill, Oregon, is a place that has baffled both visitors and investigators. Nestled in the forest is the Oregon Vortex and house of mystery. There, bottles roll uphill, broomsticks stand by themselves, and people seem to grow and shrink by changing just a couple of steps. If photographs are taken in the area, mist-like forms and

AMERICA AND AMERICANS

balls of light appear in the picture. A plane flying overhead goes through malfunctions in its instruments, suggesting the vortex travels way beyond the ground, high above the region.

- In Bovina, Mississippi, in 1894, a gopher turtle measuring 6 x 8 inches (15 x 20 cm) fell from the sky during a hailstorm.

- In 1980, the city of Detroit presented Saddam Hussein with a key to the city.

- Indiana's state nickname 'Hoosier' came from a generic southern word, meaning 'bumpkin' or 'backwoodsman'.

- Buttons were first worn on clothes in the 14th Century.

- The chain store Woolworths was originally called the 'Great Five Cent Store'.

- Men run 496 of the top 500 companies in the US.

- February 2nd is Groundhog Day in the United States.

- Since 1976, there have been over 700 executions in the United States.

- The U.S has more than twice the amount of mothers under the age of twenty than Canada.

—————— **AMERICA AND AMERICANS** ——————

* In America, black women are four times more likely than white women to die while giving birth.

* In the United States, February 7th is National Hangover Awareness Day.

* The American equivalent of English fashion's 'Sloane Rangers', are 'the Preppies'.

* Among the top twenty industrialized nations, America has the lowest voter turnout.

SHAKESPEARE

---------------- **SHAKESPEARE** ----------------

- There is no certainty that Shakespeare was born on 23 April in 1564, only that he was baptized three days later in Holy Trinity Church in Stratford-upon-Avon.

- In the Middle East, Shakespeare is referred to as Sheikh al-Subair, meaning Sheikh 'Prickly Pear' in Arabic.

- The Bard coined the phrase 'the beast with two backs' meaning intercourse in *Othello*.

- Shakespeare invented the word 'assassination'.

- There are only two authentic portraits of William Shakespeare.

- Anne Hathaway was 26 years old when William married her at age 18.

- All Uranus's satellites are named after Shakespearean characters.

- Shakespeare and his wife had eight children.

- The worst insult that Shakespeare used was 'you bull's pizzle'.

- At nearly 1,500 lines, Hamlet is the largest Shakespearean speaking part.

SHAKESPEARE

- Most Shakespeare plays employ verse and prose. But, while no play is composed entirely of prose, five plays are written exclusively in verse.

- In the 1500s, Queen Elizabeth I outlawed wife-beating after 10 p.m.

- Theatres during Elizabethan times did not have toilets, nor did the plays have intervals. Although the running times of the plays were often much shorter than they are today, audience members still felt the need to relieve themselves.

- The average American's vocabulary is around 10,000 words Shakespeare had a vocabulary of over 29,000 words.

- William Shakespeare's will is now available to the public to read online, nearly 400 years after the great playwright put quill to paper.

- There were two Shakespeare families living in Stratford when William was born; the other family did not become famous.

- The Bard crudely discusses genitalia size in *The Taming of the Shrew* where the character Curtis tells Grumio, 'Away, you three-inch fool.'

SHAKESPEARE

- William Shakespeare dabbled in property development. At age 18, he bought the second most prestigious property in all of Stratford, The New Place, and later he doubled his investment on some land he bought near Stratford.

- Shakespeare, one of literature's greatest figures, never attended university.

- Most academics agree that William wrote his first play, *Henry VI, Part One*, around 1589 to 1590 when he would have been roughly 25 years old.

- William lived through the Black Death. The epidemic that killed over 33,000 in London alone in 1603 when Will was 39 later returned in 1608.

- Elizabethan theatres would raise a flag outside to indicate what the day's feature would be: a black flag indicated tragedy; a red, history; a white, comedy.

- The play *Cardenio* that has been credited to the Bard and which was performed in his life has been completely lost to time.

- Until *The First Folio* was published seven years after his death in 1616, very little personal information was ever written about the Bard.

SHAKESPEARE

- Even Shakespeare had his critics. One called Robert Greene described the young playwright as an 'upstart young crow' or arrogant upstart, accusing him of borrowing ideas from his seniors in the theatre world for his own plays.

- Shakespeare's tombstone bears this inscription: 'Good friend, for Jesus' sake forbear to dig the dust enclosed here. Blest be the man that spares these stones, and curst be he that moves my bones'.

- The Great Bard suffered breach of copyright. In 1609, many of his sonnets were published without his permission.

- The famous playwright died in 1616 at the age of 52. He wrote on average 1.5 plays a year from when he first started in 1589.

- William never published any of his plays. We read his plays today only because his fellow actors John Hemminges and Henry Condell posthumously recorded his work as a dedication to their fellow actor.

- The Bard is believed to have started writing the first of his 154 sonnets in 1593 at age 29. His first sonnet was Venus and Adonis published in the same year.

SHAKESPEARE

- When reading horizontally from Shakespeare's original published copy of Hamlet, the furthest left-hand side reads 'I am a homosexual' in the last 14 lines of the book.

- Many expressions now taken for granted in English first appeared in Shakespeare's works, including 'elbow room', 'love letter', 'marriage bed', 'puppy dog', 'skim milk', 'wild goose chase' and 'what the dickens'.

- None of the characters in Shakespeare's plays smokes.

- Suicide occurs an unlucky 13 times in Shakespeare's plays.

- For centuries, English literary critics tried to disguise the fact that Shakespeare's sonnets were addressed to a male beloved. His Sonnet 126 contains a farewell to 'my lovely boy', a phrase now taken to imply possible homosexuality by some postmodern Shakespeare academics.

- Some believe that Hamlet, written in 1599, registers Shakespeare's grief following the death of Hamnet, his boy twin, in 1596, at the age of 11.

- William was born to a Stratford tanner named John Shakespeare. His mother Mary was the daughter of a wealthy gentleman-farmer named Robert Arden.

SHAKESPEARE

- Legend has it that, at the tender age of 11, William watched the pageantry associated with Queen Elizabeth I's visit to Kenilworth Castle near Stratford and later recreated this scene many times in his plays.

- Unlike most famous artists of his time, the Bard did not die in poverty. When he died, his will contained several large holdings of land. He left most of his property to Susanna, his first child, and not to his wife Anne Hathaway.

- Few people realize that, aside from writing 37 plays and composing 154 sonnets, William was also an actor who performed many of his own plays as well as those of other playwrights.

- As an actor performing his own plays, William performed before Queen Elizabeth I and later before James I who was an enthusiastic patron of his work.

- Of the 17,677 words that Shakespeare uses in his plays, sonnets and narrative poems, his is the first written use of over 1,700 of them.

- In the 1500s, brides carried a bouquet of flowers to hide their body odour. Hence, the custom today of carrying a bouquet when getting married.

SHAKESPEARE

- Bread was divided according to status. Workers got the burned bottom of the loaf, the family got the middle and guests got the top, or 'upper crust'.

- Houses had thatched roofs, with no wood underneath. It was the only place for animals to get warm. When it rained, it became slippery and sometimes the animals would slip off the roof. Hence the saying 'It's raining cats and dogs'.

- Those with money had plates made of pewter. Food with high acid content caused some of the lead to leach on to the food, causing lead poisoning death.

MISCELLANEOUS

MISCELLANEOUS

- Children born in the month of May are, on average, 200g heavier at birth than children born in any other month.

- The weight of a foetus increases by about 2.4 billion times in nine months.

- A human foetus acquires fingerprints at the age of three months.

- A four-month-old foetus will startle and turn away if a bright light is flashed on its mother's belly. Babies in the womb will also react to sudden loud noises, even if their mother's ears are muffled.

- Newborn babies are not blind. They have approximately 20/50 vision, and can easily discriminate between degrees of brightness.

- Most newborns cry without tears until they are three to six weeks old.

- A newborn baby's head accounts for about one-quarter of its entire weight.

- The 'spring up, fall out' phenomenon claims that children grow twice as fast in the spring as they do in the autumn (fall), while they gain more weight in autumn.

MISCELLANEOUS

* Babies have the strongest sense of smell, enabling them to recognize their mothers by scent.

* A boy's voice breaks during puberty because his vocal cords are lengthening. Up until that point, girls' and boys' vocal cords are the same length.

* Up to the age of six or seven months, a child can breathe and swallow at the same time, unlike an adult.

* Babies like pretty faces better than plain ones.

* In toddlers, most non-food-related choking accidents are caused by balloons (29 per cent), followed by balls and marbles (19 per cent). Older children are more likely to die from balloons than are toddlers.

* Six-year-olds laugh an average of 300 times a day. Adults only laugh 15 to 100 times a day.

* The common cold will delay a child's growth for the duration of the cold.

* Following a family move, boys between the ages of six and 11 tend to have problems adjusting to new environments, particularly school. Indeed, moving is potentially so traumatic for that age group that it can cause a drop in academic achievement or even IQ. The results were not conclusive for girls.

MISCELLANEOUS

---

* About 25 per cent of all children have one or more sleepwalking episodes between the ages of seven and twelve.

* Until about age 12, boys cry about as often as girls.

* Allergies cause students in the United States to miss 1.5 million school days a year, with these allergy sufferers experiencing a significantly reduced ability to learn.

* Buttons were first worn on clothes in the 14th Century.

* Methuselah was a character in the Bible, but in modern times Methuselahs are containers for champagne.

* In the Far East, rhino horns are used in medicine.

* There are men in Guam whose full-time job is to travel the countryside and deflower young virgins, who pay for the privilege of having sex for the first time, as it is forbidden for virgins to marry.

* The thirteenth of the month falls on Friday more often than on any other day of the week. In a 400-year period, there will be 688 Friday the thirteenths.

* Christian Dior launched the 'New Look', with its small waist and full skirt in the 1940s.

MISCELLANEOUS

- Men are four times more likely to attempt suicide than women.

- The coracle boat is made from a wickerwork frame covered with a leather skin.

- 45.5 per cent of all murders occur as the direct result of arguments, notably arguments between family members and friends.

- Seventy of the 3,700 death row inmates in the U.S are minors, or were when they committed their crime.

- Because of our modern diet of food preservatives, undertakers have been noticing that dead people do not deteriorate as fast as they once did.

- More babies are born in September than in any other month.

- The world's heaviest man, Robert Earl Hughes, died in 1958 aged 32. He weighed 86 stone 3 pounds. His chest measured 124in.

- A melcryptovestimentaphiliac is someone who compulsively steals ladies underwear.

---------------------- **MISCELLANEOUS** ----------------------

- If a man shaves with a razor, he uses more energy than if he uses an electric shaver because of the power required to purify and pump the water through his tap.

- Jim Bristoe, an American, invented a 30ft-long, 2-ton pumpkin cannon that can fire pumpkins up to five miles.

- Over the past 25 years, 5,000 million Smarties lids have been produced. Some rare lids are collectors' items.

- There are more people over 60 than there are under 16. By 2015, almost a quarter of the population will be over 60.

- Every weekday morning, the commuters of Los Angeles use 250,000 gallons of gas getting to work. They drive five million miles, which would be like one car driving to the moon and back 20 times, or around the earth192 times.

- Alfred the Great founded 25 towns, established schools and published a collection of laws.

- A dinomaniac is someone with the compulsive urge to dance.

MISCELLANEOUS

- Henry I nominated his daughter, Matilda, as successor. On his death, the throne was offered to his nephew, as a woman was considered unfit to rule.

- An ergasiophobe is someone who is afraid of work.

- There are more coffee drug addicts in the US than drug addicts of any other kind.

- Adolf Hitler was a vegetarian.

- In mid-2001, an estimated 8,100 Britons were aged 100 and over. By 2015, there will be three times as many men and twice as many women over 100 as there are now.

- Kathryn Ratcliffe set a world record by eating 138 Smarties in three minutes using chopsticks at the Metro Centre, Gateshead in 2003.

- American Indians used the spurs on the legs of male turkeys as projectiles on arrowheads.

- Nearly one third of all U.S. executions since 1976 were in Texas.

- John Holmes, a 1970s porn star, had a penis that measured 13.5 inches long.

MISCELLANEOUS

* Men are more likely than women to carry sexually transmitted diseases.

* In 1978, Ralph Lauren created the 'prairie look' with denim skirts worn over white petticoats.

* Ten books on a shelf can be arranged in 3,628,800 different ways.

* Bright yellow and bright blue are the safest and most visible colours for cars.

* Nearly 100 per cent of the dirt in the average home originated from outside – 80 per cent of that comes in on people, stuck to their clothes and their feet.

* The odds against a person being struck by a celestial stone—a meteorite—are 10 trillion to one.

* The world's most valuable Barbie doll is the 40th Anniversary De Beers customized doll that was worth £455,000 and wore 22 carat diamonds. At around £10,000 the second most valuable Barbie is an original prototype. Next, if in mint or never-removed-from-box condition, is a brunette 1959 ponytail Barbie that may reach up to £5250.

* The odds against flipping a coin head's up 10 times in a row are 1,023 to 1.

MISCELLANEOUS

- On average, more animals are killed by motorists than by hunters with guns.

- Monday is the favoured day for people to commit suicide.

- The odds against hitting the jackpot on a slot machine are 889 to 1.

- Deep-sea diving from oilrigs is among the world's most hazardous occupations, averaging a death rate of 1 out of every 100 workers each year.

- The manuals used for launching the first space shuttle would, if all the copies were piled on one another, reach almost twice the height of Chicago's Sears Tower.

- Virgin Atlantic discovered that it takes in an average of ten pence per passenger per flight in loose change found in the plane's seats. If that figure holds for the approximate 320 million people who fly from one country to another worldwide each year the total is about £32 million. Lost coins on domestic flights don't amount to much, however. Chicago O'Hare cleaning crews said they found only about three pence per flight. It is suggested that more travellers to other countries 'accidentally' leave foreign coins behind to avoid dealing with them once they get home.

MISCELLANEOUS

- Car accidents rise ten per cent during the first week of daylight saving time.

- Half of all murders are committed with handguns.

- There are 48 teaspoons in a cup: three teaspoons make a tablespoon and 16 tablespoons make a cup.

- The odds of someone winning a lottery twice in four months is about one in 17 trillion. But Evelyn Marie Adams won the New Jersey lottery in this period during 1985–86.

- About 66 per cent of all traffic death rates occur at night. It is believed that more fatalities occur at night because of more people driving under the influence, even though there are fewer cars on the road than during the day.

- There are more than 200 different types of Barbie doll.

- Every time you lick a stamp, you're consuming one tenth of a calorie.

- Sixty-nine per cent of accidents occur within 25 miles of home.

- Money isn't made out of paper; it's made out of cotton.

MISCELLANEOUS

- Most car horns honk in the key of 'F'.

- University studies show that the principal reason to lie is to avoid punishment.

- The colour combination with the strongest visual impact is black on yellow.

- The popular Barbie doll was without a belly button until the year 2000.

- Tablecloths were originally used as towels with which dinner guests could wipe their hands and faces after eating.

- The name of the camel on the Camel cigarettes pack is Old Joe.

- It takes 15 months of instruction at the Pentagon's School of Music to turn out a bandleader, but merely 13 months to train a jet pilot.

- Whether or not you are relaxed or braced during a car accident makes little difference to the severity of your injuries.

- The distinctive smell that you experience upon opening a box of crayons comes from stearic acid, which is the formal name for processed beef fat.

MISCELLANEOUS

* The art of map making is older than the art of writing.

* Crayola crayons come in 120 colours: 23 reds, 20 greens, 19 blues, 16 purples, 14 oranges, 11 browns, eight yellows, two greys, two coppers, two blacks, one gold, one silver and one white. In early 2001, U.S. President George W. Bush voted for his favourite colour – blue bell. Teen pop star Britney Spears chose robin's egg blue.

* The world's most valuable coin was the rare Sultan of Muscat 1804 Silver Dollar in mint condition, which sold for $4.14 million dollars at a New York City auction. The coin is thought to be one of 8 silver dollars presented as proofs to the Sultan of Muscat in 1835.

* It takes the same amount of time to age a cigar as wine.

* The 'sad' emoticon':-(' gets the same trademark protection as a corporate logo or other similar intellectual property. The mark is owned by Despair – an 'anti-motivational' company that sells humorous posters about futility, failure and repression to 'pessimists, losers and underachievers.'

* *Marijuana* is Spanish for 'Mary Jane'.

* The words 'flammable' and 'inflammable' mean the same. 'Inflammable' is grammatically correct, but it was

MISCELLANEOUS

feared that safety hazards would result when people mistook 'inflammable' to mean 'not capable of producing flames'.

- A rouleau is another name for coins wrapped in a roll of paper.

- In Ventura County, California, cats and dogs are not allowed to have sex without a permit.

- Car number plates ending in four have been banned in Beijing because they are said to be unlucky.

- Old-fashioned Chinese typewriters have 5,700 characters.

- There are more plastic flamingoes in the United States than real ones.

- For every ton of fish that is caught in all the oceans on our planet, there are three tons of rubbish dumped into the oceans.

- A misomaniac is someone who hates everything.

- In many US states the highway patrol carries two gallons of Coke in the trunk to remove blood from the road after a car accident.

MISCELLANEOUS

- Newborn babies are given to the wrong mother in the hospital 12 times a day worldwide.

- On 17 February 1930, the first flight by a cow in an airplane was recorded. The milk produced by the cow during the flight was put into containers and parachuted over the city of St Louis.

- The tradition of pumpkin carving is Irish. It started with the carving of turnips but, when the Irish immigrated to the US, they found pumpkins were easier to carve.

- A traditional Christmas dinner in early England was the head of a pig prepared with mustard.

- Superstition says, if you cry on Chinese New Year's Day, you will cry all through the year so children are tolerated and not disciplined.

- For the first time in history, the number of people on the planet aged 60 or over will soon surpass those under five.

- In Ancient Poland, it was believed that sprinkling sugar on the bride's bouquet kept her temper sweet.
- In the past, Christmas trees were only kept indoors for one night.

- The average baby spends 27.5 months in nappies.

MISCELLANEOUS

* The WD in WD-40 stands for water displacer.

* More people are born on 5 October in the United States than any other day.

* The world record for balancing people on your head is 92 in one hour.

* The wedding bouquet for Ancient Greeks and Romans, was a pungent mix of garlic and herbs or grains (garlic to ward off evil spirits and herbs to ensure a fruitful union).

* In Chinese tradition, knives or scissors should not be used on New Year's Day as this may cut off fortune.

* Seventy-five per cent of people wash from top to bottom in the shower.

* In California, you are not permitted to wear cowboy boots unless you already own at least two cows.

* The fear of Halloween is called samhainophobia.

* Methyphobia is fear of alcohol.

* Parts of the dead sea scrolls appeared for sale in the 1 June 1954 issue of the *Wall Street Journal*.

MISCELLANEOUS

- Today, an astonishing 570,000 tubes of Smarties are made every day, with an estimated 16,000 Smarties eaten per minute in the UK. There are an average of 48 Smarties in every tube.

- The Chinese symbol which looks like two women standing in one house means 'trouble'.

- The most common recipient of Valentine cards are school teachers.

- Strange college courses include advanced cereal science, amusement park administration, clay wheel throwing, fatherhood and soil judging.

- Genitofemoral neuropathy means 'Jeans are too tight'.

- US students read an average of 60,000 pages in four years.

- A 1969 Iowa state college study showed that a parent's stress level at the time of conception is a major factor in determining the child's sex. The child is usually the same sex as the less stressed parent.

- A misodoctakleidist is someone who hates practising the piano.

- Twenty-seven per cent of Americans think billboards are beautiful.

MISCELLANEOUS

* An arithmomaniac is someone who counts things compulsively.

* In Bhutan, all citizens officially become a year older on New Year's Day.

* Someone on Earth reports seeing a UFO every three minutes. In the US, reported sightings are most likely to occur in July, at 9 p.m. or 3 a.m.

* 'Wassail' comes from the Norse *ves heill*, meaning to be of good health. Wassailing is the tradition of visiting neighbours on Christmas Eve and drinking to their health.

* A suriphobe is someone who is afraid of mice.

* In the US, 26 August is National Cherry Popsicle Day.

* In California, the owners of houses with Christmas lights on them past 2 February may be fined up to $250.

* Jack-o'-lantern derives its name from British folktale character – the soul of someone barred from both heaven and hell and condemned to wander the earth with his lantern.

* An erythrophobe is someone who blushes easily.

--------- **MISCELLANEOUS** ---------

- It is estimated that 93 per cent of American children go out trick or treating for Halloween.

- In the past 40 years, the number of over-65s in Britain has doubled.

- Ninety-nine per cent of pumpkins sold in the US are for the sole purpose of decoration.

- Ukrainians prepare a traditional 12-course Christmas meal. The youngest child watches through the window for the evening star to appear, a signal that the feast can begin.

- In the US, 15 August is National Relaxation Day.

- For over 6,000 years, aboriginal people killed buffalo by driving them to jump sites. The town of 'Head-smashed-in-Buffalo-Jump' in Alberta, Canada, has among the largest of these jump sites.

- All racehorses in the US celebrate their birthday on 1 January.

- London Eye passengers reach 135 metres above the London skyline – 30 metres higher than the previous tallest observation wheel in Yokohama Bay.

MISCELLANEOUS

- Canada cancelled all national beauty contests in 1992, claiming they were degrading to women.

- People do not get sick from cold weather; it's from being indoors a lot more.

- 'Adcomsubordcomphibspac' is the longest acronym. It is a Navy term standing for Administrative Command, Amphibious Forces, Pacific Fleet Subordinate Command.

- One in twelve Americans alphabetizes their spice rack.

- An American house cat eats more beef per year than an average person in Central America.

- The Ancient Greeks called our galaxy the Milky Way because they thought it was made from drops of milk from the breasts of the Greek goddess Hera.

- Yuri Gagarin survived the first manned space flight but was killed in a plane crash seven years later.
- An algologist studies seaweed.

- Astronauts' footprints and Lunar Rover tyre tracks will stay on the moon for millions of years, as there is no wind to blow them away.

MISCELLANEOUS

* An artificial spider and web are often included in the decorations on Ukrainian Christmas trees. A spider web found on Christmas morning is believed to bring good luck.

* If the government passed a law that all the outdoor lighting in the US had to be provided by low-pressure sodium light bulbs, then they would save enough money to pay for every college student's tuition.

* The world's largest palace has 1,788 rooms. It was built for the Sultan of Brunei.

* The world's largest recorded gathering of people was at a Hindu religious festival in India in 1989. It was attended by about 15 million people.

* Abraham Lincoln went to school for less than a year. He taught himself to read and write.

* Mount Everest was known as 'Peak 15' before being renamed after Sir George Everest, the British surveyor-general of India, in 1865.

* At 7in long, the Wilson's storm petrel is the smallest bird to breed on the Antarctic continent.

* The first vending machines in the USA dispensed chewing gum and were installed in New York City train platforms in 1888.

MISCELLANEOUS

- The fragrant patchouli is a member of the mint family.

- The white half moon under your fingernail is an air pocket. No one knows why it's there.

- More shoplifters are arrested on Wednesdays in January than any other time of the year.

- The stirrup in your ear, the tiniest bone in your body, is smaller than an ant.

- In its 120-day life span, each red blood cell makes 75,000 round trips to the lungs.

- The US military operates 234 golf courses.

- Vampire bats use rivers to navigate. They smell the animal blood in the water and follow it.

- There are 556 officially recognized Native American tribes.
- A cat has 32 muscles in each ear.

- The Titanic was running at 22 knots when she hit the iceberg.

- There are 2,598,960 possible hands in a 5-card poker game.

MISCELLANEOUS

- Swans are the only birds with penises.

- When wearing a kimono, Japanese women wear socks called Tabi. The big toe of the sock is separated from the rest of the toes, like a thumb from a mitten.

- All owls lay white eggs.

- The names of the 2 stone lions in front of the New York Public Library are Patience and Fortitude. They were named by then mayor Fiorello LaGuardia.

- A broken clock is right at least twice a day.

- There are about 500 different kinds of cone snails around the world. All have a sharp modified tooth, which stabs prey with venom, like a harpoon. Most cone snails hunt worms and other snails, but some eat fish. These are the ones most dangerous to people. The nerve toxin that stops a fish is powerful enough to also kill a human.

- A pound of houseflies contains more protein than a pound of beef.

- Greater Auckland, New Zealand is the second-largest city in the world by area, the first being greater Los Angeles.

MISCELLANEOUS

- Two-thirds of the world's eggplant is grown in New Jersey.

- In Texas, it's illegal to put graffiti on someone else's cow.

- Because radio waves travel at 186,000 miles per second and sound waves saunter at 700 miles per hour, a broadcast voice can be heard 13,000 miles away before it can be heard at the back of the room in which it originated.

- The country with the biggest percentage of female heads of household is Botswana.

- Orson Welles is buried in an olive orchard on a ranch owned by his friend matador Antonio Ordoñez in Seville, Spain.

- The Bronx in New York City is actually named after the Bronx River, which is named after the first settler in the Bronx – Jonas Bronk – who settled there in 1639.

- Kermit the Frog has 11 points on the collar around his neck.

- Before they became successful in show business, Charles Bronson and Jack Palance both laboured as coal miners, as did Ava Gardner's father.

MISCELLANEOUS

* A shofar is a ram's horn used in ancient times as a signalling trumpet, and is still blown in synagogues on Rosh Hashana and at the end of Yom Kippur.

Marriage

MARRIAGE

- 'Before marriage, a man will lay down his life for you; after marriage he won't even lay down his newspaper.'
  Helen Rowland

- 'The world has suffered more from the ravages of ill-advised marriages than from virginity.'
  Ambrose Bierce

- 'Many a man owes his success to his first wife and his second wife to his success.'
  Jim Backus

- 'If you want to sacrifice the admiration of many men for the criticism of one, go ahead, get married.'
  Katharine Hepburn

- 'Bigamy is having one wife too many. Monogamy is the same.'
  Oscar Wilde

- 'Women might be able to fake orgasms, but men can fake whole relationships.'
  Sharon Stone

- 'Laugh and the world laughs with you. Snore and you sleep alone.'
  Anthony Burgess

MARRIAGE

- 'I married the first man I ever kissed. When I tell this to my children, they just about throw up.'
  Barbara Bush, First Lady, 1989

- 'No man should marry until he has studied anatomy and dissected at least one woman.'
  Honore de Balzac

- 'An archaeologist is the best husband a woman can have; the older she gets the more interested he is in her.'
  Agatha Christie

- 'The most happy marriage I can imagine to myself would be the union of a deaf man to a blind woman.'
  S T Coleridge

- 'The male is a domestic animal, which, if treated with firmness, can be trained to do most things.'
  Jilly Cooper

- 'Ah Mozart! He was happily married –
  but his wife wasn't.'
  Victor Borge

- 'If you are afraid of loneliness, don't marry.'
  Chekhov

MARRIAGE

- 'The trouble with some women is that they get all excited about nothing – and then marry him.
  Cher

- 'One survey found that ten per cent of Americans thought Joan of Arc was Noah's wife…'
  Robert Boynton

- 'For a male and female to live continuously together is… biologically speaking, an extremely unnatural condition.'
  Robert Briffault

- 'Husbands are awkward things to deal with; even keeping them in hot water will not make them tender.'
  Mary Buckley

- 'Marriage is popular because it combines the maximum of temptation with the maximum of opportunity.'
  George Bernard Shaw

- 'The majority of husbands remind me of an orang-utan trying to play the violin.'
  Jonathan Carroll.

- 'If variety is the spice of life, marriage is the big can of leftover Spam.'
  Johnny Carson

MARRIAGE

- 'Better to have loved a short man than never to have loved a tall.'
  David Chambless

- 'Marriage is an adventure, like going to war.'
  G K Chesterton

- 'Marriage is like a bank account. You put it in, you take it out, you lose interest.'
  Irwin Corey

- 'I've sometimes thought of marrying, and then I've thought again.'
  Noel Coward

- 'I feel like Zsa Zsa Gabor's sixth husband. I know what I'm supposed to do, but I don't know how to make it interesting.'
  Milton Berle

- 'Marriage is a matter of give and take, but so far I haven't been able to find anybody who'll take what I have to give.'
  Cass Daley

- 'I'd marry again if I found a man who had 15 million and would sign over half of it to me before the marriage and guarantee he'd be dead within a year.'
  Bette Davis

MARRIAGE

- 'Never go to bed angry. Stay up and fight.'
  Phyllis Diller

- 'It destroys one's nerves to be amiable every day to the same human being.'
  Benjamin Disraeli

- 'Long engagements give people the opportunity of finding out each other's character before marriage, which is never advisable.'
  Oscar Wilde

- 'Honolulu, it's got everything. Sand for the children, sun for the wife, sharks for the wife's mother.'
  Ken Dodd

- 'Any intelligent woman who reads the marriage contract, and then goes into it, deserves all the consequences.'
  Isadora Duncan

- 'A man's wife has more power over him than the state has.'
  Ralph Waldo Emerson

- 'Choose a wife by your ear rather than your eye.'
  Thomas Fuller, 1732

MARRIAGE

* 'Politics doesn't make strange bedfellows, marriage does.'
  Groucho Marx

* 'Keep your eyes wide open before marriage, and half-shut afterwards.'
  Benjamin Franklin

* 'Love is an ideal thing, marriage a real thing; a confusion of the real with the ideal never goes unpunished.'
  Johann Wolfgang von Goethe

* 'Love is blind and marriage is the institution for the blind.'
  James Graham

* 'If I were a girl, I'd despair. The supply of good women far exceeds that of the men who deserve them.'
  Robert Graves

* 'A man must marry only a very pretty woman in case he should ever want some other man to take her off his hands.'
  Sacha Guitry

* 'Women and cats will do as they please. Men and dogs had better get used to it.'
  Robert Heinlein

MARRIAGE

- 'Sometimes I wonder if men and women really suit each other. Perhaps they should live next door and just visit now and then.'
  Katharine Hepburn

- 'Bigamy is one way of avoiding the painful publicity of divorce and the expense of alimony.'
  Oliver Herford

- 'Men marry because they are tired, women because they are curious; both are disappointed.'
  Oscar Wilde

- 'Wedding is destiny, and hanging likewise.'
  John Heywood

- 'A man who marries a woman to educate her falls a victim to the same fallacy as the woman who marries a man to reform him.'
  Elbert Hubbard

- 'Marrying a man is like buying something you've been admiring for a long time in a shop window. You may love it when you get it home, but it doesn't always go with everything in the house.'
  Jean Kerr

- 'A coward is a hero with a wife, kids and a mortgage.'
  Marvin Kitman

---------------- **MARRIAGE** ----------------

- 'I don't worry about terrorism. I was married for two years.'
  Sam Kinison

- 'Marriage is a lottery, but you can't tear up your ticket if you lose.'
  F M Knowles

- 'Many a man in love with a dimple makes the mistake of marrying the whole girl.'
  Stephen Leacock

- 'Harpo, she's a lovely person. She deserves a good husband. Marry her before she finds one.'
  Oscar Levant, to Harpo Marx

- 'It's true that I did get the girl, but then my grandfather always said, "Even a blind chicken finds a few grains of corn now and then."'
  Lyle Lovett, after marrying actress Julia Roberts

- 'Marriages are made in heaven and consummated on Earth.'
  John Lyly

- 'Marriage is a great institution, but who wants to live in an institution?'
  Groucho Marx

MARRIAGE

- 'The best way to get husbands to do something is to suggest that perhaps they are too old to do it.'
  Shirley MacLaine

- 'In a novel, the hero can lay ten girls and marry a virgin for the finish. In a movie, that is not allowed. The villain can lay anybody he wants, have as much fun as he wants, cheating, stealing, getting rich and whipping servants. But you have to shoot him in the end.'
  Herman Mankiewicz

- 'I belong to Bridegrooms Anonymous. Whenever I feel like getting married, they send over a lady in a housecoat and hair curlers to burn my toast for me.'
  Dick Martin

- 'I was married by a judge. I should have asked for a jury.'
  Groucho Marx

- 'Eighty per cent of married men cheat in America. The rest cheat in Europe.'
  Jackie Mason

- 'Perfection is what American women expect to find in their husbands... but English women only hope to find in their butlers.'
  W Somerset Maugham

MARRIAGE

- 'There's a way of transferring funds that is even faster than electronic banking. It's called marriage.'
  James Holt McGavran

- 'Women want mediocre men, and men are working hard to become as mediocre as possible.'
  Margaret Mead

- 'When a man steals your wife, there is no better revenge than to let him keep her.'
  Sacha Guitry

- 'Bachelors know more about women than married men; if they didn't, they'd be married too.'
  H L Mencken

- 'I date this girl for two years – and then the nagging starts: "I wanna know your name."'
  Mike Binder

- 'I recently read that love is entirely a matter of chemistry. That must be why my wife treats me like toxic waste.'
  David Bissonette

- 'Marriage is like a cage; one sees the birds outside desperate to get in, and those inside desperate to get out.'
  Michel de Montaigne

MARRIAGE

- 'Never be unfaithful to a lover, except with your wife.'
  P J O'Rourke

- 'No woman marries for money; they are all clever enough, before marrying a millionaire, to fall in love with him first.'
  Cesare Pavese

- 'It doesn't much signify whom one marries, for one is sure to find out next morning it was someone else.'
  Will Rogers

- 'Before marriage, a man will lie awake all night thinking about something you said; after marriage, he'll fall asleep before you finish saying it.'
  Helen Rowland

- 'When you see what some girls marry, you realize how they must hate to work for a living.'
  Helen Rowland

- 'Honeymoon: A short period of doting between dating and debting.'
  Ray Bandy

- 'I think men who have a pierced ear are better prepared for marriage. They've experienced pain and bought jewellery.'
  Rita Rudner

MARRIAGE

- 'To marry is to halve your rights and double your duties.'
  Arthur Schopenhauer

- 'We in the industry know that behind every successful screenwriter stands a woman. And behind her stands his wife.'
  Groucho Marx

- 'It is most unwise for people in love to marry.'
  George Bernard Shaw

- 'By all means marry. If you get a good wife, you will become happy, and if you get a bad one you will become a philosopher.'
  Socrates

- 'Marriage: A ceremony in which rings are put on the finger of the lady and through the nose of the gentleman.'
  Herbert Spencer

- 'A husband is what's left of the lover after the nerve has been extracted.'
  Helen Rowland

- 'I think every woman is entitled to a middle husband she can forget.'
  Adela Rogers St John

MARRIAGE

- 'Wives are people who feel they don't dance enough.'
  Groucho Marx

- 'Some of us are becoming the men we wanted to marry.'
  Gloria Steinem

- 'Someone once asked me why women don't gamble as much as men do and I gave the commonsensical reply that we don't have as much money. That was a true but incomplete answer. In fact, women's total instinct for gambling is satisfied by marriage.'
  Gloria Steinem

- 'Try praising your wife, even if it does frighten her at first.'
  Billy Sunday

- 'Love is blind – marriage is the eye-opener.'
  Pauline Thomason

- 'Men have a much better time of it than women: for one thing they marry later, for another thing they die earlier.'
  H L Mencken

- 'Whenever I date a guy, I think, Is this the man I want my children to spend their weekends with?'
  Rita Rudner

MARRIAGE

- 'God help the man who won't marry until he finds a perfect woman, and God help him still more if he finds her.'
  Benjamin Tillett

- 'A successful man is one who makes more money than his wife can spend. A successful woman is one who can find such a man.'
  Lana Turner

- 'Marriage isn't a word… it's a sentence.'
  King Vidor

- 'Marriage is the one subject on which all women agree and all men disagree.'
  Oscar Wilde

- 'I guess the only way to stop divorce is to stop marriage.'
  Will Rogers

- 'In olden times, sacrifices were made at the altar, a practice which is still very much practised.'
  Helen Rowland

- 'I take my wife everywhere I go. She always finds her way back.'
  Henny Youngman

MARRIAGE

- 'Marriage is the alliance of two people, one of whom never remembers birthdays and the other who never forgets them.'
  Ogden Nash

- 'An ideal wife is one who remains faithful to you but tries to be just as charming as if she weren't.'
  Sacha Guitry

- 'I should like to see any kind of a man, distinguishable from a gorilla, that some good and even pretty woman could not shape a husband out of.'
  Oliver Wendell Holmes, Sr.

- 'It does not matter what you do in the bedroom as long as you do not do it in the street and frighten the horses.'
  Mrs Patrick Campbell

- 'A happy home is one in which each spouse grants the possibility that the other may be right, though neither believes it.'
  Don Fraser

- 'I've been asked to say a couple of words about my husband, Fang. How about "short" and "cheap"?'
  Phyllis Diller

MARRIAGE

- 'Sexiness wears thin after a while and beauty fades, but to be married to a man who makes you laugh every day, ah, now that's a real treat.'
Joanne Woodward

- 'When a girl marries, she exchanges the attentions of many men for the inattention of one.'
Helen Rowland

- 'The big difference between sex for money and sex for free is sex for money costs less.'
Brendan Francis

- 'To our wives and sweethearts... and may they never meet.'
Hugo Vickers

- 'Marriage is like putting your hand into a bag of snakes in the hope of pulling out an eel.'
Leonardo Da Vinci

- 'The appropriate age for marriage is around 18 for girls and 37 for men.'
Aristotle

- 'Instead of getting married again, I'm going to find a woman that I don't like and just give her the house.'
Rod Stewart

MARRIAGE

- 'Marriage is one of the few institutions that allow a man to do as his wife pleases.'
  Milton Berle

POLITICS

POLITICS

- Jimmy Carter once reported a UFO in Georgia.

- Almost 20 per cent of the billions of dollars American taxpayers are spending to rebuild Iraq are lost to theft, kickbacks and corruption.

- The fertility rate in states that voted for George Bush is 12 per cent higher than states that favoured John Kerry.

- The US Treasury Department has more than 20 people assigned to catching people who violate the trade and tourism embargo with Cuba. In contrast, it has only four employees assigned to track the assets of Osama Bin Ladin and Saddam Hussein.

- More than 8,100 US troops are still listed as missing in action from the Korean War.

- There are 68,000 miles of phone line in the Pentagon.

- George W Bush and John Kerry are 16th cousins, three times removed.

- Legislators in Santa Fe, New Mexico, are considering a law that would require pets to wear seat belts when travelling in a car.

- As of January 2004, the United States economy borrows £780,000,000 each day from foreign investors.

POLITICS

- During Bill Clinton's entire eight-year presidency, he only sent two emails. One was to John Glenn when he was aboard the space shuttle, and the other was a test of the email system.

- In 2004, 60.7 per cent of eligible voters participated in the US presidential election, the highest percentage in 36 years. However, more than 78 million did not vote. This means President Bush won re-election by receiving votes from less than 31 per cent of all eligible voters in the United States.

- CNN's coverage of John Kerry's acceptance speech at the Democratic Convention was marred by the accidental broadcast of expletives from a technician.

- Stalin was only five feet, four inches tall.

- Under Charles Kennedy the Liberal Democrats committed an embarrassing blunder by accidentally emailing election plans to opponents.

- One First Minister of the Welsh Assembly was mistaken for a Doctor Who villain. BBC staff thought Rhodri Morgan was an actor set to play a treelike monster on the sci-fi show.

- The day after President George W Bush was re-elected, Canada's main immigration website had

POLITICS

115,000 visitors. Before Bush's re-election, this site averaged about 20,000 visitors each day.

* Norway's Crown Prince Haakon placed Portugal on the Mediterranean in a welcome speech for the country's president.

* The day after President George W Bush was re-elected, Canada's main immigration website had 115,000 visitors. Before Bush's re-election, this site averaged about 20,000 visitors each day. Greek officials had to apologize after dropping a 113-year-old man from an electoral register because they refused to believe he was still alive.

* Cherie Blair began her controversial tour Down Under by calling her Kiwi hosts Australians.

* A Staffordshire county councillor who used civic funds to buy police a mobile speed camera was caught speeding by the same camera.

* A war veteran who got lost on his way back from the D-Day commemorations got a lift back to Paris from French President Jacques Chirac.

* About 1,600 Belgians turned out to vote in the country's elections wearing only swimming costumes or trunks.

POLITICS

- Benjamin Franklin gave guitar lessons.

- John Kerry's hometown newspaper, the *Lowell Sun*, endorsed George W Bush for president. Bush's hometown newspaper, the *Lone Star Iconoclast*, endorsed John Kerry for president.

- George W Bush, who presents himself as a man of faith, rarely goes to church. Yet he won nearly two out of three voters who attend church at least once a week.

- An NHS patient has become the holder of the new world record for the longest wait on a hospital trolley. Tony Collins spent 77 hours and 30 minutes waiting for treatment.

- The oldest person to ever be issued a driver's licence in the US was 109.

- All radios in North Korea have been rigged so listeners can only receive a North Korean government station. The United States recently announced plans to smuggle £1,000,000 worth of small radios into the country so North Koreans can get a taste of (what their government calls) 'rotten imperialist reactionary culture'.

- George Washington spent about 7 per cent of his annual salary on liquor.

POLITICS

- The French government has banned the use of the word 'email' in all its ministries, documents, publications and websites.

- Norwegian MP Trond Helleland was caught playing games on his handheld computer during a debate in Parliament.

- A Brazilian MP lost his seat over allegations that he offered voters free Viagra in exchange for their support.

- India has an estimated 550 million voters.

- UK Conservative MP John Bercow sold his 18th century home because his long-legged fiancée kept bumping her head on the low ceilings.

- The New York City Police Department has a £1.7 billion annual budget, larger than all but 19 of the world's armies.

- Television stations, including Al-Jazeera, hung banners at the 2004 Democratic National Convention before they were noticed and taken down.

- The US House of Representatives earmarked £26,000,000 to create an indoor rain forest in Iowa.

- The Oval Office is only 22ft long.

NEWS
HEADLINES

NEWS HEADLINES

- Blondes perform intelligence tests more slowly after reading jokes playing on their supposed stupidity.

- A German-based doctor has invented breast implants made from titanium.

- A Warwickshire woman married a man just a month after he stabbed her for having pre-wedding jitters.

- A pillow designed in the shape of a woman's lap became one of the best-selling Christmas gifts in Japan.

- An Englishman who shot himself in the groin was jailed for five years for illegal possession of a firearm.

- A New York woman reportedly fended off her husband's violent sexual advances by setting him on fire.

- Landlords have found the best way to get rid of drinkers at closing time at Christmas is to play a Cliff Richard song.

- A Chilean woman was horrified when she received a box through the post with a human brain inside it.

- A judge in America is reportedly facing the sack after using a penis pump while trying cases in court.

NEWS HEADLINES

- Archaeologists have dug up a 1,000-year-old padded bra in China.

- An Iranian man who struck a suicide pact with his new bride over their guilt for having pre-marital sex is being held by police after he backed out of his side of the bargain.

- Investors in Berlin are building Germany's first gay and lesbian old people's home.

- Thieves who stole a public toilet in the Belarus city of Gomel accidentally kidnapped a man still locked inside.

- A university student is auctioning his virginity on his personal website and has put a reserve of £6,000 on it.

- A female student came home to find a drunken burglar in her apartment, wearing her clothes.

- A clinic at Albury in southern New South Wales has been given permission to advertise overseas for fully paid holidays to Australia for sperm donors.

- A Russian oil company won a rare legal victory when a court ruled it could sell cannabis vodka.

- A Romanian man faces charges that he tried to blow up his kitchen because his wife was a lousy cook.

NEWS HEADLINES

- Residents of an Austrian village called F*cking have voted against changing the name.

- A German man who faked his death so he could leave his family for a younger woman has been fined £9,000.

- Police believe a US teenager who crashed a car into a telegraph pole was having sex with his girlfriend at the time.

- Shepherds in the Scottish highlands could be given free Viagra to halt a drastic drop in their numbers.

- Croatian monks have been ordered to sell off their BMWs and Mercedes.

- Romanian doctors have removed a man's wedding ring from his penis.

- A female panda named Hua Mei is pregnant after watching hours of videos showing other pandas mating.

- Subbuteo fans can now buy male and female streakers for their game.

- Two San Francisco police officers have been caught moonlighting in a hardcore-porn movie.

—— NEWS HEADLINES ——

- Prostitutes in a Dutch city say their business is being ruined by policemen turning up to watch them have sex with clients.

- A Buddhist monk decided to break his lifelong vow of celibacy with a prostitute, but picked up an undercover police officer instead.

- A company manufacturing skin cream from snail extract is exporting 20,000 bottles to the US every month.

- A mayor who set up a direct hotline for people to call with civic problems is asking bored housewives to stop inviting him round for sex.

- Scientists in Australia have found that rotten bananas could provide enough energy for 500 homes.

- A Serbian tie maker is planning to launch a new range of penis cravats for the man who has everything.

- A Danish company has given its employees free subscriptions to internet pornography sites.

- Police in Germany had to rescue a swimming-pool attendant at a hen party after the bride-to-be tried to bully him into having sex.

NEWS HEADLINES

- A groom has been given away at his wedding by his ex-wife – and his best man was his ex's new boyfriend.

- A Romanian father-of-five needed medical help after he superglued a condom to his penis.

ILLNESS AND INJURIES

ILLNESS AND INJURIES

- In 1992, 5,840 people checked into US emergency rooms with 'pillow-related injuries'.

- In 1994, there were over 420,000 accidents caused by kitchen knives, 122 thousand by drinking glasses, 29,000 by refrigerators, and 7,000 by dishwashers.

- A study published in a 1995 issue of the *Journal of Urology* estimated that 600,000 men in the United States are impotent from injuries to their crotches, about 40 per cent of them from too-vigorous bicycling.

- Pain is measured in units of 'dols'. The instrument used to measure pain is a 'dolorimeter'.

- The number-one cause of blindness in the United States is diabetes.

- About 8,000 Americans are injured by musical instruments each year.

- The earliest form of electric shock treatment involved electric eels.

- Over 90 per cent of diseases are caused or complicated by stress.

- If it is a drug, it has a side-effect.

ILLNESS AND INJURIES

* In 1898, Bayer was advertising cough medicine containing heroin. Heroin used to be a cough medicine for children. A German company (Bayer) registered the word as a trademark.

* The oldest-known disease in the world is leprosy.

* Some arthritis medicine contains gold salts which is used as an anti-inflammatory.

* In the 1800s, it was believed that gin could cure stomach problems.

* Sixty-five per cent of adolescents get acne.

* An 80-year-old London woman had a gall stone removed which weighed 13lb 14oz.

* Seventeenth century hangover cures included flogging and bleeding by leeches.

* There is no leading cause of death for people who live past the age of 100.

* President Teddy Roosevelt died from an 'infected tooth'.

* The first open heart surgery was performed in 1893.

ILLNESS AND INJURIES

- Breast reduction is the most common plastic surgery performed on American men.

- The flu pandemic of 1918 killed more than 20 million people.

- Cerumen is the medical term for earwax.

- During a kiss, as many as 278 bacteria colonies are exchanged.

- The average American kid catches six colds a year, the average kid in daycare catches ten.

- In 1992, 2,421 people checked into US emergency rooms with injuries involving houseplants.

- In 1990, in Hartsville, Tennessee, a 64-year-old woman entered a hospital for surgery for what doctors diagnosed as a tumour on her buttocks. What surgeons found, however, was a four-inch pork chop bone, which they removed. They estimated that it had been in place for five to ten years.

- In the summer of 1998, 470 Chinese people were injured by spontaneously exploding beer bottles.

- In a 1930 Quebec Junior Amateur Game, goalie Abie Goldberry was hit by a flying puck that ignited a pack

ILLNESS AND INJURIES

of matches in his pocket, setting his uniform on fire. He was badly burned before his teammates could put the fire out.

* Despite the many rat-infested slums in New York City, rats bite only 311 people in an average year. But 1,519 residents are bitten annually by other New Yorkers.

* The two steps at the top and the two at the bottom are the four most dangerous steps in a staircase.

* An Austrian woman who hid behind her boyfriend's articulated lorry so she could jump out and surprise him was taken to hospital after he reversed over her.

* Over 11,000 people are injured every year trying out new sexual positions.

* A Cuban man was struck by lightning for the fifth time in 22 years.

* In the US, 55,700 people are injured by jewellery each year.

* A Thai man who held the record for spending time with snakes died after being bitten by a mamba.

* Every year, 2,700 surgical patients go home from the hospital with metal tools, sponges and other objects

ILLNESS AND INJURIES

left inside them. In 2000, 57 people died as a result of these mistakes.

* On an average day in the United States, about 40 people are hurt on trampolines.

* Second-hand smoke contains over 4,000 chemicals including more than 40 cancer-causing compounds.

* Once a person is totally buried by an avalanche, there is only a one in three chance of survival.

* Three hundred people report to emergency rooms across the country every day due to rollerblading accidents.

* A deliveryman from Ealing crashed his van two hours after his bosses gave him a safe driving award.

* Every year, over 8,800 people injure themselves with a toothpick.

* Student Robert Ricketts, 19, had his head bloodied when a train struck him. He told police he was trying to see how close to the moving train he could place his head without getting hit.

* Several well-documented instances have been reported of extremely obese people flushing aircraft toilets

ILLNESS AND INJURIES

while still sitting on them. The vacuum action of these toilets sucked the rectum inside out.

* An 83-year-old Canadian woman was rescued after spending two days wedged behind her toilet.

* Second-hand smoke contains twice as much tar and nicotine per unit volume as smoke inhaled from a cigarette. It contains three times as much cancer-causing benzpyrene, five times as much carbon monoxide and 50 times as much ammonia.

* A woman came home to find her husband in the kitchen shaking frantically with what looked like a wire running from his waist towards the electric kettle. Intending to jolt him away from the deadly current, she whacked him with a handy plank of wood by the back door, breaking his arm in two places. Until that moment, he had been happily listening to his Walkman.

* Travis Bogumill, a construction worker in Eau Claire, Wisconsin, was shot with a nail gun that drove a 3 1⁄2 inch nail all the way into his skull. He was not killed, not even knocked unconscious. The only result from the incident was a decrease in his mathematical skills.

* Barbers at one time combined shaving and haircutting with bloodletting and pulling teeth. The white stripes

ILLNESS AND INJURIES

on a field of red that spiral down a barber pole represent the bandages used in the bloodletting.

- It is already known that Viagra can cause a form of temporary colour-blindness. But recent evidence indicates that for some people it might also be the cause of what are essentially strokes in the eyes, causing permanent damage to optic nerves, and thus permanent loss of vision.

- Second-hand smoke from pipes and cigars is equally as harmful as the smoke from cigarettes, if not more so.

- In about two in 1,000 cases where a patient is anaesthetized, the patient will awaken and be mentally alert and feel all the pain of the surgery, but be paralysed and unable to signal or communicate with the doctors.

- After assassinating President Lincoln, John Wilkes Booth jumped to the stage. As he jumped, he tripped over an American flag and broke his leg.

- According to the US Department of Transportation, an average of 550 sleep-related highway accidents occur per day.

- Nearly 60 per cent of accidents involving pedestrians aged under five happen in their own driveway when a vehicle backs over them.

ILLNESS AND INJURIES

- Of all the medicines available on the international market today, sevn per cent are fake. In some countries, the figure for counterfeit medicines can be as high as 50 per cent.

- Lead paint – linked to serious kidney problems, brain damage and learning disabilities – is found in 75 per cent of all homes, not just old, rundown houses.

- The US tops the world in plastic-surgery procedures. Next is Mexico.

- According to a Boston study of 87,000 female nurses, those who ate five or more servings of carrots a week were 68 per cent less likely to suffer a stroke than those who seldom ate carrots.

- One in every 200 people is a psychopath and they look just like everyone else.

- In medieval Japan, dentists extracted teeth with their hands.

- Mark Twain (Samuel Clemens) thought fasting was a cure for illness. He would cure his colds and fevers by not eating for one or two days.

- Ancient Egyptians believed eating fried mice would cure a toothache.

ILLNESS AND INJURIES

- Austrian physician Alfred Adler theorized that people are primarily motivated to overcome inherent feelings of inferiority. He coined the term 'sibling rivalry'.

- One of the first anaesthetics was used to help surgeons, not patients. It was developed by the Ancient Incas of Peru over 1,000 years ago. While they worked, Inca surgeons chewed leaves of the coca plant to calm their nerves. We now know these leaves contain a powerful painkilling drug.

- A Massachusetts surgeon left a patient with an open incision for 35 minutes while he went to deposit a cheque.

- Lead poisoning was common among upper-class Romans who used lead-sweetened wine and leaded grape pulp as a condiment.

- Over 2,500 left-handed people are killed each year, because they used products made for right-handed people.

THE HUMAN
BODY

THE HUMAN BODY

- There are nine muscles in your ear.

- The navel divides the body of a newborn baby into two equal parts.

- If the average male never shaved, his beard would be 13ft long when he died.

- Experts say the human body has 60,000 miles of blood vessels.

- The human eye blinks an average of 4,200,000 times a year.

- Foetuses can hiccup.

- Your brain uses 40 per cent of the oxygen that enters your bloodstream.

- Your left hand does an average of 56 per cent of your typing.

- Men without hair on their chests are more likely to get cirrhosis of the liver than men with hair.

- Blood is about 78 per cent water.

- The longest recorded sneezing fit lasted 978 days.

THE HUMAN BODY

- Sunburn seems to heal in just a few days, but the blood vessels under the skin do not return to their normal condition for up to 15 months.

- We lose half a litre of water a day through breathing.

- The screaming of an upset baby can damage your hearing. Kids can scream at levels up to 90 dB, and permanent damage can be caused at 85 dB.

- Your stomach has 35 million digestive glands.

- At the moment of conception, you spent about half an hour as a single cell.

- There are about one trillion bacteria on each of your feet.

- Side by side, 2,000 cells from the human body could cover about one square inch.

- Your body contains about 4oz of salt.

- Injured fingernails grow faster than uninjured ones.

- Jeffrey and Sheryl McGowen in Houston turned to in vitro fertilisation. Two eggs were implanted in Sheryl's womb, and both of them split. Sheryl gave birth to two sets of identical twins at once.

THE HUMAN BODY

- If you calculated the DNA length for each living person, it would stretch across the diameter of the solar system.

- Twelve per cent of the British population are left handed.

- The average heart beats 2.5 billion times in a lifetime.

- It is a medical fact that, after drinking, the last place in the body to be cleared of alcohol is the brain. We often stumble and drop things because our bodies and brains are out of synch.

- Even mild dehydration will slow down one's metabolism as much as 3 per cent.

- When you are looking at someone you love, your pupils dilate; they do the same when you are looking at someone you hate.

- It takes twice as long to lose new muscle if you stop working out as it did to gain it.

- The three things pregnant women dream most of during their first trimester are frogs, worms and potted plants.

- Your skin weighs about 3.2kg.

THE HUMAN BODY

- 55 per cent of people yawn within five minutes of seeing someone else yawn. Reading about yawning makes most people yawn.

- A blink lasts approximately 0.3 seconds.

- Seventy-five per cent of Americans are chronically dehydrated.

- In 37 per cent of Americans, the thirst mechanism is so weak that it is often mistaken for hunger.

- A mere two per cent drop in body water can trigger fuzzy short-term memory, trouble with basic math, and difficulty focusing on the computer screen or on a printed page.

- The lifespan of a taste bud is ten days.

- We forget 80 per cent of what we learn every day.

- Men get hiccups more often than women do.

- In 1991, the average bra size in the United States was 34B. Today it's 36C.

- The average North Korean seven-year-old is almost three inches shorter than the average South Korean seven-year-old.

THE HUMAN BODY

- The Amish diet is high in meat, dairy, refined sugars and calories. Yet obesity is virtually unknown among them. The difference is, since they have no TVs, cars or powered machines, they spend their time in manual labour.

- The most common phobia in the world is odynophobia which is the fear of pain.

- In a University of Arizona study, rails and armrests in public buses were found to be contaminated by the highest concentration of bodily fluids.

- A man named Charles Osborne had the hiccups for 69 years.

- An average human loses about 200 head hairs per day.

- Mexican women spend 15.3 per cent of their life in ill health.

- In 2004, one in six girls in the United States entered puberty at age eight. A hundred years ago, only one in a hundred entered puberty that early.

- Your body gives off enough heat in 30 minutes to bring half a gallon of water to a boil.

- You use over 70 muscles to say one word.

THE HUMAN BODY

- Bone is stronger, inch for inch, than the steel in skyscrapers.

- About one-third of the human race has 20–20 vision.

- In a hot climate, you can sweat as much as three gallons of water a day.

- Everyone is colour-blind at birth.

- Fingernails are made from the same substance as a bird's beak.

- A runner consumes about seven quarts of oxygen while running a 100-yard dash.

- Your teeth start growing six months before you are born.

- Your big toes have two bones each while the rest have three.

- A pair of human feet contains 250,000 sweat glands.

- Living brain cells are bright pink.

- Your ears secrete more earwax when you are afraid than when you aren't.

THE HUMAN BODY

- Your body uses 300 muscles to balance itself when you are standing still.

- If saliva cannot dissolve something, you cannot taste it.

- Your body contains the same amount of iron as an iron nail.

- You will have to walk 80km for your legs to equal the amount of exercise your eyes get daily.

- It takes about 20 seconds for a red blood cell to circle the whole body.

- Humans are born with 300 bones but, by the time they reach adulthood, they only have 206.

- The right lung in humans is slightly larger than the left.

- The average woman is 5in shorter than the average man.

- The heart beats about 100,000 times each day.

- Fidgeting can burn about 350 calories a day.

- A shank is the part of the sole between the heel and the ball of the foot.

THE HUMAN BODY

- The talus is the second largest bone in the foot.

- The attachment of human muscles to skin is what causes dimples.

- A 13-year-old child found a tooth growing out of his foot in 1977.

- A woman's heart beats faster than a man's does.

- Another name for your little or pinky finger is Wanus.

- Dogs and humans are the only animals with prostates.

- It only takes 7lb of pressure to rip off your ears.

- Wearing headphones for just one hour will multiply the number of bacteria in your ear 700 times.

- If you sneeze too hard, you can fracture a rib. If you try to suppress a sneeze, you can rupture a blood vessel in your head or neck and die.

- The total surface area of a pair of human lungs is equal to that of a tennis court.

- It takes food seven seconds to get from your mouth to your stomach.

THE HUMAN BODY

* A dog's sense of smell is twenty times better than that of a human.

* The average human dream lasts two to three seconds.

* Human thighbones are stronger than concrete.

* The tooth is the only part of the human body that can't repair itself.

* A human foetus acquires fingerprints at the age of three months.

* A four-month-old foetus will startle and turn away if a bright light is flashed on its mother's belly. Babies in the womb will also react to sudden loud noises, even if their mother's ears are muffled.

REALITY
TELEVISION

REALITY TELEVISION

- Simon Cowell reportedly made $2 million hosting 2002's *American Idol*.

- Ex-Take That singer Mark Owen won Celebrity Big Brother and relaunched his career – but after one top-ten single his comeback stalled and he was dumped by his record label.

- There are 36 cameras in the *Big Brother* house following the housemates' every move.

- *Survivor* first aired as *Expedition Robinson* in Sweden in 1997. Afraid he'd be portrayed as a fool, Sinisa Savija committed suicide after being the first contestant voted off.

- A German TV station wants men for a reality show in which they'd learn how to win estranged partners back.

- Items banned from the *Big Brother* house include writing materials, mobile phones, radios, walkmans, CDs or CD players, computers, PDAs (Psion, Palm Pilot, etc), calendars, clocks and watches, drugs and narcotics, personal medication (except in consultation with Big Brother), weapons, any electronic equipment or items requiring batteries and clothes with prominent logos.

- Simon Cowell dropped out of school at the age of 16.

REALITY TELEVISION

- A Brazilian woman is suing a TV station for the trauma she suffered after being caught up in a reconstruction of a kidnapping. The lady, from Sao Paulo, thought it was a real incident and crashed her car into a truck as she tried to escape.

- A Slovenian TV programme that tried to prove top models were brainless bimbos was scrapped after a beauty queen turned out to have a higher IQ than a nuclear physicist.

- Over the course of a *Big Brother* series, around 2,000 radio mic batteries will be used in the house.

- Creator Charlie Parsons originally pitched *Survivor* to ABC in the early 1990s but, without a pilot, they passed on the idea. Today, there are approximately 20 countries producing their own homegrown versions of *Survivor*.

- A reality show was launched in Brazil to try to find the new Pele.

- The US version of *Big Brother* may have been a flop, but the show was so popular in Spain the winner had to be airlifted from the house as frenzied fans invaded the set.

- An ambitious $40 million series called *Destination Mir* was to include launching contestants into outer space.

REALITY TELEVISION

But, after the Russian space station was ditched recently, NBC said the show – now called *Destination Space* – was put on the back burner.

- *The Real World* was originally conceived as *St Mark's Place*, a soap opera about young people in New York. But MTV balked at the cost, so creators Mary-Ellis Bunim and Jonathan Murray did some quick thinking and pitched the cheaper real-people angle. MTV thought the price was right and bought the idea on the spot.

- The UK *Big Brother* house is based in Elstree, Herts.

- Guests on *The Jerry Springer Show* have to sign contracts before they appear. One states that, if a guest isn't telling the truth, they could be liable for the cost of the show. If a guest is going on to find out a surprise they have to read and sign a list of 20 possible surprises ranging from a reunion to finding out that their partner is a man.

- Fifty kilometres of cable have been used in the technical construction of the *Big Brother* house.

- A Greek policeman was sacked after appearing on his country's version of *Pop Idol*.

REALITY TELEVISION
---

* Each Jerry Springer talk show costs around $80,000 to make.

* Over the course of a series, around 10,000 hours of tape will be recorded from the *Big Brother* house.

* David Letterman is part owner of Team Rahal auto racing team.

* A US woman whose rescue from her car during floods was shown on national television was arrested by a policeman who remembered she was banned from driving.

* David Letterman funds a scholarship at Ball State University (his alma mater).

* Simon Cowell once worked as a mail boy at RCA.

* The Jerry Springer Show airs in over 150 markets.

* Applicants for *Big Brother 3* went to incredible lengths to get noticed in their application videos. One man even pierced an intimate body part on screen while a bikini-clad woman stood on a central reservation with a sign saying: 'Beep if you want to see me on Big Brother'.

* Candid Camera began its life on radio as Candid Microphone.

REALITY TELEVISION

- A Japanese man featured in a documentary about his religious pilgrimage was arrested after police recognized him as a suspect in a decade-old stabbing case.

- A Court TV poll showed 87.3 per cent of respondents think the outcome of the original *Survivor* was manipulated.

- One couple on *Temptation Island* was recently removed from the land of debauchery when it was revealed that they have a one-and-a-half-year-old son. Fox TV did not want to be held responsible for the break-up of a family.

- Online bookies Paddy Power gave initial odds for a transsexual winning *Big Brother* of 33/1.

- In *Big Brother 3*, there were seven chickens in total, comprising three different breeds: two Boveneras, two Exchequer Leghorns and three Little Red Hens.

- *America's Most Wanted* has helped apprehend 618 criminals.

BUSINESS AND COMMERCE

────────── **BUSINESS AND COMMERCE** ──────────

* One of the richest self-made Americans who made his money under 40 is Michael Dell, chairman of Dell Computers. He is worth $18 billion.

* There are an average of 18,000,000 items for sale at any time on eBay.

* On eBay, there are an average of $680 worth of transactions each second.

* One in ten Europeans was conceived on an Ikea bed, say the company.

* The red spot on the 7up cans comes from its inventor, who was an albino.

* American office workers send an average of 36 emails per day.

* Fifty-three per cent of Americans think they are paid the right amount.

* Twelve per cent of US businessmen wear their ties so tight that they restrict the blood flow to their brain and also increase the risk of eye disease.

* Dr George F Grant received US patent number 638,920 on 12 December 1899 for his invention – the golf tee. He created it because he didn't want to get

─── **BUSINESS AND COMMERCE** ───

his hands dirty by building a mound of dirt to place his ball on.

- Dismal first-year sales of famous products: VW Beetle (US) 330; Liquid Paper (Tippex) 1,200 bottles; Cuisinart 200; Remington typewriter eight; Scrabble 532; Coca-Cola 25 bottles.

- One in six employees say they got so mad at a co-worker last year that 'they felt like hitting them but didn't.'

- Dr Guillotin merely proposed the machine that bears his name (which was rejected by the Crown) and he never made a working model. The first working model was made by his assistant years later. When the machine attained infamy in the French Revolution, Dr Guillotin protested its use and went to his grave claiming that the machine was unjustly named after him.

- Draftsmen have to make 27,000 drawings for the manufacturing of a new car.

- At General Motors, the cost of health care for employees now exceeds the cost of steel.

- According to market research firm NPD Fashionworld, 50 per cent of all lingerie purchases are returned to the store.

BUSINESS AND COMMERCE

- Dr George F Grant received US patent number 638,920 on 12 December 1899 for his invention – the golf tee. He created it because he didn't want to get his hands dirty by building a mound of dirt to place his ball on. A Bedfordshire man was sent a letter from Prudential insurance company addressed to Mr A Shagslikeadonkey.

- Dr George F Grant received US patent number 638,920 on 12 December 1899 for his invention – the golf tee. He created it because he didn't want to get his hands dirty by building a mound of dirt to place his ball on.   Twenty-three per cent of workers said they would work harder if their employer offered a '£500 shopping spree at a store of their choice'.

- A Colombian airline has promised free flights for life to a baby born on board one of their planes.

- Were the Smarties brand to be sold, its value is estimated at £73 million – up £15 million in the last four years following the introduction of spin-off products including the Smarties bar.

- More copies of the Ikea catalogue are printed each year than the Bible.

- A Sao Paulo shopping mall is offering five minutes in an oxygen mask to any customer who spends more than the equivalent of £6.

BUSINESS AND COMMERCE

- Eleven top executives of the US Direct Marketing Association (the telemarketers' group that is trying to kill the federal 'Do Not Call' list) have registered for the list themselves.

- A woman who went shopping at an Asda store in the West Midlands once found £15,000 in cash on the floor near a checkout.

- One in seven workers needs help turning their office computers on or off because of their dismal knowledge of new technology.

- A Berkshire man once sold a piece of toast on eBay which he says has the face of Joe Pasquale.

- Grocery shoppers spend an average of eight minutes waiting in line at the supermarket.

- A courier firm in Germany is on the verge of bankruptcy after an employee ran up a £20,000 mobile phone bill by calling sex hotlines.

- A Sydney man has pocketed £415 after auctioning a piece of breakfast cereal resembling ET.

- Researchers have found Britons spend more than three hours of every working day gossiping, emailing friends and flirting.

—BUSINESS AND COMMERCE—

• The drink Gatorade was named after the University of Florida Gators where it was first developed.

• Proctor & Gamble originally manufactured candles before moving on to soap.

• British people have longer relationships with some of their household appliances than with their partners.

• A US woman has sold a ten-year-old sandwich said to feature the face of the Virgin Mary for £15,000.

• A West Midlands coach company is giving older passengers a herbal spray to stop them snoring on long journeys.

• There are 1,008 McDonald's franchises in France.

• Blue neckties sell best, followed by red ones.

• The average car in Japan is driven 4,400 miles per year, in the US it is 9,500 miles per year.

• Belgians have tried to deliver mail using cats. It didn't work.

• A man once received a bill from British Gas for £2.3 trillion after a computer mix-up.

———— **BUSINESS AND COMMERCE** ————

* A massive 20.5 billion text messages were sent in the UK in 2003.

* A man believed to be the US's oldest worker has retired at the age of 104.

* Viagra became the top-selling medicine in Venezuela during the country's two-month general strike.

* Five years ago, 60 per cent of all retail purchases were made with cash or cheque. Now it's 50 per cent. By 2010, 39 per cent of purchases will be made by cash or cheque.

* The world's first bra made completely of chocolate has gone on sale in Austria.

* One of Britain's largest exam boards is introducing a vocational qualification in wheel clamping.

* Ancient Rome had a rent-a-chariot business.

* German tram passengers are having their stops announced by the voice of Gerhard Schroeder.

* Forty per cent of McDonald's profits comes from the sale of Happy Meals.

BUSINESS AND COMMERCE

- Jeans made from stinging nettles have gone on sale in the UK.

- A restaurant in west London is offering an ashtray amnesty to mark its 10th birthday.

- Great Britain has the highest European consumption of ice cream.

- The first Christmas card was printed in the US in 1875 by Louis Prang, a Massachusetts printer.

- A Berlin man is carving out a new business selling engraved toothpicks.

- George Eastman, inventor of the Kodak camera, hated having his picture taken.

- The first postage stamp to commemorate Christmas was printed in 1937 in Austria.

- In 1810, Peter Durand invented the tin can for preserving food.

- A German firm is printing novels on rolls of toilet paper to 'kill two birds with one stone'.

- There is a Starbucks in Myungdong, South Korea that is five storeys tall.

---- **BUSINESS AND COMMERCE** ----

- The first in-flight movie was shown on 6 April 1925; it was a silent film on a Deutsche Lufthansa flight.

- The Chinese airline Sichuan Airlines has paid £170,000 for the phone number 8888-8888, saying it hopes to make its customers happy, eight being a lucky number in China.

- More than two-thirds of Britain's workers never take the daily breaks they are entitled to because they are too busy.

- A survey has concluded Tesco has the easiest shopping trolleys to control.

- There has been no mail delivery in Canada on Saturday for the last 35 years.

- A German filling station is employing topless assistants in an attempt to boost trade.

- A Scottish employment quango is under fire after getting its staff to wear T-shirts saying 'Make it in Scotland' that were actually made in Morocco.

- A museum dedicated to traffic signs has opened in the Brazilian city of Sao Paulo.

BUSINESS AND COMMERCE

- A lingerie designer has created a matching bra and knickers out of human hair and is selling them for £2,000 a set.

- The Malaysian government has banned car adverts featuring Brad Pitt because they are 'an insult to Asians'.

- In 1993, the board of governors at Carl Karcher Enterprises voted (5 to 2) to fire Carl Karcher. Carl Karcher is the founder of Carls Jr. restaurants.

- A Swedish man was awarded nearly £60,000 compensation after he was sacked for telling off a colleague for breaking wind.

- Heidi Klum, once voted Germany's most erotic woman, has launched her own collection of orthopaedic sandals.

- David McConnell started the California Perfume Company (CPC) in 1886. Today the company is known as Avon, which he named after his favourite playwright William Shakespeare and Stratford upon Avon.

- Pampers disposable nappies were invented in 1961. A Leicestershire firm has been forced to stop giving workers free Christmas turkeys after a ruling by the Inland Revenue.

BUSINESS AND COMMERCE

- A Norwich sex shop had to change an advertisement after council officials objected to the use of the word 'gadget'.

- A shop has opened in London which only sells tomato ketchup.

- Delia Smith once admitted she didn't always cook everything when she used to make tea for her husband's cricket club.

- The Starbucks at the highest elevation is on Main Street in Breckenridge, Colorado.

- The US Postal Service owns 176,000 cars and trucks, the largest civilian vehicle fleet on earth.

- When Coca-Cola began to be sold in China, they used characters that would sound like 'Coca-Cola' when spoken. Unfortunately, what it ended up meaning was 'Bite the wax tadpole'. It did not sell well.

- A school has been set up in Italy to teach people how to become drag queens.

- Energy giant Powergen says it has no connection to the unfortunately named Italian website www.powergenitalia.com.

BUSINESS AND COMMERCE

- An outdoor clothing company is changing its name for the Australian market because men don't want the name 'fairy' on their clothing.

- A man who began working for a Ford dealership in West Yorkshire in 1930 was still working at the age of 92.

- A supermarket in Brazil is attracting shoppers by giving them the chance to win a job.

- A scud missile complete with its own launcher truck has been up for sale on eBay.

- A shopping centre dedicated to the gay community has opened in Brazil.

- A music channel advertised on cows at the Glastonbury Festival.

- Sainsbury's has introduced purple carrots into its range of vegetables.

- A New Zealand town once produced its own postage stamp, but put the sticky bit on the wrong side.

- The working wives of most married millionaires tend to be teachers.

──────── **BUSINESS AND COMMERCE** ────────

* In 2004, Virgin Atlantic Airlines introduced a double bed for first-class passengers who fly together.

* A Chinese department store has opened a husbands' centre for men who don't want to go shopping with their wives.

* German brothels are to be ordered to offer work experience and trainee posts if they want to continue doing business.

* *Sports Illustrated* magazine allows subscribers to opt out of receiving the famous swimsuit issue each year. Fewer than 1 per cent of subscribers choose this option.

* Workers make 15,000 calls to sex and chat lines every hour, costing UK business millions of pounds a year, according to research.

* The company that manufactures the greatest number of women's dresses each year is Mattel. Barbie's got to wear something.

* The Royal Mail once launched a search for the owner of a set of traffic lights sent in the post.

* A coffin-shaped smokers' booth has been placed outside an office in Manchester in a bid to discourage workers from lighting up.

BUSINESS AND COMMERCE

- McDonald's is turning off its trademark golden arches in New Zealand, in response to a nationwide campaign to cut electricity use by ten per cent.

- Mailmen in Russia now carry revolvers after a recent decision by the government.

- The first naked flight carried 87 passengers from Miami, Florida, to Cancun in Mexico.

- Fast-food provider Hardee's has recently introduced the Monster Thickburger. It has 1,420 calories and 107 grams of fat.

- Rizla has developed transparent tobacco rolling papers that are less than half as thin as a fine human hair.

- A Seattle taxi driver has vowed to continue wearing an Elvis-style cape for work despite being fined for breaking a dress code.

- A struggling teashop owner in China lured customers by placing lonely heart advertisements seeking a lover and then fixing the rendezvous in her cafe.

- A Georgia company will mix your loved one's ashes with cement and drop it into the ocean to form an artificial reef.

BUSINESS AND COMMERCE

- Tartan kilts have become fashionable in Austria after archaeologists claimed the country invented them.

- A Norwegian witch has won a £5,000 business grant from her government to make and sell magic potions.

- Ikea once apologized after accidentally naming a child's bunk bed after an obscene German expression. The wooden bed is called the 'Gutvik' which means 'Good f★★★' in German.

- One in three workers has come close to leaving their job because of the irritating habits of their colleagues, according to a survey.

- The busiest shopping hour of the Christmas season is between 3 p.m. and 4 p.m. on Christmas Eve.

- Sharwoods brought out a new range of curry sauces named Bundh and then realized the name translates as 'arse'.

- A Romanian taxi driver says his business has swelled since he started playing porn films in his cab for customers.

- China is the world's largest market for BMW's top-of-the-range 760Li. This car sells for £100,000 in China – more than almost all people in China make in a lifetime.

BUSINESS AND COMMERCE

- The favourite car of Premiership footballers has been revealed as the BMW X5, with 48 players owning the model.

- In an effort to raise revenue the New York City subway system is considering selling sponsorships of individual stations to corporations. Riders could soon be getting off at Nike Grand Central Station or Sony Times Square.

- The average child recognizes over 200 company logos by the time he enters primary school.

- The chip shop which came up with the deep-fried Mars Bar has launched another delicacy – fish in a Rice Krispie batter.

- Newscaster Sir Trevor MacDonald is exactly the kind of person drivers would trust to buy a new car from, according to a new survey.

- A US fizzy drinks manufacturer has issued an apology to its customers after failing to keep up with demand for its new product – Turkey and Gravy soda.

- One in four homeless people in South Korea has a credit card.

—————— **BUSINESS AND COMMERCE** ——————

* Monks in Wisconsin have set up their own online firm selling inkjet print cartridges.

* A 68-year-old US health-food executive served a 15-month sentence for labelling a 530-calorie doughnut as low-fat.

* A Russian telecoms company offers free phone calls to the White House for anyone who wants to rant at George Bush.

* Iceland consumes more Coca-Cola per capita than any other nation.

* A company in Warwickshire complained to trading standards after a 'slim, attractive' stripogram they booked turned out to be a 20-stone woman.

* They have square watermelons in Japan...
  they stack better.

* A mobile-telephone number in Bahrain is on sale for £10,000 – the number is 9111119.